RUFUS PORTER
REDISCOVERED

Fig. 1. Rufus Porter, aged about 80, when he was living in Plantsville, Connecticut. *Photograph from the Smithsonian Institution, Washington, D.C.*

RUFUS PORTER REDISCOVERED

artist • inventor • journalist   1792 • 1884

Jean Lipman

Foreword by
Gerard Piel,
Publisher, *Scientific American*

Foreword to the 1980 Edition by
John I. H. Baur,
Director Emeritus, Whitney Museum of American Art

An exhibition organized by The Hudson River Museum   April 12 - July 6, 1980

Dedicated to

Nina Fletcher Little

and Bartley A. Jackson

and all the other people

listed in the acknowledgments

Sections of Chapter One are reprinted here
with the permission of the Whitney Museum
of American Art.

Inquiries should be addressed to Clarkson
N. Potter, Inc., One Park Avenue, New
York, New York 10016

Printed in the United States of America

Published simultaneously in Canada by
General Publishing Company Limited

**Library of Congress Cataloging in
Publication Data**

Lipman, Jean, 1909–
Rufus Porter Rediscovered.

  Bibliography: p.
  1. Porter, Rufus, 1792–1884.
2. Painters—United States—Biography.
3. Inventors—United States—Biography.
4. Journalists—United States—Biography.
CT275.P6844L56   1980   759.13 [B]
79-28517

ISBN: 0-517-541157
        0-517-541165 pbk.

10 9 8 7 6 5 4 3 2 1

On behalf of the Board of Trustees of The Hudson River Museum, I gratefully acknowledge the generous cooperation of Jean Lipman, who patiently gave of her time during the organization and presentation of this special exhibition. Her collaboration allowed the Museum to present an exhibition of significance not only to art historians but to a large and diverse audience interested in nineteenth-century American art. *Rufus Porter Rediscovered: Artist, Inventor, Journalist 1792–1884* is one of the series of exhibitions in the Museum's cross-disciplinary program which features innovative presentations in art, history and science.

I particularly appreciate the important assistance and advice offered during all stages in the planning of the exhibition by Rudolph de Harak who, with his assistants Frank Benedict and Janice Bergen, provided the design for the installation at The Hudson River Museum. Special thanks are due John I. H. Baur, noted art historian and Director Emeritus of the Whitney Museum of American Art, and Gerard Piel, Publisher of *Scientific American*, who revised their contributions to the catalogue. Margaret Aspinwall contributed the text related to the exhibition installation and provided invaluable editorial assistance.

I would like to express our thanks to Jane West, Vice President and Publisher; Michael Fragnito, Managing Editor; and Pam Pollack, Production Editor; Clarkson N. Potter, Inc./Publishers who allowed The Hudson River Museum to reprint the original book, *Rufus Porter, Yankee Pioneer* (1968), in revised form for the catalogue for this exhibition.

I extend our sincere gratitude to George Bugliarello, remarkable President of the Polytechnic Institute of New York; Peter Kaufman, Assistant Director of Public Relations; Thomas Settle, Associate Professor of Social Sciences; Eleanor Adams, Assistant to President; Edward De Carbo, Jr., Dean of Student Life, the Aerospace and Mechanical Engineering, Metallurgy, Electrical Engineering and Social Sciences Departments of Polytechnic Institute of New York. Also, to the senior students of Polytechnic Institute Stephen Kurick, Hubert Figueiredo, Elliot Leyman, Mark

Ettlinger and Ed Samsen who worked long hours in the rebuilding and outdoor demonstrations of the airship in both Manhattan and Westchester County.

This exhibition could not have been realized without the generosity and participation of the following institutions and private collectors who kindly agreed to lend important works of art: American Antiquarian Society, Worcester, Massachusetts; Mr. and Mrs. R. C. Brandegee, Pittsburgh, Pennsylvania; Mr. and Mrs. John F. G. Eichorn, West Boxford, Massachusetts; Lexington Historical Society, Lexington, Massachusetts; Nina Fletcher Little, Brookline, Massachusetts; Maine State Museum, Augusta; Minnesota Historical Association, St. Paul; New York State Historical Association, Cooperstown; New York State Library, Albany; Old Sturbridge Village, Sturbridge, Massachusetts; Reading Antiquarian Society, Reading, Massachusetts; Caroline R. Stevens, North Andover, Massachusetts; Mortimer Zuckerman, Boston, Massachusetts, and an anonymous lender. We particularly want to acknowledge the cooperation of Mr. and Mrs. Charles Cobb of Hancock, New Hampshire, for permitting to be exhibited the photographic enlargements of their Rufus Porter room.

Many staff members of The Hudson River Museum worked on aspects of the exhibition: Catherine Conn, Associate Curator, provided crucial assistance as the curator responsible for the organization of the exhibition and preparation of the exhibition catalogue; Richard B. Carlson, Acting Administrator, assisted with administration related to the exhibition; Julie Lazar, Director of Development, arranged for the National Endowment for the Humanities grant and matching New York State Council on the Arts and private funding; Craig Flexner, Registrar of the Museum, supervised the details of registration; Judy Matson, Director of Public Relations, supervised national and regional promotion of the exhibition; Pauline Leontovich, Administrative Secretary, assisted with the preparation of the catalogue manuscript; Ellen Kenny, Curatorial Research Assistant, assisted Catherine Conn with organizational details; and John Holmes, Director of Exhibition Installations, who, with the assistance of Jeffrey Casper and Gary Regan, worked on the difficult technical aspects of the installation.

Rufus Porter Rediscovered: Artist, Inventor, Journalist 1792–1884 is made possible by a grant from the National Endowment for the Humanities, a federal agency. Nancy Worssam, Museum and Historical Organizations Program of the National Endowment for the Humanities, provided much appreciated encouragement and assistance. Additional funding was provided by the New York State Council on the Arts, American Can Company Foundation, Mr. and Mrs. Gregory Halpern, Mr. and Mrs. Frederick J. Stock, Mr. and Mrs. Joseph DeBlasi and Mrs. Robert S. Siffert.

Richard Koshalek
Director, The Hudson River Museum

Contents

Other Books by
JEAN LIPMAN

American Folk Painters of Three Centuries (1980)
    with Tom Armstrong

Art About Art (1978)
    with Richard Marshall

Calder's Universe (1976)

Bright Stars (1976)
    with Helen M. Franc

Provocative Parallels (1975)

The Flowering of American Folk Art (1974)
    with Alice Winchester

Rediscovery: Jurgan Frederick Huge (1973)

Calder's Circus (1972)
    with Nancy Foote

The Artist in America (Ed., 1967)

American Folk Painting (1966)
    with Mary Black

What Is American in American Art (Ed., 1963)

The Collector in America (Ed., 1961)

American Folk Decoration (1951)
    with Eve Meulendyke

Primitive Painters in America (1950)
    with Alice Winchester

American Folk Art in Wood, Metal and Stone (1945)

American Primitive Painting (1942)

Genealogy

Fig. 103. Porter coat of arms. From Joseph
Whitcomb Porter's *Genealogy of the Descendants of Richard Porter and John Porter.*

Rufus Porter—painter, inventor, journalist.
    Born: May 1, 1792, in West Boxford, Massachusetts.
    Married: October 16, 1815, Eunice Twombly of Portland, Maine, daughter
        of Anna and Daniel Twombly of Falmouth, Maine, died November 15, 1848,
        in Billerica, Massachusetts.
        1849, Emma Tallman Edgar, daughter of Thomas Edgar and Ellen Cook of
        Roxbury, Massachusetts, died 1894.
    Died: August 13, 1884, in West Haven, Connecticut.
    Children by Eunice Twombly Porter:
        Stephen Twombly, born August 16, 1816, in Portland, Maine, died October 6,
        1850, in Billerica, Massachusetts. Assisted Rufus Porter as landscape painter
        and was a partner in the *American Mechanic.*
        Mary Broadbury, born July 29, 1818, in Portland.
        Rufus King, born August 9, 1820, in Cambridge, Massachusetts.
        Twins, Sylvanus Frederick and Francis Augustus, born June 29, 1823, in Bil-
        lerica, Massachusetts; Francis Augustus died July 2, 1823, in Billerica.
        John Randolph, born December 5, 1825, in Billerica, Massachusetts.
        Edward Leroy, born July 31, 1827, in Billerica.
        Nancy Adams, born July 16, 1829, in Billerica.
        Ellen Augusta, born June 19, 1831, in Billerica.
        Washington Irving, born October 1, 1834, in Billerica, died January 7, 1836, in
        Billerica.

Children by Emma Tallman Edgar Porter:
5 children, dates of birth unknown, died in infancy.
Frank Rufus, painter, born 1859, died 1942, in Biloxi, Mississippi.

His brothers and sisters, all born in West Boxford:
Ruth, born 1780, died 1846; married Jonathan Poor, born 1771, died 1864, of Baldwin (later Sebago), Maine. Their son, Jonathan D. Poor, born 1807, died 1845, probably accompanied Rufus on one of his portrait-painting trips and was the most active of the Porter-school mural painters. He married Caroline Porter, a cousin of his mother, in 1832.

Jonathan, born 1782, died 1854. Rufus was apprenticed to him as a shoemaker in 1807.

Tyler, born 1784.

Stephen, born 1788, died 1851, in Portland, Maine.

Henry, born 1799, died 1870, in Portland.

Benjamin, born 1790. Resided for a time in Buxton, Maine; married Sarah Runnels, second cousin of Stephen Runnels who probably sailed with Rufus to Hawaii; their son named Stephen Runnels Porter.

His parents:
Tyler Porter, carpenter and farmer, born 1757, in West Boxford, served as a private in the Revolutionary War, died 1842, in Sebago, Maine.

Abigail Johnson of Andover, Massachusetts, married Tyler Porter, in 1779.

His Porter uncles and aunts, all born in West Boxford:
Lydia; Mehitable; Mehitable the second; Lucy; Jonathan; Jonathan the second; Sarah; Ruth; Mary; Susanna; David Foster who moved to Denmark, Maine; Benjamin who moved to Winthrop, Maine, in 1780 and then to Vienna, Maine, in 1788. His daughter Caroline, born 1811, died 1840, married Jonathan D. Poor.

His Porter grandparents:
Benjamin Porter, carpenter and farmer, born 1721, in West Boxford, died 1784, in West Boxford. Married 1744, Ruth Foster; 1763, Mary Sherwine.

Ruth Foster of Andover, Massachusetts, married Benjamin Porter 1744, died 1750.

His Porter great-uncles and -aunts, all born in West Boxford:
Mary; Thomas; Chadwick; Lucy; Sarah; Tyler; and Moses, who moved to Portland and whose son Aaron (1752–1837) married Pauline King, sister of the Honorable Rufus King after whom Rufus Porter named his second son. Their daughter Harriet married Reverend Lyman Beecher; she was stepmother of Henry Ward Beecher and Harriet Beecher Stowe.

His Porter great-grandparents:
Benjamin Porter, carpenter and farmer, born 1692, in Wenham, Massachusetts, married and established himself in West Boxford, in 1716, died 1778, in West Boxford.

Sarah Tyler, born 1696, in West Boxford, died 1767, in West Boxford, daughter of Moses and Ruth (Perley) Tyler of West Boxford.

His Porter great-great-grandparents:
John Porter of Wenham, Massachusetts, malster and farmer, 1658–1753.

Lydia Herrick of Beverly, Massachusetts, died 1689.

His Porter great-great-great-grandparents:
John Porter, yeoman-tanner, born 1596, in Dorset, England. He was living in Hingham, Massachusetts, in 1635, and settled in Salem, Massachusetts, in 1644 where he died in 1676. At his death he was the largest landowner in Salem Village, his lands including parts of modern Salem, Danvers, Wenham, Beverly, Topsfield and Boxford.

Mary Porter, probably born in England, died 1684 or 1685, in Salem, Massachusetts.

Foreword

"WE HAVE BEEN FREQUENTLY SOLICITED by enterprising mechanics, and others, to engage in the publication of a new scientific paper, for the advancement of more extensive intelligence in Arts and Trades in general, but more particularly in the several new, curious and useful arts, which have but recently been discovered and introduced. . . . With this encouragement, we have made arrangements to furnish the intelligent and liberal working man and those who delight in the development of the beauties of Nature, which consist of the laws of Mechanics, Chemistry, and other branches of Natural Philosophy—with a paper that will instruct while it diverts and amuses them, and will retain its excellence and value, when political and ordinary newspapers are thrown aside and forgotten."

In these engaging terms, set out on page one, Volume I, Number 1, of *Scientific American*, dated August 28, 1845, Rufus Porter made his contract with his readers. Today, *Scientific American* is one of the two oldest periodicals of general circulation in the United States (the other being *The Atlantic*) still published under its original name. Survival for 135 years is remarkable among institutions as expendable as the magazines and newspapers of the American press. The continuity of name belies, however, a discontinuity of mission, content and character that is plainly to be seen, from generation to generation, in the 242 volumes of *Scientific American* that have followed the first. A magazine—*Scientific American* as well as *The Atlantic*—is the highly personal creation of its editors. The institutional façade—ever more remote and Olympian with the years—conceals the human fallibility of the mortals whose pedagogical, political, pecuniary or other itch has brought them into the succession established by the Founder.

It is easy to distinguish the two volumes or so of *Scientific American* that Rufus Porter put out during his brief tenure as editor. For him, the façade was a proscenium. His exuberance, his innocence, his unreserved confidence that moral perfection must follow upon physical improvements (and, indeed, that physical improvements come as the consequence of moral perfection) suffuse his pages.

Even as Porter addressed his appeal to the "enterprising mechanic," however, that species was vanishing from American society. The National Trades Union had already been organized; the first injunctions had been issued against striking workingmen; and four hundred demonstrators, who had gathered at City Hall in New York to protest a cornered price on flour, had gone to jail. It was not until after Porter had sold his paper—his journeyman type boxes along with the name and goodwill—to the patent-law firm of Munn & Co. that *Scientific American* got down to the business of reporting the Industrial Revolution in America.

Here in America, as in Britain, the Industrial Revolution brought the cleaving of the sciences from the humanities. In the harsh, impersonal cruelty of the process of capital formation, sharpening the prevailing inequities in the distribution of material goods, men of letters and the arts found evidence to sustain their disposition to believe that science is inhumane or, at best, value-free. For their part, scientists and technologists were content to leave such side issues to the humanists and to get on with their consequential work. In their respective spheres of influence, each party found agreeable relief—the humanist from the obligation to submit to the discipline of verifiable knowledge, the technologist from moral responsibility for the consequences of his work.

Today it is no longer possible to live with this convenient schizophrenia. The economic, political, social and ethical consequences of work in science follow too closely upon primary discovery and invention. No responsible participant can fail his duty to try to see the picture whole.

To the editors of the present *Scientific American* (we bought the franchise from Munn & Co. in 1947), Rufus Porter speaks with a contemporary voice. We share his vision and his hope and, in good measure, it may be supposed, his innocence.

The vision is now happily affirmed with the rediscovery by Jean Lipman of Rufus Porter, painter. This enterprise in the history of American art evokes the spirit of a man who could find in Natural Philosophy and in the painting of frescoes two equally immediate routes to "delight in the beauties of Nature."

—GERARD PIEL
Publisher, Scientific American

Foreword to the 1980 Edition

IN MY PREFACE to the first edition of this book, written over a decade ago, I deplored the neglect which our public, our universities, and our historians had visited on nineteenth-century American art. That is no longer true—at least to the same extent. Today more people are collecting it, more colleges are teaching its history, and more scholars are at work in the field than ever before. There are still dark areas to be explored and worthy painters, like Porter, to be rescued from oblivion, but the process is under way.

This is gratifying and a tribute to the pioneering work of Jean Lipman and a handful of others, who taught us that early American art has virtues beyond antiquarian ones. But the damage of our original neglect can never be entirely undone. The loss of so many of Porter's lyrical and superbly decorative frescoes is beyond repair. We can only be thankful that Mrs. Lipman's book stemmed the tide and that those paintings which survived are sufficient to establish Porter as one of our finest naïve painters of the last century.

JOHN I. H. BAUR
Director Emeritus, Whitney Museum of American Art

The older America of colonial days had been static, rationalistic, inclined to pessimism, fearful of innovation, tenacious of the customary . . . it opened no doors to Utopian dreams of a golden future. The round of daily life was confined within a narrow domestic economy, with few and rare changes in social status. . . . With its expectations cramped by a drab agrarianism, it was content to remain primitively self-sufficient, not given to seeking riches by speculative short-cuts, clinging to the habitual, distrustful of change.

During the thirty-odd years between the Peace of Paris and the end of the War of 1812 that older America was dying. The America that succeeded was a shifting, restless world, youthfully optimistic, eager to better itself, bent on finding easier roads to wealth than the plodding path of natural increase. . . . The cautious ways of earlier generations were become as much out of date as last year's almanac. . . . The ideal of a static society having been put away, progress was assumed to be the first law of nature, and innovation was accepted as the sign and seal of progress.

> From the introduction to "The Romantic Revolution in America," Vol. II in Vernon Louis Parrington's *Main Currents in American Thought.*

The War of Independence energized invention and lessened the catalogue of impossibilities.

> From Thomas Paine's *The Age of Reason.*

Early American art . . . and all early American acts and deeds, are direct reflections of a mind that was pioneering in its essence. Americans pioneered in far more than a geographic dimension. They pioneered in everything.

They were always, as a people, good customers for new ideas, contraptions, inventions, time savers. They converted the one-time purely decorative love apple into a national dish: the tomato. They put grocery stores, saw mills and theatres on river boats and on road wagons.

The pioneering mind is constantly alert for new and better ways of doing things more quickly. It is the handmaiden of progress. . . . This nation was established by pioneering. It expanded by pioneering. It is where it is today because of pioneering.

The pioneer mind is not a thing of the past. It is a constant thing. It is born of freedom of speech and thought; of equality before the law; of faith and confidence; of ability to translate the hidden yearnings of people into concrete accomplishments. It is inventive and always willing to try.

> From the introductory chapter of *American Pioneer Arts and Artists* by Carl W. Drepperd.

The
Porter Puzzle

THE NAME OF RUFUS PORTER was virtually unknown when I began to research his life around 1940, and details of his amazing career had never been
published or publicized, although he was one of our great New Englanders.
It seemed important to reconstruct his life because he pioneered and made
outstanding contributions in the field of American art, and in science and
journalism as well.

Rufus Porter was born in West Boxford, Massachusetts, on May 1, 1792,
the son of a prosperous farmer who moved with his wife and seven children
to Maine in 1801. Young Rufus' higher education consisted of six months
spent in the Fryeburg Academy in Maine at the age of twelve. For the next
two years he lived as a farmer and amateur fiddler. According to an obituary
account in *Scientific American,* his family decided when he was fifteen years
old that "it would be best for him not to fiddle any longer" but to settle down
to something solid and useful, and so they apprenticed him to his older
brother, a shoemaker. Soon, however, Rufus gave up this trade and began
his itinerant career by walking to Portland, where he spent three years
playing the fife for military companies and the violin for dancing parties.
He then became, successively, a house and sign painter, a painter of gunboats, sleighs, and drums; a drummer and a teacher of drumming and drum
painting. In 1814 he was, briefly, a member of the Portland Light Infantry.
Next he taught school, built wind-driven gristmills, copyrighted a music
instruction book, moved from Portland to New Haven, and began his career
of portrait painting. Shortly after that we find him, as "Professor Porter,"
running a dancing school. There are no records of his activity for the years
from 1817 to 1819, but according to an elderly resident of West Boxford,
Porter joined the crew of a ship on a trading voyage to the Northwest Coast
and Hawaii. She remembered seeing letters written by Porter in which he
described the people and scenery of the Hawaiian Islands.

Having begun a nomadic life in his teens, Porter remained a wanderer
till his last years. He married Eunice Twombly in 1815, and she bore him ten
children. After his wife died in 1848, he remarried in 1849—a girl in her
twenties—and fathered six more children, but Porter rarely stayed at home
for any length of time. The *Porter Genealogy,* published in 1878 when Rufus
was eighty-six years old, notes: "Mr. Porter writes that he has good health,
and walked seventeen miles." At this date he is recorded as a resident of

New Haven, but he had not yet settled down and is found two years later in Bristol, Connecticut. He was still traveling in 1884, when during a visit to a son in West Haven he was suddenly taken ill and died on August 13, in his ninety-third year.

Two of his sons, Captain Rufus K. Porter and Judge John R. Porter, lived in San Diego, California, and they sent several items about their father to the *San Diego Union*. The October 5, 1873, issue mentions that "Mr. Rufus Porter, aged eighty-five years, the original editor of the *Scientific American* . . . is soliciting shares for a flying machine he has invented." The June 7, 1876, issue prints a note from Captain R. K. Porter with an accompanying letter from his father, written on his eighty-fourth birthday. The letter features a twenty-eight-line poem about himself, which mentions that his teeth, eyesight, hearing, mind, and skill have never been better. Porter ends the letter by saying that when he wrote the poem that night he was tired and sleepy, "having walked seven miles, besides working six hours in the shop."

Another letter to his son Rufus that the *San Diego Union* published, on January 16, 1880 (when Porter was eighty-nine and still did not need glasses), mentions that he has "drawings, patterns and . . . mechanical business to attend to," is planning to plant potatoes despite the cold weather, and has been digging clams. He also writes: "I have made preparations for improving the cold winter by manufacturing improved clothes-driers, and my neighbor Wooding, formerly of Bristol, sells them for me. I have a room for myself and keep my lathe for turning, sawing, boring and tenoring in the basement. I suppose I shall resume business in Meriden in three or four weeks."

Excepting his Hawaiian adventure, Porter worked steadily at the trade of itinerant artist from 1815 to around 1840. During that time he traveled throughout New England and as far south as Virginia. A versatile and productive artist, he devoted himself to the large-scale production of inexpensive portraits and murals for rural homes and country hostels. A generation before Currier and Ives had become printmakers to the American people, Porter had established a mobile one-man factory for original portraiture and interior decoration. In 1820, to speed up portrait production, he planned and constructed a camera obscura with which he could make portraits in fifteen minutes. The silhouette of the sitter was focused on a sheet of paper, the outline then sketched and rapidly filled in. These portraits, priced at twenty cents, were in great demand and sold briskly. According to his advertising handbill, Porter also produced full-face and profile watercolor portraits and ivory miniatures. A great many of the profile portraits, sensitively drawn and delicately colored, have been identified in the last few years based on comparison with the one pair reproduced in my 1968 book, *Rufus Porter, Yankee Pioneer*. A notice which Porter placed in the *Haverhill* (Massachusetts) *Gazette* for March 31, April 7, and April 14, 1821, to advertise his watercolor portraits reads:

In 1825 Porter published a book called *Curious Arts,* an art instruction manual primarily designed to give the amateur public quick and easy recipes for various types of artwork. Included in this book is a section on "Landscape Painting on Walls of Rooms"—and in the following years Porter devoted himself chiefly to mural painting. His frescoes were executed in large scale on dry plaster walls in a combination of freehand painting and stenciling, some in full color, others in monochrome, the foliage occasionally stamped in with a cork stopper instead of being painted with a brush. These methods, as well as stencil work, had long been used for decorating plaster, woodwork, and furniture, but Rufus Porter was the first to popularize them for landscape painting. His rapid technique and stock stencils reveal the inventive Yankee introducing time- and labor-saving devices and mass-production methods for art as he did for industry. His simple murals provided a popular substitute for the elaborate, imported scenic wallpapers that were fashionable at the time, and though somewhat related to wallpaper designs, Porter's scenes always have a fresh native flavor.

A mural signed *R. Porter* in the Dr. Francis Howe house in Westwood, Massachusetts, was recorded by E. B. Allen in a 1922 *Art in America* article on New England frescoes. Starting with this, I researched and published the full story of Rufus Porter's amazing career in my 1968 book, recording 160 houses in rural Massachusetts, New Hampshire, Vermont, and Maine decorated with wall paintings executed by Porter, often with the help of assistants. These included his son Stephen Twombly Porter, his nephew Jonathan D. Poor, and several others. Always eager to instruct, Porter was quite literally a "master" of mural painting with a "school" of pupils. Since publication of my book, dozens more Porter murals have been brought to my attention, and it is safe to assume that a great many others remain undiscovered or were destroyed during the past hundred years. The Howe house murals were saved when the house was torn down, and they are now privately owned.

Attributing the frescoes presents few difficulties, since the Porter and Porter-school murals are distinguished by typical style and content. Their most obvious characteristics are their large scale; clear, bright colors; and bold design and execution. The three most frequently recurring scenes are harbor views, much like Portland harbor as seen from Munjoy Hill, with houses, ships and islands, mountains in the distance, and large "featherduster" elm trees and small shrubs in the immediate foreground; mountain-climbing or hunting scenes used for stairway decorations; and farm village scenes, most often used for overmantel frescoes, with buildings, fields, fences, roads, and again the large elms and small stylized shrubs in the foreground. The trees invariably occupy almost the entire height of the painted wall and establish the first plane of the picture. Other earmarks of his murals include billowing round clouds, clear reflections of objects in water, sharp shading of the darkened sides of houses and trees, and the use of stencils for many details, including houses and boats. Occasional exotic details such as tropical trees and vines, possibly based on recollections of Hawaiian scenery, are also characteristic. Examples of mantelpieces, overmantel panels, and fireboards decorated with similar painted landscapes have recently been attributed to Porter or his assistants. In a number of the houses with walls painted by Porter, he evidently also decorated the woodwork. (A pair of signed oil landscapes has just been brought to my attention, as well as some oil portraits found in the attics of houses Porter frescoed. Attributing the latter to Porter is problematical, but the signed landscapes confirm that Porter painted in oils. As he painted landscapes, it is also very possible that he painted some oil portraits and the many miniature watercolors of his clients while he was decorating their houses.)

In a series of articles published in 1845 in the first volume of *Scientific American*, Porter discussed the mural painter's approach to his art. Here we find him enthusiastically recommending, for subject matter, American farm scenery; for style, deliberate abstraction. This was indeed a revolutionary combination for a mid-nineteenth-century artist to have advanced.

In finishing up landscape scenery, it is neither necessary nor expedient, in all cases, to imitate nature. There are a great variety of beautiful designs, which are easily and quickly produced with the brush, and which excel nature itself in picturesque brilliancy, and richly embellish the work though not in perfect imitation of anything.

Rufus Porter's outstanding trait was his total independence of the more conventional ideas and fashions of his day. He felt himself free to live, to think, and to paint as he wished. This accounts both for the bold originality of his ideas as an inventor and for his free approach to the art of painting. Oblivious of academic realism, he developed a personal, deliberately abstract style, with unconventional designs and color schemes that he rendered in rapid, bold brushwork.

During the years of Porter's work as an itinerant artist he actively practiced a subsidiary profession—that of inventor. Porter's inventions were generally directed toward saving time and labor, and his liking for the itinerant life apparently caused him to specialize in devices that would improve means of locomotion. He visualized the possibilities and drew up plans for an automobile, an elevated train, and a passenger plane. After he had designed a "flying ship" and exhibited machine-driven working models that were flown in New York, Boston, and Washington (the largest model was twenty-two feet long), Porter published in 1849, neatly timed for the gold rush, a book called *Aerial Navigation, the Practicability of Traveling Pleasantly and Safely from New York to California in Three Days.* Porter tried, unsuccessfully, to promote his invention. He first offered, in *Mechanics' Magazine,* half of his patent claims to any company or person who would build a full-scale model. He subsequently stated in the *New York Mechanic* that he would accept ten percent of the profits if anyone would promote his invention. He next petitioned the Senate for an appropriation to enable him to demonstrate the practicability of his airship. Then, in 1852, he formed the Aerial Navigation Company, which issued stock at five dollars a share, and as late as 1873 he is recorded as still soliciting shares. Rufus Porter never flew, but he was the first man in the world to plan and try out the possibilities of a power-driven passenger plane.

Porter also concentrated on developing portable mechanisms, and "portable" is prominent in the newspaper titles of his published inventions. We find plans for "Porter's Portable Horse Power," a portable fence and a portable boat, a pocket chair, and even a car for moving houses. There was nothing stodgy or static in Porter's scheme of things. A forward-looking devotee of variety, change, and speed, his life, art, writings, and inventions are entirely consistent; all typify the changing trends of his times and predict to an amazing degree the tempo of twentieth-century life.

Throughout his life Porter was interested not only in doing but also in teaching. He had the instincts of the leader, the promoter, and sought at every turn to propagate the ideas and skills which he developed. During his career as an artist he was an active teacher, publishing a popular art primer, writing a series of articles on the art of painting, and working with a small "school" of pupils who learned and practiced his methods of mural painting.

In 1845 Porter's quarter-century career as an itinerant landscape and portrait painter in rural New England had come to an end, and he began a new life in New York City, first in the electrotyping business and then as a journalist. As a magazine editor and pamphleteer, Rufus Porter sought to instruct and lead public opinion. The several scientific journals which he founded and edited covered everything from education to politics. In the 1840s he published and edited the *New York Mechanic, American Mechanic* and *Scientific American.* The latter, which he founded in 1845, was one of the most important journals of its time, as it is today. Porter's journals, representing the interests of mechanics and farmers, were boldly independent and progressive. Porter was a freethinker and a severe critic of organized churches; the religious articles that he wrote and published in his latter days can only be termed revolutionary. As journalist and commentator on his times, Rufus Porter strengthened the ideals of freedom, equality, and progress in the young democracy in which he had played so varied and active a part.

In *Main Currents in American Thought,* Vernon Louis Parrington characterizes Mark Twain as "an authentic American—a native writer, thinking his own thoughts, using his own eyes, speaking in his own dialect—everything European fallen away, the last shred of feudal culture gone . . . 'the very marrow of Americanism' "; a man who "with all his shortcomings—because of them indeed—is an immensely significant American document." This characterization of the great Yankee writer could well be applied to our Yankee pioneer, Rufus Porter.

That Porter's picturesque career and manifold achievements should have remained virtually unknown seems a strange phenomenon but not an unprecedented one. As in the case of many great lives that have emerged from obscurity into the limelight, it will merely take time to bring about a proper evaluation. Before I wrote the essays on Porter's wall paintings (published in 1942 in *American Primitive Painting* and in greater detail in 1950 in *Art in America*), the entire publicity given Rufus Porter was to be found in a couple of obituaries; in several brief newspaper and magazine articles; and in a few paragraphs in three biographical dictionaries. He might have been mourned as one of the great men of his time. Not so. Three New Haven newspapers devoted a few lines to an account of his death; the *New Haven Evening Register* bit about the funeral was headed "Few Present." The *San Diego Union,* to which Porter had contributed articles when he was in his eighties, printed a brief obituary in which the entire description of Porter's career read: ". . . the deceased was the founder of the *Scientific American* and also an inveterate teetotaler, not having made use of tea, coffee, wine, cider or beer for the last forty years." *Scientific American* published a couple of unsigned accounts of his life, and from then on he was virtually forgotten. There were a few small items about him in a book on aeronautics; a few contemporary comments on his airship; and a modern reprint of his *Aerial Navigation.* To date very little has been added to this bibliography, and neither the current *Encyclopaedia Americana* nor the *Encyclopaedia Britannica* includes Rufus Porter. In the last five years, however, interest in Rufus Porter has been accelerating: hundreds of letters about his murals, portraits, and inventions were sent to me; a poem about him was included in *Discover America,* a Bicentennial booklet published by San José State University; and a room-size ceramic sculpture by Malcolm Cochran (in the collection of Dartmouth College Galleries and Museums)—a group of life-size ceramic portrait busts of Porter—was exhibited as a traveling show in 1977.

The extraordinary lack of interest in Porter's life, however, can be accounted for. Although he made detailed mechanical drawings and models for quite a number of machines that have been mass-produced in the twentieth century, he was a visionary rather than a practical inventor. His lack of fame in his (and our) time came about primarily because his art activities were carried on with almost total anonymity and because he drew up and sold the majority of his inventions without patenting them. A brilliant artist and inventor, Porter was an ineffectual businessman who never successfully merchandised or profited by his inventions.

It is interesting to find that he sold one of his inventions, the revolving rifle, to Samuel Colt for one hundred dollars; the revolver Colt developed became famous but its inventor did not. It is also significant that an exhibition at the New York Public Library in 1967 showing "The Rise and Fall of the Elevated Railroad" did not include Porter's detailed proposal published, with a drawing, in the January 1, 1846, issue of the *Scientific American* (see Fig. 25), although this preceded by two years the "first" practical proposal, and preceded the first elevated railroad actually constructed by two decades. Porter's surviving murals, all but three of which were unsigned, were never postcards and calendars, and discussed in articles and books—as anonymous works—and the owners of the houses he had frescoed knew nothing about the painter. The books Porter wrote were published in small editions and the few remaining copies are in the treasure rooms of libraries and universities, known only to bibliophiles. His scientific journals were published in an erratic manner, and the now great *Scientific American* was sold within assembled under his name. Individual examples were reproduced on picture a year of its origin for eight hundred dollars. The result of Porter's fickle management of his journals is that the *New York Mechanic* is known as the first scientific newspaper in this country, but few link it with the name of Porter; and when the *Scientific American* proudly celebrated its hundredth anniversary in 1945, Rufus Porter was almost forgotten. An editorial on the centenary of the *Scientific American* in the *New York Times* recounted every pertinent detail about the history of the journal except the name of its founder and first editor.

Another reason for Porter's strange obscurity is that, like many pioneers, he was somewhat too advanced for even his very progressive times. In the nineteenth century men looked forward to the future, but they still thought in small steps and slow stages. Roger Burlingame remarked in his *Engines of Democracy* that to the nineteenth-century man the fact that the submarine cable worked successfully for twenty-five miles did not make the first proposal that it should work successfully for a thousand less ridiculous. Thus, Porter's more progressive contemporaries could envision the directed balloon flight but seriously questioned his sanity when he thought of a trip from New York to California in three days. This was a twentieth- and not a nineteenth-century approach to the subject of mechanical flight. Porter's ideas were disparaged in his time because his prophetic vision leaped over small obstacles and spurned small calculations.

Evidently Rufus Porter was not so much ignored as actively blackballed in his own day. In the large tome *The History of Boxford,* published in 1880, during his lifetime, there is a final chapter dealing in detail with "Distinguished and Professional Natives." Here several dozen Boxford personages are discussed, but Porter is not included. Even a section listing the important descendants of Benjamn Porter, Rufus' grandfather, does not mention him in any way. He was obviously in actual disrepute in his town, and his name was effectively obliterated from Boxford history. As we continue into the twentieth century we see that the chief speaker at the annual meeting of the Boxford Historical Society in 1944, who was an old-time resident, read an address on "Boxford's Most Unforgettable Characters," and in this reminiscent account Jonathan J. Porter, Rufus' cousin, played a large part, but Rufus was not mentioned. When I addressed the same meeting with a sketch of Rufus Porter's life and achievements, I was amazed to find that few of the Society's members had ever heard of him or had seen the examples of his murals in West Boxford houses. And Boxford was at that time a historically minded town of less than a thousand inhabitants!

When in 1834 Porter first presented to the public his plans for a power-propelled airship, Count Zeppelin and the Wright Brothers were not yet born. Mrs. John A. Andrew, whose family has lived in Porter's birthplace for generations and whose house in West Boxford contains some of his frescoes, said in a letter to me that after *Aerial Navigation* was published "people lost confidence in him as N.Y. to California in 3 days was a crazy idea and he was looked upon as being a little bit queer." She added that Porter was so far ahead of his time that he was discredited by his contemporaries, and she hoped that we might perhaps make up for that now.

Interestingly enough, the only perceptive contemporary account of Rufus Porter appeared in an English journal. An anonymous Englishman, who wrote an obituary estimate of Rufus Porter for the English journal *Invention* (reprinted in the *Scientific American* obituary, November 8, 1884), paid tribute to the energy, ingenuity, and versatility of the American inventor and contrasted his character and career with that of the typical Englishman. Though considering Porter solely as an inventor, the author of this brief article coupled his name with that of Benjamin Franklin and defined the significance of his life in terms of fundamentals, seeing him as a great American who both typified and transcended an era of American history. From across the Atlantic the English journalist wrote of Rufus Porter as "a living representation of the genius of American invention for over three-quarters of a century." He described him as "the true type of the smart American Boy," as the typically American Jack-of-all-trades. He remarked that in this new country hardiness, ready adaptability, and versatility were everything, unlike the older England where well-defined and strictly preserved paths of industry prevailed. He stated that Porter's was a memorable contribution to the great task of saving human manual labor and claimed that he "will live as one of the brightest examples of the versatility of American invention." One can add a twentieth-century postscript to the effect that he will surely live, too, as a pioneer journalist, and, perhaps most importantly, as one of the foremost New England painters.

Young Jack-of-all-Trades

BY THE 1790s THE AMERICAN REVOLUTION and the Declaration of Independence had made surprisingly little impression on the inland towns of New England. The solid New England citizen did not regard himself as the fortunate member of our great new democracy, but continued to lead the life of an English Crown colonist. America, the land of the free in which all men were proclaimed equal, was still largely a feudal aristocracy. Slave-owning was taken for granted. Mechanics were considered vulgar. In New England towns the old families and the clergy were the people of established importance, the fixed ruling class; and this class, federalist and autocratic, looked with distrust and fear on the growing republicanism. Ideas and rank and occupations were settled, subject to change only under the most drastic circumstances. While Washington and Jefferson were busily organizing the Great American Experiment the staid New Englanders were viewing these goings-on with gloom and suspicion. The rumblings of change were faintly audible in the distance, but in eighteenth-century New England maintaining the status quo was the order of the day.

Boxford, in Essex County, Massachusetts, was a moderately prosperous town in 1792, the year Rufus Porter was born, and his was a typical example of the best old New England families. These people led quiet, orderly, industrious lives. They were contented within the confines of their small town, living simply, getting ahead slowly. The merchants of nearby Newburyport, Salem and Boston were already engaged in large-scale trade. The lifting of Crown restrictions on manufacturing after the Revolution had made way for the first stirrings of industry. But the inland Boxford community was still untouched by these new vistas and continued in its placid, contemplative, religious life. Eighteenth-century Boxford, still steeped in English tradition, and the eighteenth-century Porters in their powdered tiewigs and smallclothes were at the opposite pole of the bold new times and adventurous ideas destined to revolutionize nineteenth-century

America. Colonial Boxford represents the exact reverse of what Rufus Porter was to stand for and symbolizes all he left behind when, at the turn of the century, he moved with his family to Maine.

Rufus Porter was born on May 1, 1792, the son of Tyler and Abigail (Johnson) Porter. He was descended from John and Mary Porter who came from Dorset, England, to Salem, Massachusetts, in the early seventeenth century. This pilgrim Porter, born in 1596, was a tanner. He is recorded as living in Hingham, Massachusetts, in 1635. In 1644 he moved to Salem where he prospered and made large purchases of land. At the time of his death in 1676 he was the largest landowner in Salem Village, his lands lying in what is now Salem, Danvers, Wenham, Beverly, Topsfield and Boxford. He was a man of energy and influence, well known in the Colony and held many official positions, among which was deputy to the General Court in 1668.

The descendants of John Porter were mostly hardy, long-lived people of more than average ability and prosperity, and an impressive number of them were distinguished and important personages. On the Topsfield side of the family we find the Reverend Nathaniel Porter, one of the founders of Fryeburg Academy in Fryeburg, Maine. A branch of the family founded the town of Danvers and produced General Moses Porter, who distinguished himself at Bunker Hill and served under Washington all through the Revolution, as well as one Zerrubbabel Porter, the first large-scale shoe manufacturer in the United States. Another descendant, Benjamin Porter, resided in Wenham and in 1716 married and established himself in West Boxford (originally part of Topsfield) where he became one of the most prominent townsmen. This was Rufus' great-grandfather. The eighteenth- and nineteenth-century descendants of this first Boxford Porter include several well-known ministers, doctors, lawyers, merchants, an army colonel, a ship's captain, a professor of mathematics and a member of the Maine legislature. We find other Boxford Porters related by marriage to families of importance such as that of Henry Wadsworth Longfellow; the Honorable Rufus King, first minister to England, after whom Rufus Porter named his second son; and the Beechers. Harriet Porter Beecher, the wife of Reverend Lyman Beecher and stepmother of Henry Ward Beecher and Harriet Beecher Stowe, was Rufus Porter's third cousin.

The first Benjamin Porter was one of the wealthiest men in Boxford. He owned more slaves than any one in town in the mid-eighteenth century—a fair indication of his position. When he married and moved from Wenham to West Boxford in 1716 he bought the old Blake place—a hundred acres on the Ipswich Road near the Andover town line—for which he paid five hundred pounds. An able carpenter, he built his dwelling over the old cellar of the George Blake home which had housed Rebecca Blake, famous in Boxford history as "the Witch of 1692." The Benjamin Porter farm eventually descended to the second Benjamin and from him to his son Tyler. It remained the family homestead until 1801 when Tyler Porter, Rufus' father, sold it to Simeon Foster of Andover and moved to Maine. It has been a cellar-hole for many years now.

In 1796 four-year-old Rufus Porter (as reported in the *Scientific American* obituary) "was in school learning Noah Webster's spelling book." He attended the Fifth District schoolhouse in the West Parish of Boxford. Here, in a one-room frame building, under the jurisdiction of the first school committee in Boxford, young Rufus started his brief education (see Fig. 2). The year before he entered school the committee had introduced English grammar into the curriculum but this was reported as "only used to a slight extent." The three R's were drilled into the young pupils' heads during all the school hours, and school exercises opened and closed with prayer.

At this time the entire family spent all day Sunday at the meetinghouse, the Second West Parish Church, built in 1774. It was in this church (Fig. 3), seated on a rough plank bench, looking up to the high pulpit which the minister reached by a flight of stairs, that young Rufus, aged eight, might have heard the Reverend Peter Eaton deliver what Sidney Perley described in his *History of Boxford* as "a well adapted oration in commemoration of the sublime virtues of General George Washington." This was in December 1800, the first anniversary of the President's death.

In 1801, when Rufus was just nine years old, Tyler Porter sold his home and, leaving behind him colonial Boxford and its aristocratic eighteenth-century traditions, removed with his family to the village of Flintstown, Maine. This little settlement, incorporated in 1802 as the town of Baldwin (the area where the Porters lived became the town of Sebago in 1826), was a raw, sparsely inhabited lumberman's village, very different from the old farming town of Boxford. It adjoined the Maine territory of what is now Bridgton, which had been given to a number of Boxford people as a grant in 1766. Two of Tyler Porter's brothers had migrated to this section of Maine in the late eighteenth century, which accounts for the general locality chosen by Tyler Porter. Early Baldwin contained not much more than a gristmill, sawmills, church, school and store, and was surrounded by wild timberland.

By 1804 the Porters had already made another move, to the even smaller settlement of Pleasant Mountain Gore in the northwest part of the present town of Denmark. Despite some family precedent for homesteading in Maine, Tyler Porter's move from the old Porter farm and the established society of Boxford to the backwoods of Maine must have seemed at the time a daring thing to do; and it inevitably strikes us as significant of the changing times to find the Porters, settled for three generations in eighteenth-century Boxford, venturing forth to a pioneer life in the first years of the new century.

In 1804 Rufus, now twelve years of age, was sent to Fryeburg Academy, a preparatory school for Dartmouth College which had been founded in 1792. One of the founders of the academy and a member of the first Board of Trustees was Reverend Nathaniel Porter, a distinguished relative;

his connection with the Academy was undoubtedly the reason for Tyler Porter's choice for his son.

It was for Rufus, painter-to-be, a fortunate one. The beautiful town of Fryeburg, set on a high plateau overlooking the White Mountains, must have made an indelible impression on the lad's mind. Views of the mountains were later to become a stock item in Porter's frescoes, and we can imagine that the impressive beauty of Mount Washington and of the long range of snowcapped mountains as seen in his school days was never forgotten. Here, too, in Fryeburg Rufus probably had an early taste of mountain-climbing which he later used as the subject of exciting scenes painted up and down many New England stairway walls. Certainly the rocky ascents from Fryeburg to the summit of Jockey Cap or Carter's Dome seem the exact prototypes of those mural mountain-climbing scenes (see Fig. 81), and in one of the murals (Fig. 66) we find the Old Man of the Mountain of Franconia Notch.

In the old records of Fryeburg Academy there is an item under the Schedule of Entries giving Rufus Porter's name as entered by Tyler Porter on November 8, 1804, for one quarter and recording the fee of $1.50 paid for tuition. Rufus attended the Academy for two quarters, the total expense for his tuition coming to just three dollars. Let's see what he got for his money.

During Rufus Porter's term at the Academy the Reverend Amos J. Cook was Preceptor—and the only teacher for the thirty-foot-square one-room school building (Fig. 4). Mr. Cook followed a worthy predecessor for in the year 1802–1803 Daniel Webster, just graduated from Dartmouth, had served as Preceptor. Mr. Cook, also a Dartmouth graduate and personally recommended for the post by Daniel Webster, seems to have been an energetic and progressive young man. At the Academy he started a museum of objects of curiosity and interest which included letters to himself from George Washington, John Adams and Thomas Jefferson; geological specimens; old firearms; some Indian relics. As Preceptor he taught all the subjects—English, Latin, Greek and mathematics—to the thirty-odd boys, cared for the building and acted as secretary to the Board of Trustees. He was also appointed teacher of music; the trustees had voted, as quoted in the Academy's records, "That as the cultivation of Music has a direct tendency to soften the ferocious passions, ameliorate the manners etc., instrumental and vocal music be attended to by those students who have talent and inclination to improve therein." At the same time "two good flutes and two good violins" were provided by the trustees. Under the Reverend Cook's tutelage Rufus undoubtedly had his first and probably his only musical instruction.

Fryeburg Academy, when Rufus Porter attended, was modeled after the typical English grammar school. The character of the school was strongly religious and still archaic from an academic point of view. Yet the trustees and the Preceptor showed a fair degree of progressive tendency. And the life the scholars led—boarding independently with Fryeburg fam-

Fig. 2. The one-room school Porter attended in West Boxford probably looked much like this—a detail of the frontispiece of *The Only Sure Guide to the English Tongue* by William Perry, 1788.

Fig. 3. Church in West Boxford, Massachusetts, as Porter saw it in his childhood. Engraving from Sidney Perley's *History of Boxford*.

THE OLD FRYEBURG ACADEMY
IN WHICH WEBSTER TAUGHT

Fig. 4. Fryeburg Academy, Fryeburg, Maine, as it looked when Porter attended for six months in 1804–1805. From *The Illustrated Fryeburg Webster Memorial*.

Fig. 5. Porter, as a shoemaker's apprentice in West Boxford, Massachusetts, in 1807, would have worked in a cobbler's shop much like the one in the woodcut by Nathaniel Dearborn, c. 1815. *Worcester Art Museum.*

Fig. 6. House and sign painters (Porter worked at this trade in Portland in 1810–1811) learned their trade in shops such as this, and then often took to the road, as Porter did.

ilies, attending the small simple school, coasting or mountain-climbing in the free hours—was certainly healthful and sound.

Rufus was kept at Fryeburg Academy only six months and after the age of twelve he had no formal education whatsoever. His lack of consistent schooling partly explains both the virtues and vices of his mature habits of life and thought. On one hand, it may have contributed to the lack of stability and of practical disciplined action which prevented the successful consummation of so many of his ideas and enterprises. On the other hand, Porter, graduating early from dull routine and strict discipline into the care-free world of his personal inclinations, profited from the independence of the self-taught. Little was dictated from without and so he was free to develop from within. He could devote his life to pursuing original channels of thought, and he was strikingly independent of the narrow prejudices and conventions of his time. He was an innovator in art and journalism, and his career as an inventor epitomizes this pioneering tendency. He became, in short, one of the most progressive Americans of the nineteenth century.

In Porter's time the rigid classical education of the eighteenth century was to be relaxed, and in our day quite abandoned. Rufus Porter, however, threw it to the winds in the first years of the nineteenth century and taught himself in much the same spirit as that of twentieth-century "progressive education." As we shall see, set ways and formal rules were abhorrent to him in his youth, and in his mature life he actively opposed the influence of academicism in every field of his activity. Had Rufus completed his secondary education at Fryeburg Academy he would probably have gone on through Dartmouth and might have emerged a conventional preacher, statesman, doctor or lawyer rather than the footloose painter, journalist and inventor he became.

After leaving Fryeburg in April 1805, Rufus went home to Pleasant Mountain Gore where he seems to have done a variety of things for the next two years without showing any inclination to settle down to any of them. In the editorial of the first (1847) issue of the *Scientific Mechanic*, Porter mentions that he was "originally a farmer" and this probably refers to these years. Perhaps the boys took charge of the farming while the father devoted himself to carpentry. But Rufus was evidently not much of a farmer. During his early teens, according to the 1884 account in the *Scientific American*, he had already become adept in making all sorts of mechanisms such as water wheels, windmills and lathes. He also wrote poetry and played the fife and the violin. The Porters, however, did not like the idea of their son becoming a mechanic or a poet or a musician. The sort of haphazard existence Rufus was leading was frowned upon by his family, who thought he had frittered away enough time and should settle down to one of the solid, accepted trades.

Rufus' older brother Jonathan had remained in West Boxford and was established as a shoemaker, so when Rufus was fifteen years old his family apprenticed him to his brother and sent him to West Boxford to learn the business of shoemaking (see Fig. 5). According to the apprentice system of the time he would earn his keep the first year while he was learning, then receive fifty cents a week for the next five years. After that he would be a master shoemaker in his own right, ready to practice his trade and to have apprentices of his own. This apprentice system, still in effect in early nineteenth-century America, was a carry-over from the old guild system and was soon to be outmoded. It was natural that Rufus Porter's eighteenth-century family would still take for granted the long period of apprenticeship culminating in a reliable profession which could be practiced for a lifetime and then passed on to a son. But it was equally to be expected that Rufus, an alert and independent lad, might question this drab cycle which the older generation considered normal and sound. The prospect of six years of apprenticeship and then a cobbler's shop certainly did not appeal to him, and within a few months he deserted and gave up all thought of learning to be a shoemaker.

Carrying his fife and his fiddle he set out on foot for Portland, 106 miles away, where his second cousin, Aaron Porter, was established as a successful physician. This was the year 1807. Thomas Jefferson was President; Henry Wadsworth Longfellow was born in Portland; Fulton's *Clermont* made her famous trip from New York to Albany; the Pennsylvania Academy of Art was celebrating its first anniversary in Philadelphia; Gilbert Stuart was painting in Boston. At the age of fifteen Rufus Porter was ready to begin life on his own terms.

Portland, Rufus' headquarters until he moved to New Haven in 1816, was his legal residence until 1820. It may be stated here, however, that during Porter's entire life no address was ever really more than an expedient stopping place.

Samuel Longfellow, in his *Life of Henry Wadsworth Longfellow*, recreates the Portland young Henry knew, and the views from the Longfellow windows which he describes closely resemble the scenes we see in some of Porter's later murals. "In summer," Samuel Longfellow writes, "it was pleasant enough to look out from the upper windows; those of the boys' room looked out over the cove and the farms and woodlands toward Mount Washington, full in view on the western horizon; while the eastern chambers commanded a then unobstructed view of the bay, White Head, Fort Preble, and the light-house on Cape Elizabeth."

The very year Rufus arrived in Portland was the year the Portland Observatory was built on the summit of Munjoy Hill, overlooking Casco Bay. Porter's fondness for observatories, which we find prominently placed in many of his later paintings (all looking very much like the Portland Observatory—see Fig. 45), undoubtedly originated with his first introduction to this brand-new tower. The Observatory was the chief "sight" of the year, and the place from which one had the best view of the harbor. It was this view of Portland harbor, specifically as seen from the Observatory or from the Eastern Promenade on Munjoy Hill, that became Porter's most often painted landscape. We find this harbor scene in a Portland house that Porter decorated in the twenties, and on the walls of many inland farmhouses in Maine, New Hampshire and Massachusetts.

When Rufus came to Portland in 1807 he had no thought of becoming a painter. He was a musician, and until 1810 he practiced his profession playing the fife for military drills and the violin for dances. These dancing parties were held in the ballrooms of the popular taverns and were gay affairs indeed. The musician, seated in the raised fiddler's seat, would play his tunes—"Boston Fancy" or "Steamboat Quickstep," jigs, waltzes and reels— and as he played he would call out the changes for the sets. The dance would continue late into the night and end with trays of mulled wine or cider passed among the company by the tavern host.

In 1810 Porter made an important change of occupation, becoming a house and sign painter in Portland (see Fig. 6). This was not routine and mechanical work in the early years of the nineteenth century as it is today. House painting involved grinding and mixing paints, making and applying sizes, constructing brushes of various kinds. The painter had to know how to apply paint to floors, woodwork and plaster, and he was also expected to know how to decorate baseboards and doors with painted graining and mantels with two-tone "marbleized" designs. He might even have been asked to finish the painted plaster walls with a decorative freehand or stenciled frieze, or to paint an allover stencil design on the floor. As for sign painting, the lettering was the least of the matter. A butcher's sign might have been ordered adorned with the picture of an ox, a hatter's sign with a scene showing the inside of the shop. The tavern signs of the day, designed to attract the traveler, featured pictures of Indian chiefs, horsemen, sailboats, animals, coaches, American eagles, portraits of George Washington or similar eye-catching subjects.

Countless talented eighteenth- and nineteenth-century artists started their careers as craftsmen. Joseph Badger, Matthew Pratt, Edward Hicks, James Frothingham and John Neagle are among those who began as house, coach or sign painters, and who as artisans learned all the fundamentals of design and the proper use of paints and brushes. In this sound fashion eighteen-year-old Rufus Porter embarked on his long career of portrait and fresco painting. Certain details, such as the stenciled horsemen found in Porter's early frescoes of the thirties (see Fig. 61), look as if they might have been lifted bodily from the designs of early tavern signs. His idea of covering the walls of ordinary rooms with inexpensive landscape paintings undoubtedly originated in his early house painting days when he found it dull work to decorate vast areas of plaster with one-color washes. These murals were cheap and attractive substitutes for the imported scenic wallpapers that Porter very likely had seen in some of the finer houses.

Rufus Porter left Portland and his painting early in 1812 to join the militia in West Boxford. At this time he and his brothers Stephen and Jonathan are recorded as privates in the West Parish company of foot, which formed a part of the third regiment of the state militia. The captain of the company was John Tyler, a distant cousin and father of the Tylers whose portraits Rufus painted in 1819. Before war was openly declared in June 1812, men were being drafted to guard the seaports all along the coast. In accordance with an order from the lieutenant-colonel commandant, Rufus' company met at the West Parish meetinghouse on May 25, and he was among eight soldiers drafted for this seacoast duty. He was evidently sent to Portland, possibly at his request, but somehow he seems to have managed to evade soldiering almost immediately. When we next hear of him in Portland, still in 1812, he had returned to his old job of painting—adapted to wartime by painting gunboats instead of houses.

The following year found Rufus Porter near his family in Denmark, Maine, the home of his uncle, David Porter, playing the drum for Denmark soldiers, painting sleighs and drums and teaching drumming and drum painting. This decorative painting, which he now practiced and taught, was related to sign painting but involved more highly specialized techniques and designs. The sleighs and drums were first painted in a solid background color and then elaborate freehand or stencil designs were applied in various colors over a varnish sizing. The process of applying colored paint or metallic powders to a stencil was a delicate one in which the "velvet finger"—the index finger of the right hand wrapped in a piece of velvet—was used to transfer a touch of paint or a few grains of metal powder to the stencil pattern. Sleighs were ornamented with subtly shaded designs of vines, leaves, conch shells, birds and grapes, just like those commonly found on Hitchcock chairs. The drums were painted with brilliantly colored and gilded eagle designs and other patriotic emblems, which were also popular for sleighs. This work—combining stenciling and freehand painting in a purely decorative and highly stylized manner—was at the farthest pole from realistic painting; and it may have had a good deal to do with Rufus Porter's later liking for a formalized rather than illusionistic style.

In September 1814, Rufus was back in Portland, serving as fifer and drummer in the Portland Light Infantry which, like his former Boxford company, formed a part of the third regiment of the Massachusetts Militia. (Maine was part of the state of Massachusetts until 1820.) During the next two months Porter served briefly in two other companies, in one as a private, in the other as a musician (see his signature on a Portland Light Infantry roster, Fig. 7).

The War Department records provide the following details of Rufus Porter's service in the War of 1812:

No official record of service prior to 1814.

Sept. 7–Sept. 19 and Sept. 26–Oct. 3, 1814, Musician in Capt. Nathaniel Shaw Jr.'s Company, 3rd (Nichols') Regiment, Massachusetts Militia. Raised at Portland. Service at Portland. This organization known as Portland Light Infantry, organized June 6, 1803.

Oct. 16–Nov. 5, 1814, Private, Capt. Bailey Bodwell's Company, Ryerson Regiment, Massachusetts Militia, stationed at Portland.

Fig. 7.   Detail of an 1814 roster of the Portland Light Infantry with Porter's signature. *Maine Historical Society, Portland.*

Figs. 8, 9.   Soldiers in the uniform of the Portland Light Infantry, in which Porter served as private and musician in 1814, are seen in a detail from his mural in the Coburn Tavern, East Pepperell, Massachusetts, c. 1824. (A similar military drill is featured in a number of overmantels by Jonathan D. Poor—see Fig. 99.) Note also the item from Porter's *Scientific American*, most likely engraved by him (August 13, 1846).

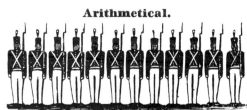

Arithmetical.

A file of soldiers consists of twelve men; each man is capable of assuming four different positions in each of the twelve places.   How many positions are the twelve collectively capable of assuming?: Rule first—Multiply four into itself twelve times the product will show the number of positions the file is capable of without changing places; second —multiply each of the twelve numbers by the next, thus: 1 by 2, this product by 3, and that by 4, &c., the last product will show how many positions the file may assume by changing places allowing one position in each.   Third—multiply the two grand products into each other which will give the answer required, viz., 7,811,788,426,600.

Nov. 6–Nov. 25, 1814, Musician, Lieut. Oliver Bray's Detachment, Artillery, Massachusetts Militia, under supervision of Maj. Gen. Alford Richardson. Raised at Portland. Service at Fort Burrows, Fish Point, Portland, "for the protection of the forts, ordnance and munitions of war and other property belonging to the Commonwealth."

The veteran, applying for pension in 1878, states that he could not remember the exact dates of his service. Allowed pension for service of 33 days, receiving $8 per month from 1878–1884.

Up to the time of the Civil War the state militia was as much a social as a military institution, and it was considered a special honor to be a member of the Portland Light Infantry. This company, in which Porter began his Portland service in 1814 and of which he was the last surviving veteran of the War of 1812, was extremely popular. Many of the young men of Portland's best families sought admission to its ranks and no event of any importance was complete without the presence of the Light Infantry in full uniform.

The uniform consisted of a black cap with a brass comb edged with red worsted as a fringe, and a red plume; red coat faced with black; black stock; white waistcoat and pantaloons with black cord in the seams; and black half-gaiters with red tops. We recognize this as the uniform in the military drill scenes which Rufus Porter and his pupil Jonathan D. Poor later featured in their frescoes (see Figs. 8, 9, 99).

The Portland Light Infantry company-trainings and musters were held on Munjoy Hill at the edge of the bay. If we visit Portland we can see today, much as it was in the early 1800s, the high Eastern Promenade bordering Munjoy Hill, a narrow strip of land planted with evenly spaced elm trees which frame views of the bay. This was the panorama Rufus had seen from the Munjoy Hill Observatory seven years before when he first came to Portland, and this was the view he saw regularly as a soldier at drill. The islanded harbor, glimpsed through the spaces between spreading elms, huge and prominent in the foreground, is the very scene of a number of Porter's most interesting frescoes (see Color Plates 1, 4, 7, 12). The large elms became, in fact, a sort of trademark for Porter murals, and the dramatic change of perspective from great foreground trees to a distant scene was to become the dominant motif of his landscape designs.

Until recently there hung in the room of the Portland Light Infantry in the Portland Armory on Milk Street an historic document—the muster roll of men who took part in the War of 1812 in Captain Nathaniel Shaw, Jr.'s Company, Third Regiment, Massachusetts Militia. Listed there was Rufus Porter's name coupled with that of one John Fay, "Musicians." This faded document recording Rufus Porter's military service has been lost; the enduring records are his mural paintings of military drills, Portland harbor scenes, and the various mechanical devices of a military nature which he invented in his later years.

Rufus Porter's brief participation in the War of 1812 ended just a month before peace negotiations were concluded on Christmas Eve, 1814.

But before that time Rufus was already engaged in a new profession—a surprising one for a young man who had ended his schooling at the age of twelve—as teacher of one of the six district schools in Baldwin, Maine. Perhaps he had gone to visit boyhood friends in Baldwin after his military discharge and casually filled a winter term vacancy in one of the schools. The position did not last, in any case. Within a few months he was teaching in nearby Waterford, the town in which the Squire Cushing family of Boxford had settled some time before; the Cushings and Porters had undoubtedly been acquainted in Boxford, and this might account for Porter's move.

Rufus Porter did not long remain a schoolmaster. He gave up his Waterford post at the end of the term and again took to the road for Portland where he now earned his living by building wind-driven gristmills.

On January 24, 1815, he registered a music instruction book for copyright in the District Court of Maine. This book (Figs. 10, 11), of which only a manuscript title page was deposited, was titled *The Martial Musician's Companion, containing Instructions for the Drum and Fife, together with an Elegant Collection of Beats, Airs, Marches and Quick steps: to which is added, Instructions for the Bass-drum.* Rufus Porter had undoubtedly planned to publish this book, which he must have written during or soon after his period of drum teaching in Denmark in 1813. But no copy of the printed book has ever been found, and the only mention of the title occurs in *A Bibliography of the State of Maine* whose author, Joseph Williamson, collected a number of other titles from the Maine copyright entries. The book was most probably never printed or set up in type at all. Had it been, a printed rather than manuscript title page would surely have been filed for copyright. A corroboration of this assumption is the fact that in Reginald Webb Noyes's *Bibliography of Maine Imprints to 1820* the book is not included though the author mentions that he drew on Williamson's bibliography. The dropping of Porter's volume by Noyes almost certainly means that the book was not printed.

There seems to be ample explanation for Porter's abandoning plans for publication of a music book, for during the course of that same year in Portland he also worked as a builder and married, and soon thereafter moved to New Haven and started portrait painting.

On October 16, 1815, the Reverend Joshua Taylor married Rufus Porter to Eunice Twombly of Portland. Between 1816 and 1834 ten children were born of this marriage, but that did not mean that Rufus had settled down. Quite the reverse, the pace of his roving life seems to have accelerated from that date.

The gristmill building business may have petered out or perhaps Rufus just wanted to be free of family life. Whatever the reason, he left for New Haven within a year of his marriage, leaving his wife in Portland. A letter written by Frank Rufus Porter in 1940 tells that his father traveled via packet and canal from Portland to New Haven where he worked as a portrait painter, and about 1816 "opened a dancing school furnishing his own

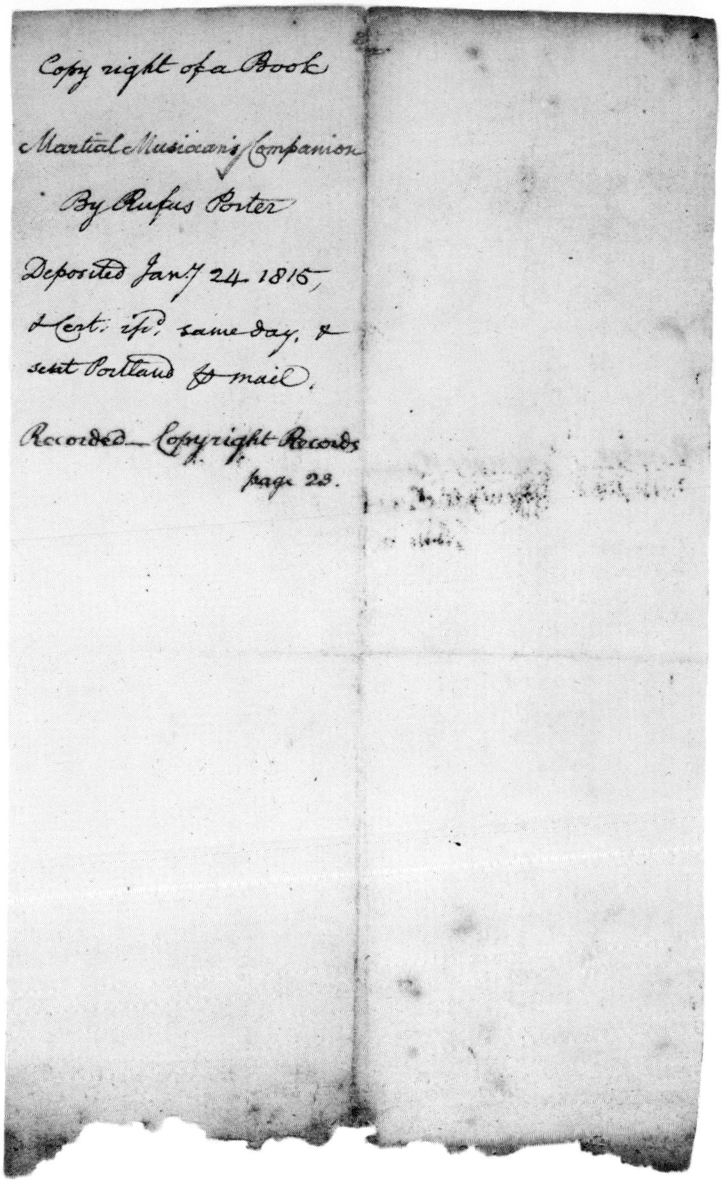

Copy right of a Book

Martial Musican's Companion

By Rufus Porter

Deposited Jany 24 1815,
& Cert: ifd same day, &
sent Portland by mail.

Recorded Copyright Records
page 23.

Figs. 10, 11. Copyright and manuscript title page for *The Martial Musician's Companion*, a music book which Porter registered for copyright in Maine in 1815, but evidently never published.

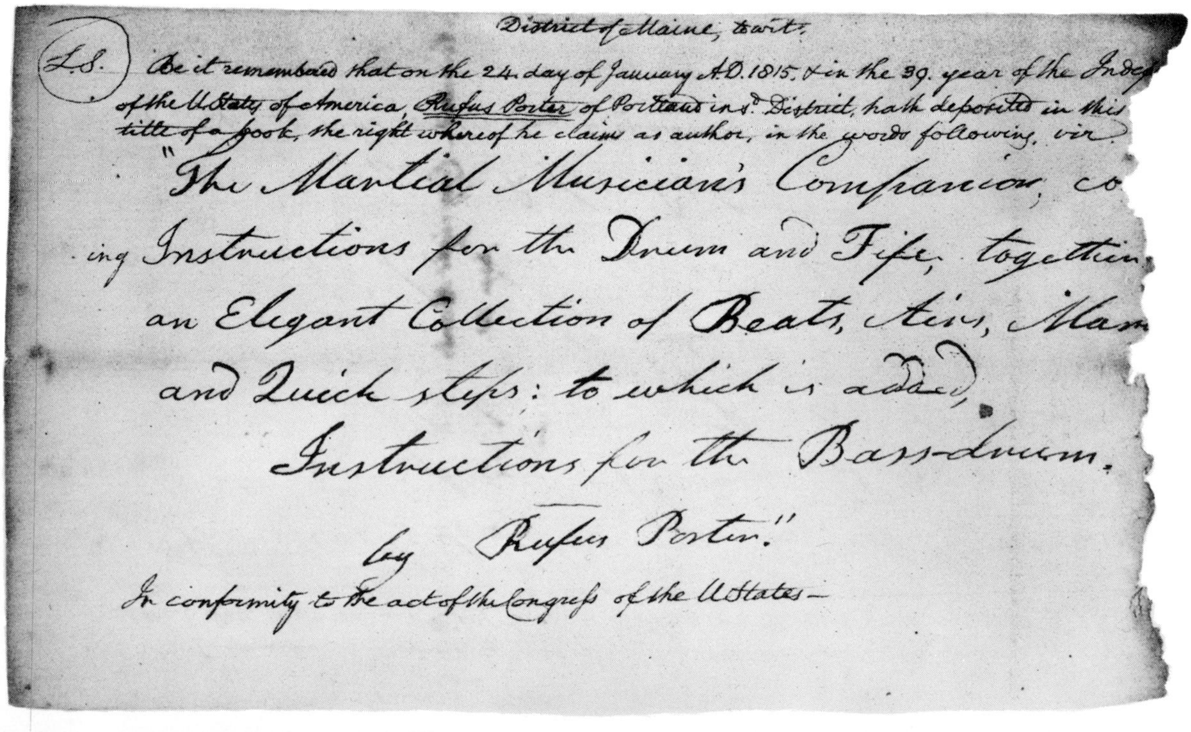

District of Maine, to wit:

L.S. Be it remembered that on the 24. day of January A.D. 1815. & in the 39. year of the Indep of the U.States of America Rufus Porter of Portland in sd District, hath deposited in this titile of a book, the right whereof he claims as author, in the words following. viz

"The Martial Musician's Companion, co
ing Instructions for the Drum and Fife, together
an Elegant Collection of Beats, Airs, Mar
and Quick steps: to which is added,
Instructions for the Bass-drum.

by Rufus Porter."

In conformity to the act of the Congress of the U States—

Fig. 12. "Prof. Porter" conducted a dancing school in New Haven in 1816. An early engraving gives an idea of what his classes may have looked like, with Porter at the violin.

Fig. 13. Three-masted ship like that on which Porter presumably sailed on a trading voyage to the American Northwest and Hawaii, c. 1817–1819. He is said to have spent some time painting in Hawaii before returning to New England. This is a detail from a Porter fresco, c. 1825–1830, in the Wagner house, Lyme, New Hampshire.

music on the violin where he became known as Prof. Porter." It is worth noting that by the time Rufus Porter was in his early twenties his taste for teaching was already marked. He had been a teacher of drumming and drum painting, planned a music instruction book, taught children in two rural schools and become a professor of dancing in New Haven. Here in 1816 we have Professor Rufus Porter aged twenty-four, veteran of the War of 1812, ex-farmer-shoemaker-fiddler-drummer-painter-teacher-builder, and now professional portrait painter and master of a New Haven dancing school!

Professor Porter's dancing school (see Fig. 12), like many early Porter projects, seems to have lasted less than a year and Rufus returned to Portland sometime in 1817 to visit his wife. There is no written account of his activity for the next two years, that is, from the fall of 1817 to 1819, but verbal tradition makes it reasonable to assume it was during this period that he went to sea on a trading voyage and spent some time in Hawaii (see Fig. 13).

Mrs. John A. Andrew of West Boxford, for whose husband's great-grandfather Porter painted the frescoes still preserved in the Andrew house there, has recalled a great many anecdotes about Rufus Porter's life which have, when checked, coincided exactly with recorded biographical data. The seafaring phase of Porter's life is not mentioned anywhere in writing but is commonly recalled in West Boxford and was related in detail by Mrs. Andrew; she said that as a young man he set sail on a trading voyage to the Northwest Coast and Hawaii, staying awhile in the Sandwich (Hawaiian) Islands where he paid his expenses by painting. (As a daughter of Porter's was born on July 29, 1818, he must have sailed at the end of the year 1817.) Mrs. Andrew had seen a number of letters written from Hawaii by Rufus Porter to her husband's great-grandfather Andrew in which Porter described the people and scenery of the Islands. Another resident of West Boxford, Mr. Frank A. Manny who privately published a number of pamphlets on early Boxford history, pointed out that Boxford was one of the Massachusetts towns early associated with Hawaiian affairs, that many Hawaiian relics are preserved in West Boxford, and that in the first quarter of the nineteenth century a number of Boxford boys sailed from Boston on trading voyages to the Northwest Coast, Hawaii and China. More specifically, he recalled a traditional connection between Rufus Porter, Hawaii, a trading voyage to the Northwest Coast and one Stephen Runnels (later spelled Reynolds) also of West Boxford, whose journal of the 1810–1813 trading voyage of the *New Hazard* was published by the Peabody Museum. (Sarah Runnels, a second cousin of Stephen Runnels, married Rufus' brother Benjamin Porter; their son Stephen Runnels, Rufus Porter's nephew, is the only blood relative recorded in the National Archives file on Rufus Porter.) It seems likely that Porter and Runnels were shipmates on a later trading voyage.

Yankee boys went to sea in the early years of the nineteenth century because seamen's wages were high but above all because seafaring offered a free, adventurous life, an exciting way to get about and see the world. Their fathers had mostly spent monotonous lives at home on the farm, but these lads might board a ship bound halfway round the world—fighting Indians on the Northwest Coast, seeing the picturesque Sandwich Islands and wooing the glamorous native girls, sailing to China for a cargo of tea and silk—and return home with a sack of silver dollars and a lifetime's recollection of adventure on the high seas.

These early voyages—like the itinerancy on land and the experiments going on in politics, science, the arts and religion—are part of the story of a restless, inquisitive era in which young Americans, looking beyond their narrow horizons, were bursting the bounds of established convention and familiar geography. They were eagerly exploring new ideas and new lands. A typical newspaper advertisement of a trading voyage assured the public that all "wishing to adventure" or to join a voyage of "observation and enterprise" would be assured of the fulfillment of their desires.

It is easy to understand how young Porter would have impulsively decided to go to sea and how, after many months of confinement on one small ship, he would have been eager for a shore visit in colorful Hawaii. With his fiddle and his paintbrushes he was well prepared to earn his keep on the Islands before working his way home as a seaman again in his own good time.

Like William Williams (the delightful eighteenth-century English-American painter, who began his career as an amateur), Rufus Porter's chief profession was "Painting in General," which meant anything from the side of a house to a miniature portrait. He undoubtedly painted a number of portraits in the Hawaiian Islands, which may still be preserved there, and when he returned to New England he took with him recollections of Hawaiian scenery which found their way into many of his New England frescoes. His interest in ships colored the rest of his life, and it had a good deal to do with the subject matter of both his later inventions and his fresco paintings. More specifically, we see a typical Hawaiian landscape in a Massachusetts fresco representing the sacrifice of Isaac (Fig. 91), volcanic mountains in a number of landscapes, and other details specifically related to tropical scenery. E. B. Allen (in *House Beautiful*, March 1929), discussing an anonymous fresco in Amesbury, Massachusetts (one of Porter's, see Figs. 73–75), comments on the "exotic appearance" of some of the trees. The exotic character of the decorative shrubs and the vine patterns found in a number of Porter's frescoes, as well as some definitely tropical-looking trees, give to these New England landscapes a strange accent which can be attributed to his stay in the Sandwich Islands.

Inventor

WE HAVE SEEN RUFUS PORTER EMERGING from the static, aristocratic society of the late 1700s into the dynamic democracy of the nineteenth century. This was the new era of the common man, of unbounded optimism, free experiment and awareness of unlimited opportunity. Alexis de Tocqueville, in his *Democracy in America* written just before the middle of the nineteenth century, explains nineteenth-century America as an age of practical invention in which every man was able and eager to better himself and attain wealth and position through his own efforts. In such a society anything that will further and improve the effectiveness of those efforts is of the utmost importance. Hence the significance of invention and inventors in the young American democracy. De Tocqueville states that practical science and democracy go hand in hand, and speaks of the "clear, free, original and inventive power of mind" which he considers a national characteristic of the nineteenth-century American. Here we have Rufus Porter in a nutshell, a striking personification of his times. Rufus the adventuresome lad, the inventive artist, the daring journalist, the visionary inventor—in all of these roles we sense that "clear, free, original and inventive power of mind."

Porter's lifetime career as an inventor—which paralleled his other major activities as journalist and painter—seems the inevitable result of personal inclination allied with a constant awareness of and response to the everyday needs of his age. Time was becoming the commodity of major importance in the new step-lively era, and we find Porter inventing an alarm clock. He invented a washing machine, clothes drier, and sewing machine to save the housewife's time; a rotary plow (Fig. 14), a double hand rake and many other implements to save time for the farmer (see Fig. 15); a copying machine for the artist; a color-printing machine for the printer. Life in the nineteenth century was actively on the move; nothing was static; and Porter's device for moving houses (Fig. 16) epitomizes the spirit of the times. The Porter portables, which range from his "Portable Horse Power" to a tricky folding chair-cane, have already been mentioned (see Figs. 17,

18). The dawning era of rapid communication and transportation is reflected in his improved "American Telegraph," "Horse Power Boat" (Fig. 19), paddle wheel steamboat, automobile, elevated railroad and airship. His "Steam-Carriage for Common Roads" (Fig. 20) introduced in the *Scientific American* (October 2, 1845), is described as costing five hundred dollars, weighing six hundred pounds, and capable of going ten miles per hour. "There can be no doubt," says the inventor, "of its ultimate complete success."

In a long letter written to William Markoe from Washington, D.C., in 1857, Porter lists and describes in detail—with the hope that Markoe, who had invested in Porter's airship, would help to secure investors—a number of inventions: "An Engine of Defense," "A Self-operating Marine Pump," "The Sonorific Beacon," "An Aerial Marine Light," "A Simple and perfect self-regulating and independent Pump," "A Steam Farmer."

Porter evidently promoted some of his inventions by forming small stock companies whose shareholders contributed to the cost of producing the machines and shared in the profits. The promotional circular for his "Steam Farmer" (Fig. 21) is mentioned and enclosed in the letter, quoted before, to William Markoe; Porter says that the invention "met with no encouragement here [Washington, D.C.], because it was known that I was the proprietor of a plan for aerial navigation, which did not succeed." The most interesting part of this eight-page letter, in the collection of the Minnesota Historical Society, St. Paul, is the inventor's account of his prefabricated "portable dwelling house, elegant, warm and comfortable, and which can be constructed, painted and finished for less than $200." (See Fig. 104.) He had built one in Baltimore the previous summer, he says, "sold it for cash before it was finished, and afterward took it down and removed it four miles, without unhinging a door, or unshipping a window." The house consisted of five rooms and a pantry, with nine glass windows and five paneled doors. "It is composed of sections of convenient size for packing in boxes for transportation, and may be taken down, or set up ready for occupancy, in two hours." After selling the house in Baltimore, according to this letter, more were wanted and Porter "contracted with a party to carry on the business: but they disappointed me." He then began to construct another "by the aid of a rich man," and states that "there is a prospect that a hundred more will be wanted here [Washington, D.C.], but, my patron has failed to pay my workmen, for want of cash, and the probability is that I shall not be able to finish it." The house was two-thirds done, and Porter ends this part of the letter by offering to send it to Markoe, who lived in St. Paul, Minnesota, for one hundred dollars.

He then goes on with "An Extraordinary Statement" which he had prepared to present "to the Head of Departments, and perhaps the President" to describe his career as an inventor—"having done more to achieve the progress of useful improvement in the United States, than any other man living."

THE ROTARY PLOUGH.

Fig. 14. Porter's "Rotary Plough," presented in *American Mechanic*, April 21, 1842.

Fig. 15. Porter's "Field Engine," presented in *Scientific American*, August 6, 1846.

THE FIELD ENGINE;
A MACHINE FOR HARROWING, SOWING AND ROLLING AT THE SAME TIME

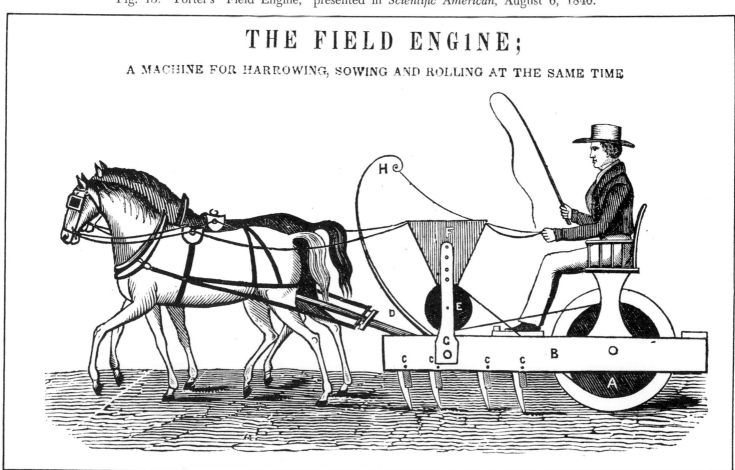

Fig. 16. Porter's "Car for Removing Houses," presented in *American Mechanic*, May 28, 1842.

Fig. 17. Porter's "Portable Horse Power," presented in *New York Mechanic*, February 6, 1841.

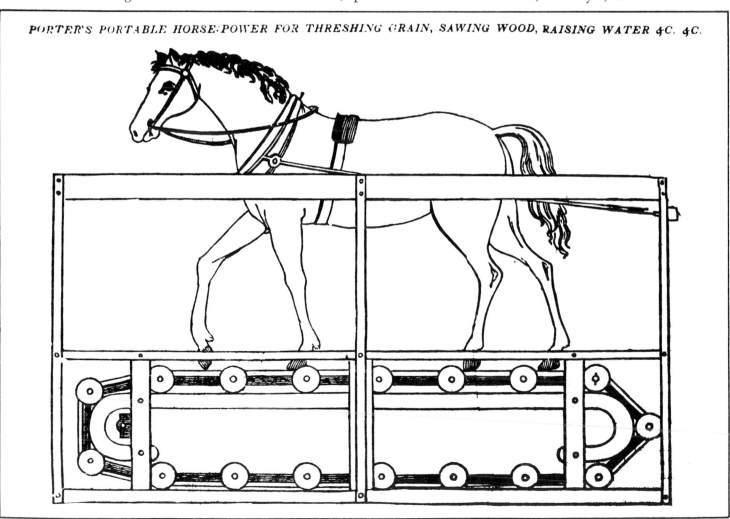

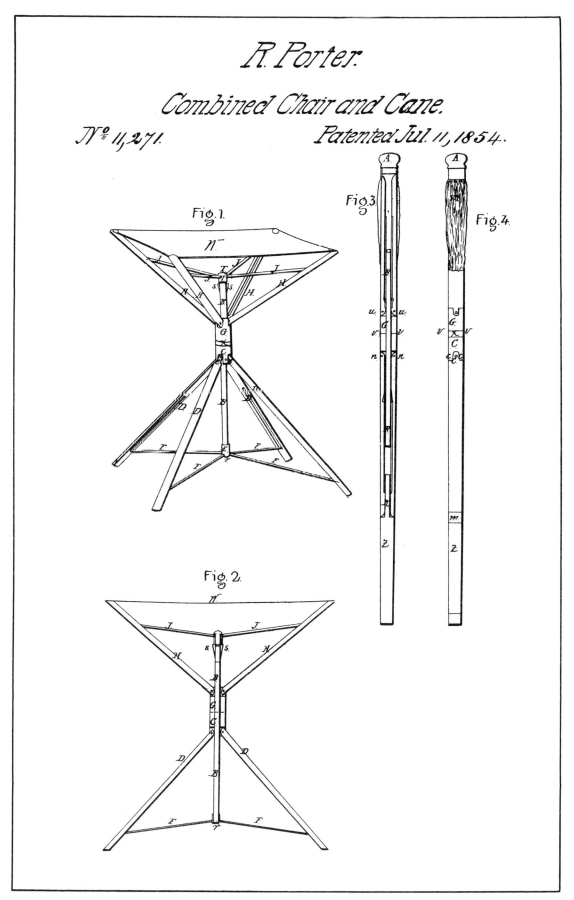

Fig. 18.   Porter's "Combined Chair and Cane," patented July 11, 1854.

Fig. 19. Porter's "Horse Power Boat," presented in *American Mechanic*, September 24, 1842.

Fig. 20 Porter's "Steam-Carriage for Common Roads," presented in *Scientific American*, October 2, 1845, was to cost $500, weigh 600 pounds, speed 10 m.p.h.

LIBERAL AND INTERESTING PROPOSITION.

There is no subject of mechanical improvement so much in demand, and so much enquired for, as a machine that will perform common farm work by steam power—such a machine would enhance the value of lands, and reduce the price of produce throughout the United States. With this view the writer has invented a very perfect machine, which embraces a combination of five different patentable inventions, and is denominated the STEAM FARMER. It will ascend or descend hills with safety and facility, and will plow, harrow, sow, reap, rake, mow, cart hay, thresh grain, shell corn, saw wood, make fence or go to market. The entire weight of the machine is only 800 pounds, and its cost, less than $500; and the expense of working it only 15 cents per day, for each horse-power.

This machine has been constructed and put in successful operation some years since, but the inventor having subsequently discovered several excellent improvements, has abandoned the original machine, and now proposes to construct a new one, with the various improvements in combination.

It had become obvious to the inventor, (as perhaps, to all scientific engineers) that the main difficulty in the way of working steam carriages on farms, or on common roads, consisted in the excessive weight of the cylindrical boiler: he therefore invented a tubular boiler that produces more than four times as much power, in proportion to its weight, as any other boiler in use; and will sustain fifteen times as much steam pressure, as is required in ordinary service. This boiler has been thoroughly tested by severe actual service, under various circumstances.

The original and peculiar points of excellence in this machine, are

1st. The boiler produces four times as much power in proportion to its weight, as any other kind, and is perfectly safe with regard to explosion.

2d. The boiler is furnished with a self-regulating pump, that will invariably supply the boiler with the water required, without any attention from the engineer, whether the engine is in motion or at rest.

3d. The machine is furnished with an equalizing device, whereby the power of the engines is applied equally to both driving wheels, whether running in straight lines or in curves.

4th. It has also, an arbitrary speed-changer, by means of which, either the speed or the force may be varied as occasion may require; so that, with a two-horse power engine, the machine will draw a load equal to the draught of four, or even eight horses.

5th. The entire machine is so light and manageable as to run rapidly on common roads, or work freely on every soil on which horses can travel.

The drawings and illustrations of this extraordinary invention have been attentively examined and investigated by many of the first practical engineers in Washington and Baltimore, not one of whom has discovered anything objectionable, but most of them have highly commended its excellent devices and arrangements, which are in advance of anything of the kind hitherto projected. And it is freely admitted by the most intelligent, that if the machine will operate as represented, (and being constructed upon well known and established principles, there appears no grounds for doubt or uncertainty) the patent right will be worth at least $1,000,000; and in view of the fact that Woodworth's Patent Planing Machine, though embracing very little science, produced upwards of $5,000,000 to its proprietors,—this will admit of a much higher estimate.

Now the inventor, having expended at least $1,000 in bringing this invention to its present perfection, and being anxious to bring the machines into immediate and general use, proposes to put one half of the exclusive right of the invention into the form of stock, to consist of 100 shares of $1,000 each, (one-fifth of the estimated value) and on the condition that only five per cent. shall be paid when twenty shares shall have been taken, (for it is not the intention of the inventor to sell any more shares than sufficient to enable him to construct one first rate machine, and establish the manufacture of them) and the balance of the price to be paid from the next proceeds of the invention, after the share-holders shall have received $500 per share: (or if preferred, the share-holders may receive $1000 per share from the first proceeds, on condition that they will then relinquish their titles). Each share-holder will be furnished with a full title deed, neatly printed and duly executed, and which will entitle him to draw a proportionate share of the proceeds monthly. The money is to be paid to Messrs. W. F. Ellis & Brother, (responsible and scientific engineers of Washington,) who will act as agents for the stock-holders, and superintend the construction and introduction of the said machines, and distribute the proceeds to share-holders as above stipulated.

RUFUS PORTER.

We, the undersigned, believing that the prosperity of the United States would be advanced by the introduction of efficient machinery, for the cultivation of land by steam power, hereby agree to take the number of shares affixed to our respective names, in R. Porter's Steam Farmer, on the terms and conditions above specified.

NAMES.	RESIDENCE.	NO. OF SHARES.

Fig. 21. Porter's "Liberal and Interesting Proposition" was circulated c. 1857 for prospective shareholders in his "Steam Farmer." *Minnesota Historical Society, St. Paul.*

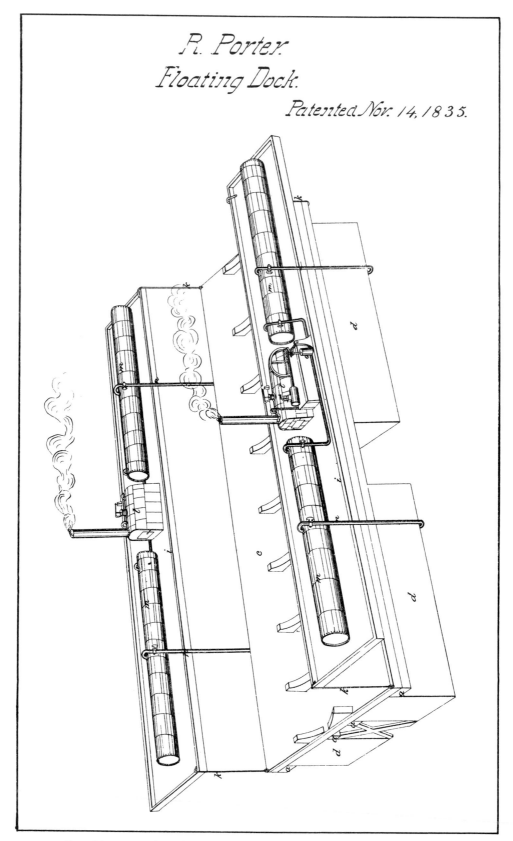

R. Porter.
Floating Dock.
Patented Nov. 14, 1835.

Fig. 22. Porter's "Floating Dock," patented November 14, 1835.

Rufus Porter seems never to have lost confidence in his inventions; he regarded as temporary their failure to achieve recognition.

He originated mechanisms of various sorts all his life and patented several dozens of them. He is described by a native of West Boxford as having had a passion for inventing anything newfangled, from a washing machine to a flying machine. In his first journal, the *New York Mechanic*, he advertised as an inventor and promotor, and in his *Scientific Mechanic* it was mentioned that he had "introduced upwards of one hundred new mechanical inventions." These ranged from a pocket lamp, trunk lock, vise and wire cutter, to a floating dock, a vehicle for traveling on ice, bullet engine, automobile, elevated railroad and airship (see Figs. 20–25 and 30).

His son Frank Rufus Porter, in a letter written in 1940 to the *Scientific American*, talks about the Colt revolver (see Fig. 26): "Then there was the six hole revolving cilinder or barell which preceded the revolving cilinder of Colt's revolver that idear was sold to Colt before it was patented."

Porter was considered an important inventor in his time, and had he not so inadequately promoted his innovations and so casually disposed of them he would surely have gone down in history as one of the greatest American inventors. Instead, he became a kind of mechanical Johnny Appleseed, sowing the seeds of new and ingenious ideas as he traveled his way through New England and scattering them abroad through his journals.

A number of Porter's most important inventions were introduced by a newspaper diagram followed by a detailed explanatory caption and promotion or purchase offer. The announcement of the "Hot Air Ventilation System" in the *New York Mechanic* ends with the statement that "the plan is entirely original, and promises immense advantage, which the Inventor is disposed to share with any person who will aid him in introducing the invention to general use." Appended to the cut and explanation of the "Fog Bell Boat," also in the *New York Mechanic*, is the statement that "the author, being deeply engaged in other business, liberally offers a joint interest in the invention to any person who will take charge of introducing it." Many of Porter's inventions were patented, but selling them outright seems to have presented problems. A few of these devices seem quite fantastic today—the "New Method of Rowing Boats" and the "Life Preserver" (Figs. 27, 28) look like Rube Goldberg cartoons—but more of them have come to be of basic importance. When one realizes that among Porter's inventions were a washing machine, revolving rifle, rotary plow, trip hammer, ice-making machine, municipal fire alarm system, chain-stitch sewing machine, revolving almanac (Fig. 29) and many others in common use today, it becomes evident that regardless of who bought and promoted them Porter must rank as one of our foremost inventors.

Rufus Porter, according to his son Frank, was "very improvident" but his "prolific brain or inventive mind" always managed to save the day. In one of Frank Porter's vivid, illiterate letters (which he wrote over a period of

THE BULLET ENGINE.

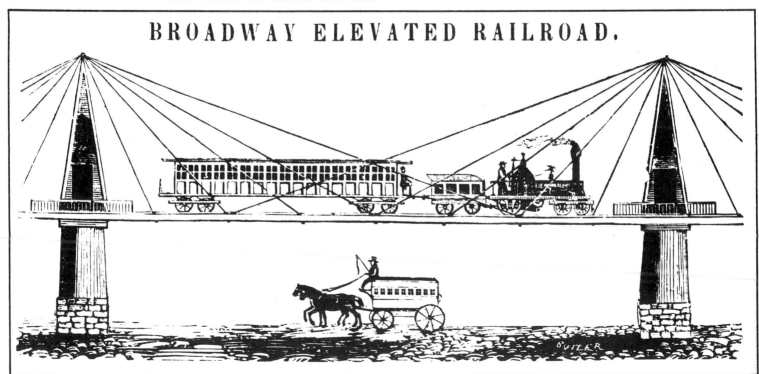

Fig. 23. Porter's "Bullet Engine," presented in *Scientific American*, August 6, 1846. (Note military uniforms.)

Fig. 24. A Porter vehicle planned for the skating season, as seen in *Scientific American*, March 6, 1847.

Fig. 25. Porter's "Broadway Elevated Railroad" was proposed in the January 1, 1846 issue of *Scientific American*, two decades before the first El was built.

Travelling on Ice.

SKATES have been in use a long time, and may still be found in abundance, of elegant paterns and finish, at most of our hardware shops; but we think they may be in some measure superseded by an invention more in accordance with modern modes of locomotion, and requiring less skill in its management.

BROADWAY ELEVATED RAILROAD.

Fig. 26. A lithograph of the Colt Arms Manufactory as it looked about 1855. In 1844 Porter sold Colonel Colt his invention for a revolving rifle, the antecedent of the famous Colt revolver. *Library of Congress, Washington, D.C.*

Fig. 27. Porter's "New Method of Rowing Boats," presented in *American Mechanic,* June 11, 1842.

Fig. 28. Porter's "Life Preserver," patented May 25, 1840.

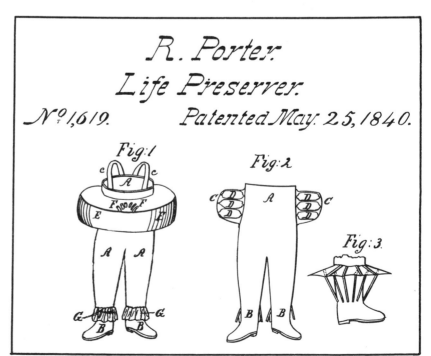

Fig. 29. Porter's "Revolving Almanack," which he invented and sold in Billerica, Massachusetts, in 1822. *Old Sturbridge Village, Sturbridge, Mass.*

years to the editorial department of the *Scientific American*) he writes, in a fashion reminiscent of a Victorian melodrama:

Allow me to recall one outstanding incident of this nature in the winter of 1872 he was living at Plantsville Conn. the weather for a week had been hovering around the zero mark yes! bleak and cold the cubboard was bare the rent was due no old time acquaintance to borrow even two bits from for Rufus Porter seldom in his latter days stopped over a year in the Town well when he was apprized of the situation he stopped his writing which proved to be of a religious nature set up straight drummed his feet turned his thoughts from theory to facts. Yes! he surveyed what was practically the last hod of coal in the house then he jumped up pulled on his over coat and went down into the bascment there with his hammer and saws, chisells and saws he soon shaped out the cam lever vice he worked on that model until 11 P.M. that night the following P.M. he was ready with his model he stepped over to Plants foundry and machine shop, within 4 hours he returned with a lot of crispy green backs, he had sold his ide for he was a salesman.

The most dramatic story of Rufus Porter's career as an inventor is that of his "aeroport." In 1820, traveling on foot as an itinerant portrait painter, Porter first thought of the practical aspects of flying; he claimed to have invented the main details of his revolutionary airship in that year. Many years later he recalled that the inspiration for his steam-powered dirigible, a forerunner of the modern dirigible balloon, was the possibility of liberating Napoleon from the prison island of St. Helena. Rufus Porter was actually the first man in the world to plan and try out the possibilities of a power-driven airship. The *Encyclopedia Americana* shows the "first" proposed "aerial carriage" of 1843; Porter published his plans in 1834. Also shown is the "first" power-driven model of 1848; Porter's model was flown in 1847. The tale of Porter and his airship makes strikingly apparent that nineteenth-century combination of optimism, vision and practical ingenuity that created our twentieth century. It illustrates what Roger Burlingame so well describes in *March of the Iron Men* as the peculiarly American imagination that could jump details into a vision beyond the horizon—and could so clearly and factually create that vision as to make it take shape as eventual reality.

In 1834, when Rufus Porter published and illustrated in the November 8 American edition of *Mechanics' Magazine*—an English periodical which was the prototype for Porter's scientific newspapers—the first specifications for his "Travelling Balloon, or Flying Machine," his plan of the machine was based on a spindle-shaped vessel three hundred and fifty feet long and thirty-five feet in diameter containing hydrogen gas to sustain it in the air. There would be on board an apparatus for the production of gas to keep the balloon constantly inflated. A propeller driven by a steam engine, with charcoal as fuel, would make it possible to carry one hundred passengers with their baggage and provisions at a speed of at least fifty miles per hour. The passengers would occupy a saloon suspended directly under the balloon by cords or wires. A combination vertical and horizontal rudder with ball-and-socket control would enable the machine to move in any direction as well as to easily ascend or descend. Provisions for safety would include the construction of the saloon with cylinders of air of sufficient buoyancy to support it and the passengers if it should be forced to descend on the water. Each passenger, moreover, would be furnished with a parachute. The expense of the materials was estimated at less than three thousand dollars; the engine, two thousand dollars; construction costs, five thousand dollars; the total of ten thousand dollars being less than the cost of an ordinary ferry boat. "Such," concludes Porter, "is my plan for flying."

This plan was again published in the forties in Porter's *New York Mechanic* and *Scientific American*. The specifications and the illustrative cut are substantially the same, with only slight differences in the details of construction and some variations in cost estimates. In these articles Porter enlarges on the practicability and safety of traveling by air, and assures his prospective airborne passengers that in case of accident they would land safely by parachute and that even the baggage "would all come to land in due time." The most important change is an estimated possible velocity of one hundred instead of fifty miles per hour.

The gold fever of '49 made New England intensely speed conscious and accelerated the use of high-speed clipper ships. The gold diggers had been traveling by the overland trail in mule wagons, by the Panama route which crossed the Isthmus, or by sailing around the Horn to San Francisco. It took more than five months for either the land or sea voyage. The clipper ships were expected to make the voyage in three. Rufus Porter, unimpressed with the goal of a mere three months to the West Coast, promptly wrote a sixteen-page booklet designed for the gold-seeking forty-niners describing the practical possibilities of his airship for a cross-country trip from New York to California in three days!

This was *Aerial Navigation*, published in 1849 by H. Smith, New York (Fig. 30). The subtitle gives the gist of its content: "The practicability of traveling pleasantly and safely from New–York to California in three days, fully demonstrated: with a full description of a perfect aerial locomotive, with estimates of capacity, speed, and cost of construction." On the back cover is an engraving of the airship with a caption reading "Best Route to California." Under the cut is the announcement that "R. Porter & Co., . . . are making active progress in the construction of an Aerial Transport, for the express purpose of carrying passengers between New York and California." Fifty to one hundred passengers were to be carried at a speed of sixty to one hundred miles per hour. The machine was to be in operation about the first of April 1849, and the Company proposed to carry a limited number of passengers for fifty dollars including board. The transport was expected to make a trip to the gold region and back in seven days. More than two hundred passage tickets had been engaged and the books were still open to subscribers, up to three hundred reservations. All this is detailed in brisk (close to Madison Avenue) style in promoter Porter's back-cover advertisement. In the body of the book Rufus Porter, scientist, details specifications and plans. In the conclusion the imaginative itinerant visualizes a delightful jaunt from New York to the scenic Connecticut River Valley and then back to New York to dine, or a low-flying sightseeing cruise above the Rocky Mountains. "We have discovered no apparent difficulty," he says, "in passing over the Atlantic to London or Paris." He concludes the practical specifications and visionary plans for his "aerial locomotive" with a dramatic prophecy: "These things are indeed but fancies at present, but in a few months these fancies may become pleasant realities in America, while the proud nations of Europe are staring and wondering at the soaring enterprise of the independent citizens of the United States." Porter's little book describing the possibility of a trip from New York to California in three days to search for gold carried to an early extreme the Horatio Alger attitude of the time. Nothing was impossible, opportunity was infinite, and in this new America it would be easy indeed to reach the end of the rainbow.

Only three copies of *Aerial Navigation*, one of the most remarkable Americana items in existence, are known to have survived. One is in the library at Yale University, one at Harvard and one in the Minnesota Historical Society. The book was, however, reprinted privately in an edition of two hundred in San Francisco in 1935. Commander H. V. Wiley comments in the introduction on the many things forecast by Porter that have been incorporated in a modern airship, and on the safety of commercial airships as a means of transportation, which is so vividly pictured in the book. In the San Francisco edition, Lawton Kennedy, its printer, describes *Aerial Navigation* as "Porter's triumphant essay in advertising." He concludes by saying: "While I deplore the great man's failure to accomplish his purpose, now that the realm he aspired to conquer is traversed daily by ships he hoped would be actualities in his lifetime, I feel that with his then-chimerical scheme today a fact, this little book may serve as a tribute to his colossal and fertile imagination."

Thomas Lask, in reviewing the 1968 edition of *Rufus Porter: Yankee Pioneer* for the *New York Times*, mentioned that Porter's announced intention, as published on the back cover of *Aerial Navigation*, "to carry a limited number of passengers—not exceeding 300—for $50 including board," quite accurately anticipated the twentieth century. The fully booked flights with inflight meals is interesting, and updating the fifty dollars' cost to 1980 would arrive at a quite appropriate fare for the trip from New York to California.

A twelve-page booklet titled *An Aerial Steamer, or Flying Ship*, published in Washington, D.C., in 1850 (Fig. 31), was a sequel to *Aerial Navigation;* it's aim was, again, to explain and promote Porter's flying machine. "The only circumstances which has [sic] hitherto prevented this invention from successful operation," states the inventor, "has been the want

BEST ROUTE TO CALIFORNIA.

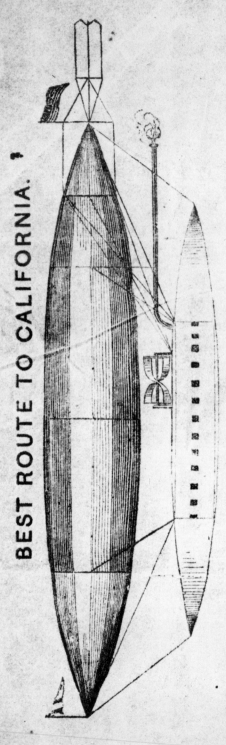

R. PORTER & CO., (office, room No. 40 in the Sun Buildings,—entrance 128 Fulton-street, New-York,) are making active progress in the construction of an Aerial Transport, for the express purpose of carrying passengers between NewYork and California. This transport will have a capacity to carry from 50 to 100 passengers, at a speed of 60 to 100 miles per hour. It is expected to put this machine in operation about the 1st of April, 1849. It is proposed to carry a limited number of passengers—not exceeding 300—for $50, including board. and the transport is expected to make a trip to the gold region and back in seven days. The price of passage to California is fixed at $200, with the exception above mentioned. Upwards of 200 passage tickets at $50 each have been engaged prior to Feb. 15. Books open for subscribers as above.

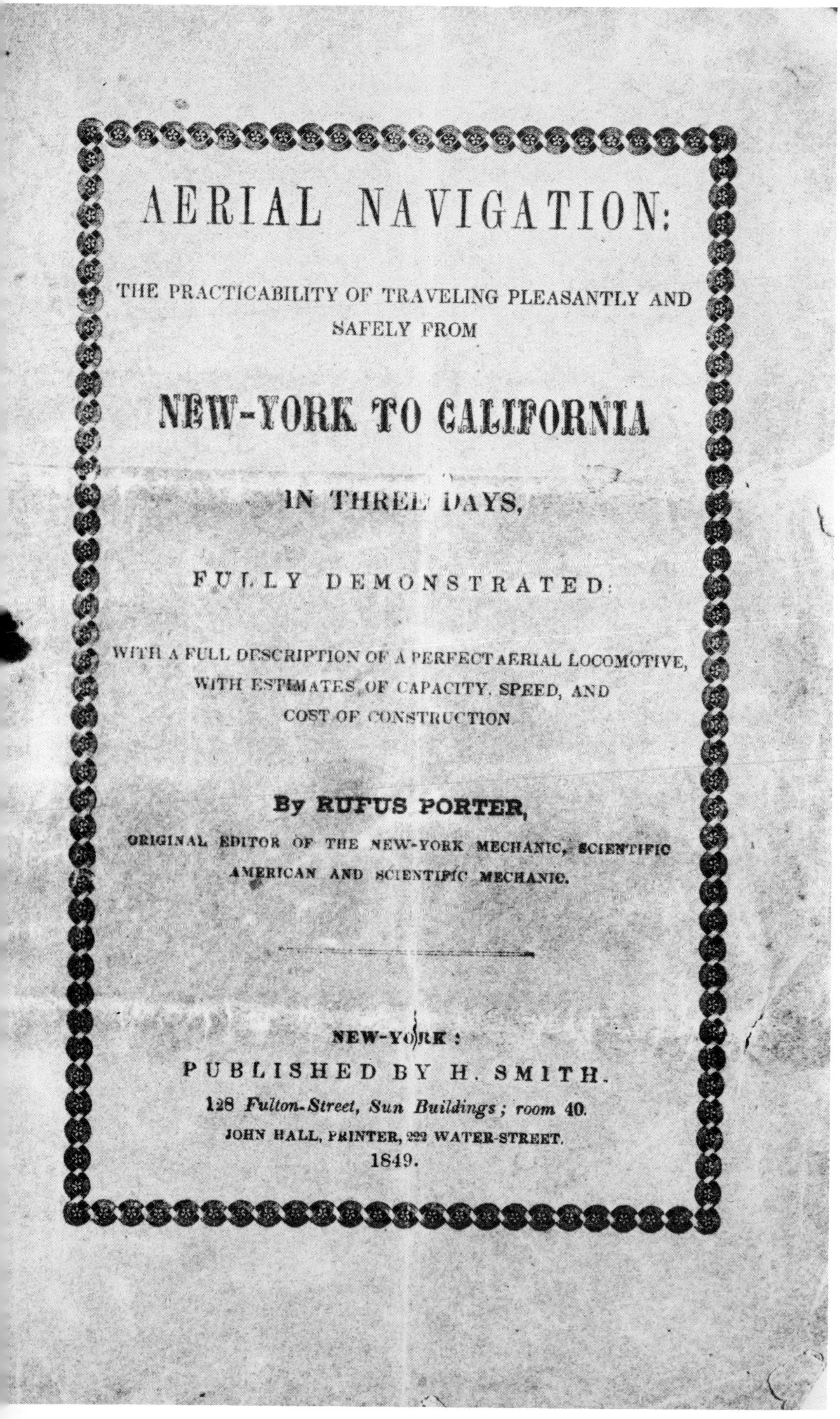

AERIAL NAVIGATION:

THE PRACTICABILITY OF TRAVELING PLEASANTLY AND

SAFELY FROM

NEW-YORK TO CALIFORNIA

IN THREE DAYS,

FULLY DEMONSTRATED:

WITH A FULL DESCRIPTION OF A PERFECT AERIAL LOCOMOTIVE,
WITH ESTIMATES OF CAPACITY, SPEED, AND
COST OF CONSTRUCTION

By RUFUS PORTER,

ORIGINAL EDITOR OF THE NEW-YORK MECHANIC, SCIENTIFIC
AMERICAN AND SCIENTIFIC MECHANIC.

NEW-YORK:

PUBLISHED BY H. SMITH.

128 Fulton-Street, Sun Buildings; room 40.

JOHN HALL, PRINTER, 222 WATER-STREET.

1849.

Fig. 30. Back and front covers of Porter's *Aerial Navigation,* published in 1849. The book was timed for the Gold Rush, presenting the possibility for a New York to California trip in three days; the clipper ships were aiming at covering the distance in three months. *Minnesota Historical Society, St. Paul.*

of the requisite funds." Appended to the last page are brief excerpts from newspaper accounts to "show that Mr. Porter's experiments on a small scale, have been successful."

Porter had constructed his first model in 1833. By 1841 he had built a machine-driven model which he described in his *New York Mechanic* as a measure "to secure the right of priority in this invention." In 1847 and 1849 he exhibited a small working model in New York, in 1850 a larger and improved model in Boston and New York, and in 1853 he demonstrated a twenty-two-foot model in Washington. Professor Porter, as he was now known, was a clever showman, and the large model displayed in Washington was evidently eye-catching as well as scientifically constructed. The airship, according to a later description in the *Scientific American* (November 20, 1869), was furnished with flags and gaily painted, and gazing out of the row of open windows on each side of the saloon were many happy-looking passengers.

A few contemporary editorial comments on Porter's models record both skepticism and enthusiasm as to the possibilities of practical aviation. Ironically, it was the early editors of the journal Porter originated, the *Scientific American,* who were most caustic in their remarks. In the issue for March 3, 1849, they state: "Just think of it—to see a vessel 800 ft. long flying thro' the firmament to California, or to England. . . . We wish [the inventor] all success. We intend to put down our name for the *second* trip." The *Scientific American* for January 15, 1853, advises Porter to take his first trip to Paris where Napoleon III might make him *Président du Département de Grand Ballon* out of gratitude for his having thought of rescuing Napoleon from St. Helena by means of a dirigible balloon. In the issue for May 28, 1853, an editor speaks of Professor Porter's lectures on the aeroport being "as clear as *mud*" and the project of the Aerial Navigation Company "so grand and vast, it is enough to make Mount Vesuvius burst out in fiery laughter." The *Scientific American* also quoted other newspaper statements about the invention. *The Philadelphia Bulletin:* "Though every man of sense is, or ought to be aware of the impossibility of steering a balloon, or any other aerial machine, yet it seems there has been found, in New York, a fellow who was knave or fool enough to advertise, for exhibition, a Flying Machine. . . . We have heard of nothing more ridiculous since a theater was once filled to see a man get into a pewter pot." The *Boston Bee:* "Mr. Porter's 'flying machine' did all it promised on Wednesday evening [at Temple Hall]. It rose above the audience and went around the hall, exactly as he said it would, and the spectators gave three cheers for the successful experiment." The *New York Sun:* "The aerial steamer model was again tried at the Merchant's Exchange yesterday afternoon, and with brilliant success. It described the circle of the rotunda eleven times in succession, following its rudder like a thing instinct with life." The *Washington Evening Star* comments on the performance at Carusi's saloon in 1853: "Never before the introduction of Mr. Porter's model aeroport has anything appeared upon which creeping humanity could base a rational anticipation of the long desired art of flying."

Porter's constant stumbling block was the practical promotion of his invention. As early as 1834 he had offered through *Mechanics' Magazine* half of his patent claims to "any person or company who will be at the expense of building such a balloon on a scale sufficient to test its ability." In an 1841 issue of the *New York Mechanic* he says that he will be satisfied with 10 percent of the profits if anyone will promote his invention.

In 1851, after having tested the main principles of his invention on a small scale in New York and Boston, Rufus Porter petitioned the Senate for an appropriation to be made to enable him to demonstrate to the world the practicability of his airship. His petition to the Senate states that for twenty years he has devoted much of his time to the subject of aerial locomotion, has constructed several models which have successfully demonstrated the workability of his aeroport, and has frequently explained the machine at public gatherings to the entire satisfaction of all present. He expresses great confidence as to the practicability of aerial navigation and points out that to make possible rapid travel across the country and transportation of the mails the invention should be worthy of national encouragement. He ends by praying that an appropriation of five thousand dollars be made "to enable him to extend his experiments, and apply his invention on a scale of practical utility." The sad end of this attempt was that the matter was referred to the Committee on Commerce, from thence to the Committee on Naval Affairs, and that was the last heard of the petition.

The following year, in 1852, Porter took the matter of financial support into his own hands by forming the "Aerial Navigation Company" which issued stock (Fig. 32) at five dollars a share. The prospectus for the venture, published in the *National Intelligencer* for March 20, 1852, describes "A chance to secure a cash income of $10 to $20 per week for twenty years by the investment of five dollars in advance." Here the practicability of aerial navigation is again stressed, with specifications for a large "Pioneer" aeroport to carry 150 passengers at a speed of ninety miles per hour, with total cost of construction fifteen thousand dollars and running expenses under twenty-five dollars a day. Simultaneous with the launching of the Aerial Navigation Company Porter started a newspaper called the *Aerial Reporter* which was published biweekly in Washington in 1852 and 1853. This journal discussed various aspects of aeronautics and reported to the shareholders on the sale of shares and the progress of the aeroport.

After about six hundred shares were taken the aeroport was finally begun in Washington in 1852. Countless disasters, however, interfered with its successful completion. A severe storm damaged the framework when it was almost finished, vandals slashed the balloon, the varnish used caused disintegration of the canvas, and the funds available proved inadequate to the needs. (This and the following accounts of the aeroport were relayed from the *Aerial Reporter* to the New York public via the *Scientific American*

Fig. 31. Cover of Porter's *An Aerial Steamer,* published in 1850. *Minnesota Historical Society, St. Paul.*

Fig. 32. Porter's Aerial Navigation Company was organized and issued stock in 1852 (No. 779) to promote his airship. *Smithsonian Institution, Washington, D.C.*

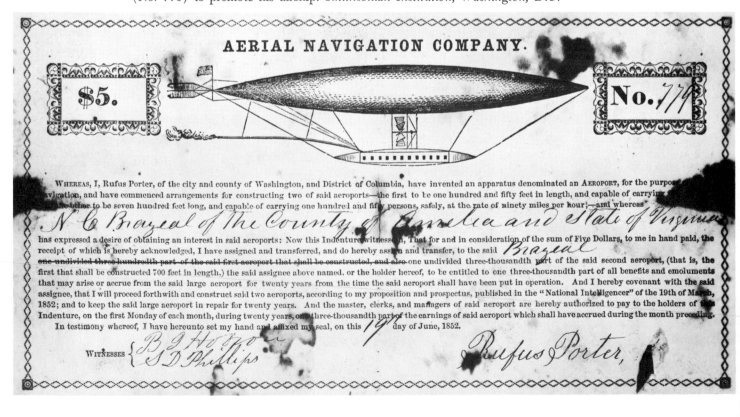

in 1852–1853. As only one issue of the *Reporter* has been found, such excerpts are especially valuable.) In one issue of the *Aerial Reporter* the inventor entered among expense items twenty-one dollars due him for his personal services for twelve days. The budget was evidently slim! But Porter's Yankee optimism and tenacity did not waver, and he continued work on the aeroport. He lamented the want of funds but prophesied in the *Reporter* that "this important invention is destined to succeed eventually and constitute the principal and general instrument of transportation of merchandise, as well as mails and passengers, throughout the world." (This was the concluding sentence in Porter's *Aerial Steamer.*) In 1869 the *Scientific American* announced that Mr. Porter thought "there would be no difficulty in constructing an aeroport capable of carrying 500 passengers safely to any part of Europe, in three days or less," and that he intended to complete a passenger aeroport as soon as he could command the requisite funds. Porter was then seventy-seven years old, and had been planning and working on his aeroport for just half a century. Although the full-scale model was never launched, this half-century of experimental effort the inventor put into it played a significant, though now almost forgotten, part in the history of aerial navigation.

In 1911 A. F. Zahm stated in his book entitled, like Porter's, *Aerial Navigation* that until after the middle of the nineteenth century there was no substantial advance in aeronautics—as no one had conceived of a practical motor balloon with a light engine—with one notable exception: "the invention of Porter in America." Zahm comments on the modernity of Porter's design and says that "it might well be copied now by a promotor of that identical project." Zahm remarks that at this time (1911) the most successful European experiments have not yet attained half the speed contemplated by that "ambitious and chimerical Yankee." It is only within the present generation that Porter's plans for practical air travel and transportation are being achieved, and his vision of carrying five hundred passengers to Europe is still to be realized. (Lockheed's design for a three-hundred-passenger airbus was published in 1967.) A. J. Philpott, in an article on Porter's airship published in the *Boston Globe* for September 20, 1936, states unequivocally that Rufus Porter "knew more about aerial dynamics than any other man of his time." We may well end the story of Porter's aeroport with a small item printed in the *New York Sun* for December 7, 1913:

Perhaps you don't know who Rufus Porter was, and if that be the case, you, as a patriotic American, will be interested in learning that he has some right to be described as the father of the dirigible airship. It is not necessary to emphasize that he was of the genus Yankee, for his imaginative powers stamped him with that hallmark.

Rufus Porter, born in the eighteenth century in Washington's presidency, contributed a great deal to the art and journalism of the nineteenth, and he did as much as any single American to create our modern machine age. It seems extraordinary that the lives of two Porters, Rufus and his son Frank, spanned one hundred and fifty years of our country's history from 1792 to 1942. Picture Rufus Porter in 1800 listening at church in West Boxford to an oration commemorating the first anniversary of Washington's death, and writing for the *Scientific American* from Washington during Polk's presidency in 1847 that "the progress of mechanical improvements has never been more rapid in this country than at present"; while in 1938 his son Frank Rufus Porter comments on Roosevelt's New Deal in a letter to the *Scientific American* and complains that "things are getting pretty badly messed up with their new labor saving contraptions."

Frank Rufus Porter (1859–1942) was born in his father's sixty-eighth year and was in a sense a twentieth-century projection of his father's life and work and ideas. Frank, who signed himself "F. Rufus Porter," was extremely proud of his father, was fundamentally much like him and was obviously influenced by him. Like Rufus Porter he had little formal education but was bursting with vigorous and original ideas, and his career as a sign painter, artist and amateur scientist is right in the Porter tradition. Judging from his letters he was, though quite illiterate, very much of a philosopher, and in his comments on some of the articles in twentieth-century volumes of the *Scientific American* we have a significant sequel to Rufus Porter's pioneer experiments.

An article printed in a 1939 issue on visualizing "hyperspace" drew from F. Rufus Porter a concrete plan for making the fourth dimension simply understandable. This plan, confidently presented in the Rufus Porter style for describing innovations, solves the problem of the fourth dimension through a simple experiment in which a mule's head is immersed in water contained in a three-foot-square strong-box and then withdrawn to create a vacuum! Porter ends his exposition by remarking, without punctuation but with a good deal of punch, that in discussing the fourth dimension "we will have nothing to go by until we establish a zone of our own for our private use something with a limit say a trillion mile radius of the center of the earth then we could go ahead with our dimention [sic] stuff and know just what we are talking about, we have no business calling on space or time to help settle our little problems."

A remark by Walter B. Chrysler quoted in the *Scientific American* regarding the need for superior men and machines provoked this comment: "Let the Machines come on but make them our dumb servants not masters. plenty of thinking to be done right here and now and we had better start today. Yes! we need the super man all right but get him in the right place. . . ."

Journalist
and Pamphleteer

RUFUS PORTER'S JOURNALS dealt with all the areas in which he worked and thought. As there was no major interest of nineteenth-century America with which he failed to concern himself, his articles provide a valuable cross section of the ideas and trends of his times. Porter's theories on art and his how-to-do-it instruction (as they appeared in these journals) are of primary interest and will be considered in following chapters. The journals also give us a broad view of the literature, religion, science and invention, politics and current events of Porter's day. Most important, we clearly sense, as we skim through these periodicals, the spirit of the American people in the mid-nineteenth century. During this period we see Rufus Porter as an inventor and journalist, contributing to and critically commenting on the evolution of the great political experiment. In his journals we see a functioning democracy in terms of broad communication by the press, telegraph and railroad, of large-scale production of goods, of free religious discussion. We are aware of the new tempo of life, the optimism, the exhilarating sense of great opportunity. This spirit of the time—so different from both the stolidity of the eighteenth century and the nervous pessimism of the twentieth—is captured in a poem which Rufus Porter published in the April 9, 1849, issue of the *Scientific American*. The first two stanzas are almost martial in their clarion call to action:

> Men of thought! be up and stirring
>   Night and day;
> Sow the seed—withdraw the curtain,
>   Clear the way!
> Men of action, aid and cheer them,
>   As ye may.

There's a fount about to stream,
There's a light about to beam,
There's a warmth about to glow,
There's a flower about to blow;
There's a midnight blackness changing
            Into gray.
Men of thought, and men of action,
            Clear the way!

Once the welcome light has broken,
            Who shall say,
What the unimagined glories
            Of the day:
What the evil that shall perish
            In its ray!
Aid the dawning, tongue and pen;
Aid it, hopes of honest men;
Aid it, paper—aid it type—
Aid it, for the hour is ripe,
And our earnest must not slacken
            Into play.
Men of thought, and men of action!
            Clear the way!

This editorial poem calls on paper and type to "clear the way" for the future. Porter's scientific journals were planned to do just this. The press was becoming an important factor toward the middle of the century, and Porter's New York newspapers were among the pioneers of American journalism. New York was not a center of intellectual life and aristocratic culture such as Philadelphia and Boston, but as a commercial port it attracted enterprising young men ambitious to rise in the world of affairs. In becoming America's economic and financial capital, its press became the focus of progressive thinking. William Cullen Bryant from Massachusetts was setting forth the best liberal ideas of the times in the *Evening Post*. Horace Greeley from Vermont made the *Tribune* the spokesman of the plain people—the wage earners and the farmers. Rufus Porter was one of this group of native New Englanders who migrated to New York and founded the liberal press that pointed the way to new opportunities in America, clothed with new dignity the laboring classes, and definitively replaced any remaining feudal habits of thought with those of a progressive democracy. As a journalist Porter was vehemently liberal rather than conservative, oriented toward the future rather than the past. In his articles on painting he was consistently unacademic and experimental; and in his discussions of religion, as of art and politics, he was a "freethinker" in the literal sense of the word.

The *New York Mechanic*, the first of Porter's New York journals, was a workman's weekly in which he had bought an interest in 1840. Starting with a "new series" in January 1841, it was published by Rufus Porter and M. J. Smith, and, after the first two months, by "Rufus Porter & Co." and edited by Porter. This was the first scientific newspaper in the country. Its very subtitle seems to symbolize its time: "The Advocate of Industry and

Enterprise, and Journal of Mechanical and Other Scientific Improvements" (Fig. 33). The periodical prospered but for some reason the office was moved to Boston. There Porter's interest was diverted to the trade of electroplating and he immediately sold the paper. Beginning with Volume 2, 1842, the name of the journal was changed to *American Mechanic,* and the new proprietor, J. M. Vanosdel, and S. T. Porter (Rufus' son Stephen) were now listed as publishers with Rufus Porter as editor. In an 1842 issue the editor announced his intention of "giving the pith and substance of the story in as few words as possible"—a very advanced "spot news" concept at a time when long-winded reporting was the accepted journalistic style. In the October 22, 1842, issue, the name of "S. G. Deeth, Editor and Proprietor" appeared on the masthead. The issues immediately after Porter's editorship ended were noticeably lacking in variety and vigor; and, despite Editor Deeth's announced circulation "ranging from 3000 to 4000 copies per week," a few months later publication ceased.

During the period of Porter's control we find that diagrams and descriptions are a featured item, with Porter's own inventions invariably occupying page one, top center (and this continued in the *Scientific American*). Porter also used the *New York Mechanic* as a means for publicizing the "general patent agency" which he ran in connection with the paper. He describes in glowing terms the opportunity for buying rights in "new inventions now on hand" which Rufus Porter & Co. is authorized to sell in whole or in part, and states that "we are confident that we can furnish to enterprising young men, better facilities for making money than can be found elsewhere in the United States." Another announcement calls attention to the fact that operating models of the inventions can be seen at the office of the *New York Mechanic.* The inventions offered were, without doubt, largely of Porter origin. Other features of the newspaper were Porter's columns devoted to "Curious Arts," including "Landscape Painting on Walls of Rooms," and to "Aerial Navigation" (*Curious Arts* had been published as a book in 1825, *Aerial Navigation* was to be published in 1849); articles on religion, including one on "Millerism," which was to be expanded into a series in the *Scientific American,* appeared as well as tidbits of information, poems and articles. There are interesting news items from the Sandwich Islands, in which Porter must have been especially interested since his visit there, and statistics on the trade of the Islands. Most significant for the times are the editorials on the advantages of railroads. A number of illustrated articles for young people—one, for instance, on ornamental kites—are pleasant minor features. There is a remarkable editorial titled "Rational Toys" which, in the exact spirit of the twentieth-century progressive education, advocates the promotion of playthings that will "instruct while they amuse."

Rufus Porter was working as an electroplater in New York in 1845, and that year he invested one hundred dollars in cash to start the folio journal which he called the *Scientific American.* The four-page paper was

// THE //
NEW YORK MECHANIC

THE ADVOCATE OF INDUSTRY AND ENTERPRISE, AND JOURNAL OF MECHANICAL AND OTHER SCIENTIFIC IMPROVEMENTS.

VOLUME 1—NUMBER 16,—New Series. NEW YORK, SATURDAY APRIL 17, 1841. PUBLISHED AT NO. 7 ANN STREET, N. Y.

THE NEW YORK MECHANIC

IS PUBLISHED EVERY SATURDAY MORNING, AT NO 7 ANN STREET, NEW-YORK, (*near Broadway*,) BY

RUFUS PORTER & Co.

The publishers of this paper are pledged to furnish each number with a full description of at least one new mechanical invention, with an ENGRAVING. Also, General notices of the progress of mechanical and other scientific improvements; American and Foreign Discoveries and Inventions; catalogues of American Patents; Scientific Essays, illustrations of mechanical principles; Useful information and instruction in arts and Trades, Curious Philosophical Experiments; General miscellaneous intelligence, foreign and domestic, with occasional literary notices, Poetry, Anecdotes &c &c.

TERMS.—To city Subscribers, Three Cents per copy, payable on delivery to the carriers To distant Subscribers, who receive the paper by mail, $1,50 per annum, of which, one dollar is required in advance, and the balance in eight months

Four copies will be forwarded to one address for five dollars in advance. Any person who may procure five subscribers and forward to the proprietors a current five dollar bill, will receive the sixth copy gratis.

TERMS OF ADVERTISING.—For eight lines or less 50 cts.—sixteen lines for 75cents, for the first, and half price for each subsequent insertion.

From the Knickerbocker.

The Happy Home.

I love the hearth where evening brings
Her loved ones from their daily tasks,
Where virtue spreads her spotless wings,
And vice, fell serpent, never basks;
Where sweetly ring upon the ear
The blooming daughter's gentle song,
Like heavenly music whispering near,
While thrilling hearts the notes prolong.

For there the father sits in joy,
And there the cheerful mother smiles,
And there the laughter-loving boy,
With sportive tricks, the eve beguiles;
And love, beyond what worldlings know,
Like sunlight on the purest foam,
Descends, and with its cheering glow,
Lights up the Christian's home.

Contentment spreads her holy calm
Around a resting place so bright,
And gloomy Sorrow finds a balm,
In gazing at so fair a sight;
The world's cold selfishness departs,
And Discord rears its front no more,—
There pity's pearly tear drop starts,
And Charity attends the door.

No biting scandal, fresh from hell,
Grates on the ear, or scalds the tongue;
There kind remembrance loves to dwell,
And virtue's meed is sweetly sung;
And human nature soars on high,
Where heavenly spirits love to roam,
And Vice, as stalks it rudely by,
Admires the Christian's happy home

Oft have I joined the lovely ones,
Around the bright and cheerful hearth,
With father, mother, daughters, sons,
The brightest jewels of the earth;
And while the world grew dark around,
And Fashion called her senseless throng,
I've fancied it was holy ground,
And that fair girl's a seraph's song.

And swift as circles fade away
Upon the bosom of the deep,
When pebbles, tossed by boys at play,
Disturb its still and glassy sleep,
The hours that sped in pure delight,
And wandering feet forgot to roam,
While wave and banners of the night
Above the Christian's happy home.

The rose that blooms in Sharon's vale,
And scents the purple morning's breath,
May, in the shades of evening fail,
And bend its crimson head in death;
And earth's bright ones, amid the tomb,
May, like the blushing rose, decay;
But still the mind, the mind shall bloom,
When time and nature fade away.

And there, amid a holier sphere,
Where the archangel bows in awe,
Where sits the King of glory near,
And executes his perfect law,
The ransomed of the earth, with joy,
Shall in their robes of beauty come,
And find a rest without alloy,
Amid the Christian's happy home.

From the Utica Democrat.

My Home, I'll Think of Thee.

BY F. B. AUSTIN.

I'll think of thee, my youthful home,
Yes, ever think of thee;
And when I'm singing other songs,
Oh then I'll sing of thee.
For why should not thy memory live,
And highest, holiest be,
Of all the thoughts that in me dwell,
My childhood's home, of thee.

'Twas there I first was taught to speak,
To know and meditate,
Of all I saw above, below,
And God their maker great—
'Twas there my senses first were charmed
With songs of melody,
That ever calm and soothe my mind,
Like tears of sympathy

'Twas there I heard my mother sing,
The songs of other times,
And listened while my father told
Of lands and distant climes:
And there I first was taught the ways
Of truth and holiness,
That are engraven on my mind,
As guides to usefulness.

'Twas there the happiest of my days
Were pass'd so sweetly by,
While setting 'round the cheerful hearth,
With friends of nearest tie;
But, oh! how sad the memory—
There's nothing now the same;
Time, the destroyer, hath been there,
And wraught a wondrous change.

A few short years have pass'd away,
And with them they have taken
Many of my youthful friends,
And many scenes forsaken;
Nor has my youthful home escaped—
A broken band are we;
For time and death have both been there,
Whose tracks I plainly see.

Yet, I'll think of thee, my youthful home,
Yes, ever think of thee,
And when I'm singing other songs,
Oh then I'll sing of thee.
For why should not thy memory live,
And highest, holiest be,
Of all the thoughts that in me dwell,
My childhood's home, of thee.

Utica, January, 1841.

CURIOUS ARTS.

To make a strong water proof glue.—Dissolve common glue in water in the usual way, and dip into it some clean paper, sufficient to take up an ounce or more of the glue. When the paper is nearly dry, roll it up, or cut it into strips and put them into a wide mouthed phial or flask, with about four ounces of alcohol; suspend this over a fire so as to boil it gently for an hour, having the cork set in slightly to prevent its taking fire, but not so as to prevent the vapour entirely.

Then take out the paper (the only use of which is to give the glue more [illegible] the action of the alcohol) and add one [illegible] shellac in powder; continue the heat, [illegible]ing the mixture till the shellac is dissolved. Then evaporate it to the proper consistence for use. *Note.*—Many experiments have been made, in order to discover some aqueous size, that when dry, would resist moisture: and some have recommended skimmed milk, and others vinegar, as a menstruum for the glue. But it does not appear from trial, that either of these are but very little better for this purpose than water; nor is it probable that any similar composition of size will resist moisture much better than common glue, especially if it be mixed with sulphate of lime, or some similar substance by way of support.

To render wood, cloth or paper fire-proof.—Dissolve one ounce of alum, half an ounce of subborate of soda, and half an ounce of cherry tree gum, in half a pint of vinegar. Dip any cloth or piece of paper, or wood, in this mixture, and let them dry;—they cannot afterwards be ignited so as to blaze, but may be considered safe with regard to their taking fire by accident. *Note.*—Though this composition is a very powerful preventive against fire, it is too complex for common use, and has too much colour for white cloths or papers; but a solution of one ounce of sub-borate of soda in a pint of water is very transparent and harmless, and will answer in most cases nearly as well.

To make good brilliant carmine.—To eight gallons of water add one lb. of pulverized cochineal and half an ounce of salt of tartar: boil them half an hour, and then add half an ounce of alum. Let this settle, and pour off the clear, which boil again with a little isinglass glue. Stir with a wooden spatula. When the colour is precipitated, pour off the water, and dry the precipitate, which is carmine.

Remarkable Chain of Events.—It is justly mentioned in the Washington correspondence of one of our contemporaries, that the several gradations by which Mr. TYLER, the new President of the United States has reached his present exalted station, are among the most remarkable that have ever distinguished the progressive elevation of any public man. He has for the third time stepped into a high public trust by the death of the incumbent. He was made Governor of Virginia by the death of his predecessor, he being Vice Governor; he was made Senator by the death of one before his time expired; and now he becomes President by the death of one to whom he was Vice President. If the hand of Providence is in all things, it is assuredly in this, and inscrutable as its designs appear, they are doubtless those of beneficence and wisdom.

Aluminous Salts.—We find in the last number of Silliman's Journal, an illustration of the preservative properties of aluminous salts—properties which have long been known, and were not unfrequently resorted to by the ancients. That distinguished officer, General Wayne, died thirty or forty years ago, at Erie, (Pa.) and was buried in the vicinity of the lake. The body was not long since disinterred, and removed by his son, who was astonished to find it in so perfect a state of preservation; and on examination, it was discovered to have been deposited in argillaneous soil strongly impregnated with a solution of alum. The features were at once recognised by those who had known General Wayne.—*Mer. Journal.*

PNEUMATIC LAMP.

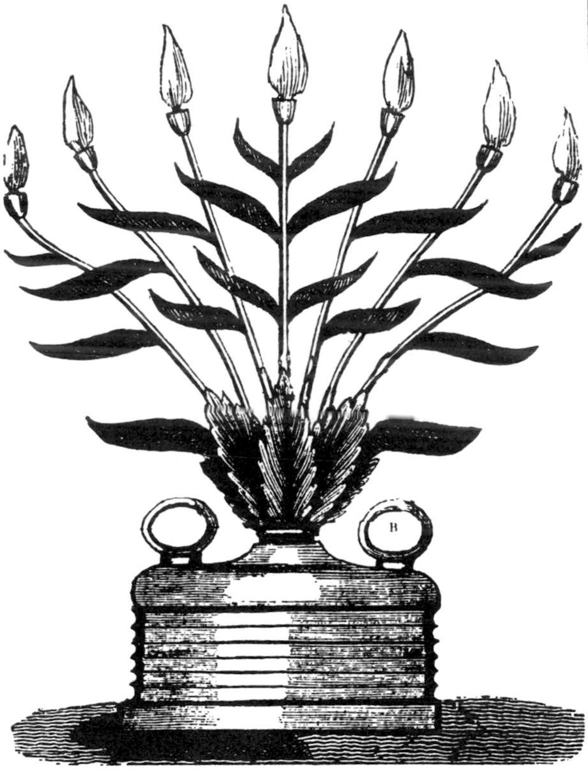

This cut represents one of the many fancy forms and figures of which the Pneumatic Lamp is susceptible. The principal peculiar advantage of this lamp, consists in having the oil-vessel, and consequently, nearly the whole weight of the lamp at the bottom, which effectually secures it against danger of being overturned, and at the same time allows the light to radiate more perfectly, especially in a vertical direction, than it does from other fashioned lamps. For common service, the pneumatic lamp has but a single plain tube, rising vertically from the fountain (oil vessel,) with a short wick and full flame at its top.—Either common oil or camphine may be used in this lamp, and the quantity of light may be regulated to the convenience of the illuminated. The following description of the Pneumatic Lamp, may be sufficient without sectionals, or full references.

A cylindric vessel, three inches in diameter, and two inches high, is made of glass, brass or britannia,—closed at the top, with a slight elevation in the centre. One or more tubes, or hollow copper wires are inserted and fixed in a vertical position in the centre of this fountain, extending downward very nearly to the bottom of the vessel, and upward six inches or more from the top. At the top of each tube is a small socket for receiving a short piece of wick. This vessel is filled about half full of oil or other combustible liquid, which by means of a super-atmospheric pressure on its surface, is forced up into the hollow tubes and furnishes the requisite supply to the flame. For the purpose of producing this pressure, a minute air pump is fixed in the top of the fountain, the piston of which is worked by the finger, by means of the ring A. There is nothing peculiar in this pump; the valves are simple like the common forcing pump. This piston being occasionally moved with the finger, a quantity of air is forced into the fountain, which by its elasticity and expansive force, presses on the surface of the oil, and thus keeps the burners supplied sufficiently to support a clear and brilliant flame, without having the wick project from the socket so as to be consumed by the flame or produce any degree or quantity of smoke. Another ring B, on the opposite side of the lamp, is attached to a cork or metalic stopper to the aperture by which the oil is occasionally replenished. The leaves represented in the above cut, are made of tinfoil and laquered of a green color; but as before observed, this principle is susceptible of a great variety of fancy forms and figures: the fountain may be made in the fashion of an urn or flower-basket, and the stems or tubes may be fancifully braided and interwoven together, without affecting the lamp with regard to convenience or utility.—The inventor would be pleased to contract with some person to take the agency, charge and management of constructing and vending these lamps on very liberal terms.

To the Ladies.—The following *true* anecdote is respectfully dedicated to the ladies, being a practical and forcible illustration of their celebrated faculty of keeping secrets: "P. is a little, pretty, reckless brunette; the idol of her father, and the spoiled child of her mother. Every body scolds at her quizzical and odd sayings, and all love her for her frankness and open heart. One day she was walking with a friend arm in arm, and she was teasing her friend to tell her something, which was not proper to be universally circulated. Her friend answered her, 'Tell you, P. no, indeed. I shall do no such thing. You never kept anything twenty-four hours in your life.' She flung her arms around her friend's neck in a very *convincing* manner, and exclaimed, 'Oh! Miss X, I can keep a secret, indeed I can. There was Miss A. told me six months ago that she was engaged to be married, and I never told any one of it, and *I never will*.' It was not until her friend burst into a fit of laughter, that she was aware her secret was out.—*Providence Journal.*

Interesting to the Curious.—In digging a deep vault near Pine and Third streets, the workmen lately came to a stratum containing pieces of trees and roots, at the depth of 28 feet. They passed through ten feet of limey soil eleven of coarse gravel, four of red clay, and then went three feet into a sort of marsh mud containing trees and roots. The wood, though far decomposed, still retained its original structure, and the bark and roots their distinct forms. It appears at first sight to belong to the pine, though others skilled in dendrology might decide differently. As the river in its present state could never have deposited the superincumbent strata, we must apparently refer the deposite of the wood to some deep ravine, which has long since been filled up; or to the general cause which deposited the alluvium over a large part of our country, when streams were larger, or the land much lower than at the present day. The bottom of the vault is about the level of the surface of the river at this time.—*Phil. North Amer.*

Currents of the Mediterranean.—Some years ago, Capt. Smyth, having procured specimens of sea-water at different depths from the Straits of Giberaltar, submitted them to Dr. Wollaston, who examined them, and published the results of his experiments in the Philos. Trans. 1829. Part 1. From these he concluded that there is a current setting into the Straits and an under current setting out to the Atlantic.—Mr. Lyell, without refering to Ray, offers some objections to this opinion. But if he had quoted the 'Pirysico-Theological Discourses,' we should have been supplied with a full discussion of the interesting topic; for, says Ray, 'I do not understand how waters can run backward and forward in the same channel at the same time; for, there being but one declivity, this is as much as to affirm that a heavy body should ascend. It is a crossing of proverbs, *ano potamon*, making rivers ascend to their fountains, affirming that to be done, which all the world hath hitherto looked upon as absurd and impossible.' Ray was also well aware of the arguments adduced in favor of an under current at the Propontis and Baltic Sound, which he likewise discusses at great length, and with great ability.—'M. Marsilly,' he observes, 'affirms that the lower water in the channel of the Thracian Bosphorus is driven northward into the Euxine Sea, while the upper flows constantly from the Euxine southward; and that that which flows from the south is salter and heavier, which he found by letting down a vessel close shut up, fitted with a valve to open at pleasure, and let in the lowest water, which being brought up and weighed, was found to be ten grains hevier than the upper. That the upper and lower flow contrary ways he found by the fisherman's nets which being let down from vessels that were fixed were always by the observation of the fishermen by the force of the current driven towards the Black Sea, and by the letting down of a plumet; for if it were stopped and detained at about five or six feet depth, it did always incline towards the Mamora or Propontis.' It is obvious that Dr. Wollasten must have been unacquainted with these facts, otherwise he would not have considered it necessary to have submitted a paper to the Royal Society, the contents of which had been so obviously anticipated by upwards of a century; the three localities alluded to being so analogous that Ray applies the same reasoning to them all.

Railway Accidents.—The report of the Railway Commissioners which has recently been presented to the English Parliament, gives some interesting results of an elaborate examination into the character of the accidents which have occured on English railways in the course of a few months previous. A report of this character from a Commissioner established on this side of the Atlantic, would doubtless present a curious result, and might prove of great advantage to the public:

1. Out of thirty-five railway accidents which have occured in the course of the last five months, twenty-one are attributable, among other causes, to "defective arrangements."

2. Eighteen are attributable to "misconduct of servants;" and

3. Six are attributable to "mechanical causes," among which the breaking of axles occupies a prominent place.

With reference to these results, the following observations suggest themselves:

1. The inherent danger of railway travelling is very small, and even under the present system, less than that of other modes of conveyance.

2. It is not, however, by reference to comparative, but to absolute safety, that the question must be considered. The public have a right to expect that the *maximum* degree of safety which the nature of the case admits should be attained without reference to the safety of other modes of travelling. This is the more necessary, as railway accidents, when they do occur, are frequently of a frightful character, and calculated to cause a panic in the public mind, which materially diminishes the benifit which the country would [illegible] derive from this improved mode of conveyance.

3. The *maximum* degree of safety is far from being attained in practice, as appears from the fact, that a great majority of the accidents above referred to have arisen from causes not in any respect inherent in the nature of locomotive travelling, and which might have been avoided by the adoption of a better system of arrangement.

The following details of the accident which occasioned the death of Mr. Farnham, will be read with interest as history, years hence.

The severe snow storm of March 13 impeded the regular passage of the cars. The first train due at 10 o'clock, did not arrive until noon. The second, due at 4 o'clock, did not leave the Boston depot until 3, and in about an hour was followed by the evening train. At Haverhill the forward train was about 30 minutes in advance of the other. The plough, a machine to clear the snow from the track, was attached to it, and its progress was comparatively slow. About half a mile south of the depot in this village, there being a slight ascent in the road, and the snow laying deeply and compactly in the track, the engine was not of sufficient power to force itself along, and it stuck in the drift. This was about 7 o'clock in the evening; and knowing that the other train must be near, Mr. Farnham, the conductor, took a stand between the passenger and baggage cars—the baggage car being in the rear—and swung his lantern as a signal to apprise the engineer of the other cars of his proximity and danger. A passenger stood awhile with Mr. Farnham, and hearing the cars approaching, he leaped from his stand, and urged the conductor to do so too; but Mr. F. thinking it impossible that his signal should be unnoticed or neglected, kept his post. The engineer of the last train did not observe the signal until so near it, that apprehending it impossible to arrest the crash, he leaped from his stand to the ground and left the cars to their fate. The engine run furiously into and through the baggage car of the forward train, and struck Mr. F. upon the breast and forced him through the end of the passenger car wounding him so severely that he survived but a short time. He was carried to his family in this village and died about 10 o'clock in the evening.

Turn him out.—According to the last census returns there is but one individual in Massachusetts unable to read or write.—*Star.*

published weekly with the principal office at 11 Spruce Street, New York—also at 16 State Street, Boston, and 21 Arcade, Philadelphia. Subscriptions were two dollars a year. Porter continued editing this publication until 1847, but within a year of its origin had sold it to Alfred Ely Beach and Orson D. Munn for eight hundred dollars. At that time it was printed as a quarto, with a circulation of two hundred and less than a page of advertising. By 1848 the circulation was ten thousand and thirty thousand by 1860. O. D. Munn and Company with Orson D. Munn, his son and then his grandson as president, owned and edited the *Scientific American* until 1947, when the magazine came under its present ownership and editorial direction. With Gerard Piel as publisher and Dennis Flanagan as editor, *Scientific American* today has a circulation exceeding seven hundred thousand. In addition, it is published in six translated editions—Italian, Japanese, Spanish, French, German, and Chinese—which brings its worldwide circulation to a grand total of one million.

The *Scientific American* was one of the most important journals of its time, as it is again today. Roger Burlingame, in his *March of the Iron Men*, speaks of the early *Scientific American* as "a sign of the changing times . . . a prophet of a world enlightened by a new publishing era based on new communications." The first volumes are basic and much quoted source books for the history of American invention. In its own time the *Scientific American* was the most important source book for the inventors themselves, and Burlingame emphasizes this: "Perhaps no other single factor has been a greater boon to old-school inventors than the *Scientific American* with its up-to-the-minute lists of patents, its lucid illustrations and diagrams, its sometimes over-enthusiastic articles about innovations, some of which came to naught but most of which stimulated some amateur mechanic or incipient engineer."

The *Scientific American* had essentially the same policy, format and content as the *New York Mechanic,* and the identical subtitle. The first issue (Fig. 34) announced that besides reporting the progress of science and industry the paper would include "useful information and instruction in various Arts and Trades; Curious Philosophical Experiments; Miscellaneous Intelligence, Music and Poetry." The newspaper was not so much an objective scientific journal as an enthusiastic presentation to the public of all of Porter's richly varied interests—a *Curious Arts* in newspaper form with emphasis on science and invention, presented, to borrow a Porter phrase, with "a full share of independence."

The material on "Aerial Navigation" reappears. A series of articles on "The Art of Painting" and a column entitled "Interesting Experiments" are expanded from "Curious Arts," which feature also continues as such. A regular column on religion is an important addition, as well as one entitled "Latest News." Other prominent items are the engravings, undoubtedly

53

Fig. 33.   A front page of *New York Mechanic,* the first of Porter's New York journals, published in 1841.

designed and executed for the most part by Porter himself, which include illustrations for the inventions here presented to the public, and odd pieces such as a "Phrenological Chart" and a diagrammatic "Plan of the City of Jungo . . . situated about 95 degrees East of the North Pole." (This Plan of the City of Jungo had appeared five years before in the *New York Mechanic*.) It is worth noting that Porter's engraving was closely related to his painting style. A sure, strong line distinguishes both his landscape painting and his draftsmanship as an inventor and journalist.

Bits of original music add further variety to the amazingly diversified contents. The poems which are scattered among the scientific articles include such titles as "Man's Mind is Free," "Never Look Sad," "At Home: Sweet Home" and "The Drunkard's Dream." In one issue an essay by Longfellow on "Rain in Summer" is printed next to an item on "A New Material for Roofing."

In addition to the sizable one-man job of editing, publishing and circulating the *Scientific American*, Porter continued active work as an inventor. He regularly presented, solicited production support for and promoted the finished product in the editorial and advertising pages of the *Scientific American*. He also was engaged in writing patent specifications for inventors, a business which he continued all during the latter part of his life, and which was developed by the next owners of the *Scientific American* into a highly lucrative patent department, with a branch office in Washington. Porter was also on call as an expert consultant to examine and give opinions on new inventions. He further advertised in the *Scientific American* "drawings of machinery, engravings on wood, and lithographic drawings, neatly executed, at the lowest prices, at this office."

Porter's critical journalism is in complete accord with his creative activities—invention and painting. His constant political belief was that of a homespun republicanism founded on the inherent dignity and value of the ordinary man rather than on the inherited privilege of aristocracy. As an editor Rufus Porter was a militant crusader for the rights of his fellows; as an inventor he worked for the economic improvement of the people; and as an artist he painted down-to-earth landscapes on the walls of rural houses and taverns for the enjoyment of the so-called "common man." Porter's paintings are pictorial expressions of his conviction that the simple countryside is at the heart of the nation, and of his feeling for the dignity and beauty of the everyday scene. In an editorial letter in the July 31, 1845, issue of the *Scientific American*, written to describe a trip from Worcester to Boston, Porter expresses in vigorous terms his respect for the spirit of the New England villages through which he passed. It is interesting to read of his admiration for the social and economic security of rural New England whose modest, serene beauty he pictures in his frescoes. He has this to say about the American farm villages:

They are not like many towns in other parts of the country, in which a herd of

Fig. 34. Page 1 of the first issue of *Scientific American*, published by Rufus Porter in New York, August 28, 1845.

SCIENTIFIC AMERICAN.

THE ADVOCATE OF INDUSTRY AND ENTERPRISE, AND JOURNAL OF MECHANICAL AND OTHER IMPROVEMENTS.

VOLUME I. | NEW-YORK, THURSDAY, AUGUST 28, 1845. | NUMBER 1.

THE

SCIENTIFIC AMERICAN,

PUBLISHED EVERY THURSDAY MORNING, AT NO. 11 SPRUCE STREET, NEW YORK, NO. 16 STATE STREET, BOSTON, AND NO. 21 ARCADE, PHILADELPHIA,

(THE PRINCIPAL OFFICE BEING IN NEW YORK,)

BY RUFUS PORTER.

Each number will be furnished with from two to five original Engravings, many of them elegant, and illustrative of *New Inventions, Scientific Principles,* and *Curious Works;* and will contain, in addition to the most interesting news of passing events, general notices of the progress of Mechanical and other *Scientific Improvements;* American and Foreign Improvements and Inventions; Catalogues of American Patents; Scientific Essays, illustrative of the principles of the sciences of Mechanics, Chemistry and Architecture; useful information and instruction in various Arts and Trades; Curious Philosophical Experiments; Miscellaneous Intelligence, Music and Poetry.

This paper is especially entitled to the patronage of Mechanics and Manufacturers, being the only paper in America, devoted to the interests of those classes; but is particularly useful to farmers, as it will not only apprise them of improvements in agricultural implements, but instruct them in various mechanical trades, and guard them against impositions. As a family newspaper, it will convey more useful intelligence to children and young people, than five times its cost in school instruction. Another important argument in favour of this paper, is that it will be worth two dollars at the end of the year when the volume is complete, (Old volumes of the New York Mechanic, being now worth double the original cost, in cash.)

TERMS.—The "Scientific American" will be furnished to subscribers at $2,00 per annum,—one dollar in advance, and the balance in six months.

Five copies will be sent to one address six months, for four dollars in advance.

Any person procuring two or more subscribers, will be entitled to a commission of 25 cents each.

Wife, Children and Friends.

If the stock of our bliss be in stranger hands vested,
The fund, ill secured, oft in bankruptcy ends;
But the heart issues bills which are never protested,
When drawn on the firm of—wife, children and friends.

Though valour still glows in life's dying embers,
The death-wounded tar, who his colours defends,
Drops a tear of regret as he, dying, remembers
How blest was his home with—wife, children and friends.

The soldier, whose deeds live immortal in story,
Whom duty to far distant latitude sends,
With transport would barter whole ages of glory
For one happy day with—wife, children, and friends.

The day-spring of youth, still unclouded by sorrow,
Alone on itself for enjoyment depends;
But drear is the twilight of age, if it borrow
No warmth from the smile of—wife, children, and friends.

Let the breath of renown ever freshen and nourish
The laurel which o'er the dead favourite bends,
O'er *me* wave the willow, and long may it flourish,
Bedewed with the tears of—wife, children, and friends!

Attraction.

Attraction is a curious power,
That none can understand;
Its influence is every where—
In water, air and land;
It keeps the earth compact and tight,
As though strong bolts were through it;
And, what is more mysterious yet,
It binds us mortals to it.

You throw a stone up in the air,
And down it comes—ker-whack!
The centrifugal casts it up—
The centripetal—back.
My eyes! I can't discover how
One object 'tracts another;
Unless they love each other, like
A sister and a brother.

I know the compass always points
Directly at the pole;
Some say the north star causes this,
And some say—Symm[illegible]
Perhaps it does—prehaps it don't
Prehaps some other cause;
Keep on *prehapsing*—who can solve
Attraction's hidden laws?

A fly lights on a 'lasses cup—
Attraction bids him woo it;
And, when he's in, attraction keeps
The chap from paddling through it.
Attraction lures the sot to drink,
To all his troubles drown;
But when his legs give way, he falls,
And 'traction keeps him down.

Attraction is a curious power,
That none can understand:
Its influence is everywhere—
In water, air and land.
It operates on every thing—
The sea, the tides, the weather;
And sometimes draws the sexes up,
And binds them fast together.

IMPROVED RAIL-ROAD CARS.

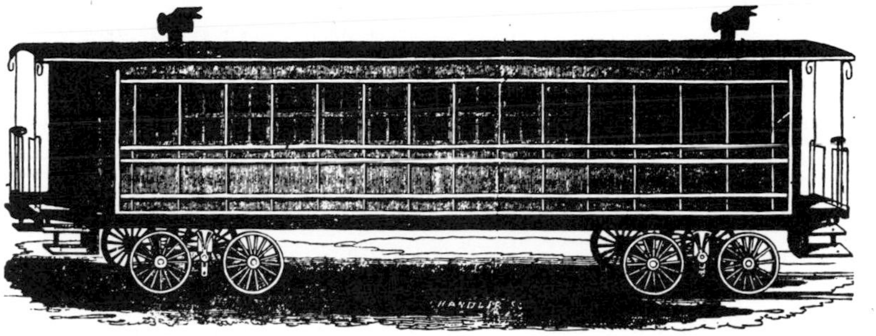

There is, perhaps, no mechanical subject, in which improvement has advanced so rapidly, within the last ten years, as that of railroad passenger cars. Let any person contrast the awkward and uncouth cars of '35 with the superbly splendid long cars now running on several of the eastern roads, and he will find it difficult to convey to a third party, a correct idea of the vast extent of improvement. Some of the most elegant cars of this class, and which are of a capacity to accommodate from sixty to eighty passengers, and run with a steadiness hardly equalled by a steamboat in still water, are manufactured by Davenport & Bridges, at their establishment in Cambridgeport, Mass. The manufacturers have recently introduced a variety of excellent improvements in the construction of trucks, springs, and connections, which are calculated to avoid atmospheric resistance, secure safety and convenience, and contribute ease and comfort to passengers, while flying at the rate of 30 or 40 miles per hour. We purpose to give a particular description of these improvements, accompanied with suitable engravings, in our next number, that our readers may be enabled to appreciate more fully the progress of improvements in this important branch of mechanism.

LOWELL AS IT WAS AND AS IT IS; By Rev. HENRY A. MILES, is a neat 18mo of 234 pages just issued by Powers & Bagley, Lowell. It is full of facts of general interest. We learn from it that the Merrimac Company (whose dividends are so often quoted) employs 1250 women, whose average earnings considerably *exceed* $2 each per week above the cost of their board. The laboring men average 85 cents per day above their board; fifty-six overseers receive $2 each per day with occasional premiums. [These are the *reduced* wages we hear of.] None are employed under fifteen years of age. No woman is retained a day after she is known to be guilty of licentious conduct, but not one in a hundred is ever discharged for any such cause. The average running time is 12 hours 10 minutes per day, which is too long and should be shortened, but the average working time of each hand is but ten hours and a half. In the Boott Mills, a careful account of working time has been kept, and it appears that 106 girls averaged 267 days each in a year and 10 hours 8 minutes per day, each being paid according to her work, and ☞ all are paid in cash every month,—not one farthing in store orders, or barter of any kind. The average earnings of the women in all the factories, including novices, is $1,93 per week besides their board. Many girls who have been school teachers gladly take places in the mills, as the pay is higher here, and the work lighter, though the hours are longer. No one has lost a sixpence of her earnings in the Lowell factories since the first was started. The girls have about $100,000 in the Savings Bank.

—Such is the condition of the Laboring Class in the principal Manufacturing town in America. Granted that it is not all it should be—that it might and should be improved—it is still true that no where else does a Laboring class of equal numbers earn so much, year by year; no where else are they so constantly employed, comfortably situated and adequately rewarded. Let those who would overthrow this state of things go to work and build up something better, or show how it may be done. Until they have some crude notions of this sort, ought they not to cease their incessant warfare on American Manufactures?—*Tribune.*

MAKING ARTICLES IN HORN.—The handles for knives, razors, and other articles moulded in horn, are thus made: The horn is first cut into appropriate pieces with the saw, and when heated, these are prepared with a knife or spoke-shave, to the general form and size required; after which the pieces are pressed into moulds. An idea of the mould will be conveyed by imagining two dies or pieces of metal, parallel on their outer surfaces, and with a cavity sunk entirely in the one, or partially in each, according to circumstances: it is made either straight, curved, twisted, rounded, bevelled, &c., or it is engraved with some device, according to the pattern of the work to be produced. The pressure is applied to the dies by enclosing them in a kind of clamp made with a strong pair of nut crackers, but with a powerful screw at the end opposite to the joint; the mould, dies, and horn, are dipped into boiling water or a few minutes, and then screwed as fast as possible immediately on removing the same, and in about twenty minutes the work is ready for finishing; some handles are made of two pieces joined together.

A SMOKE FILTER FOR LOCOMOTIVES.—An invention, which promises to be one of great utility, has been recently made by Mr. J. P. Dempfil, a French gentleman, of much scientific talent.—The invention consists of "an attachment" to the chimney of a locomotive, dividing it by a partition in two parts or passages, upward and downward, with a fly-wheel at the bottom of the downward draft, and a layer of gravel or sand underneath the wheel. The top of the chimney is closed, and the smoke and cinders pass upward through one passage to the top, then descending through the other, (a strong draught being made by the revolution of the fly-wheel, which is put in motion by the steam,) and all the refuse of the smoke pipe is retained by the grand filter, and the heated air again passes into the furnaces.

BURNING WELL.—A correspondent of the Cleveland Plain Dealer, gives an account of a burning well that may be seen at Southington Centre, in Trumbull county, Ohio. The well is 91 feet deep, all but 24 feet through sand-stone, quick sand and hard rock, which the augur used for boring could not penetrate. When it was withdrawn, a peculiar odor, accompanied by a rushing sound, was perceived. Suspecting the presence of inflammable gas, Mr. Wannemaker, the owner of the well, lowered a lamp into it. A violent explosion, that did some injury to the by-standers, was the consequence, and the gas still continues to burn. It is doubtless carburetted hydrogen.

NEW ARTICLE OF EXPORT.—We are told that a Yankee broom maker in Ohio has leased some twelve hundred acres of bottom land, on the Scioto river, near Columbus, and planted the entire plot in broom corn, with a view to export the crop to England, where he intends to proceed himself, and engage extensively in the manufacturing of brooms, taking with him the wood for the handles, and the machinery used for the purpose. Brooms made from the American broom corn are so much superior, for various uses, to any thing to be had in England, that they have become, within a few years past, quite a favorite in that country and are now exported thither in large quantities.—*Ex. paper.*

EXTRAORDINARY PHENOMENON.—The inhabitants of the village of Moulton were greatly astonished on Saturday last, at observing a considerable quantity of hay (from a field where it was in cocks for stacking) rise rapidly into the air. There was not the slightest breeze of wind perceptible at the time: however the hay continued to ascend until it apparently passed through the clouds, which were sailing high at the time. After the lapse of a few minutes it again appeard like a small black streak in the cloudy vapour, where it continued to form a most novel and extraordinary sight for ten or fifteen minutes, when it gradually descended again to the earth.—*Lincolnshire Chronicle.*

IMPROVEMENT IN OREGON.—Already has a canal been commenced around the dangerous falls in the Columbia river, at Willamette, by Dr. McLaughlin, an American citizen. Its length will be about half a mile, part of the way through a solid bed of primitive rock, and the fall in the entire distance will be about thirty-five feet. The projector expects to complete the work in two years, at a cost of thirty thousand dollars. His charter, procured from the Oregon Legislature is for twenty-one years. It is said that the improvement which will be effected in the navigation of the Columbia, by this construction of the canal will, of itself, fully reward the community for the privilege conferred by the Legislature.

PORTRAIT PAINTING.—A portrait painter in large practice might write a pretty book on the vanity and singularity of his sitters. A certain man came to Copely, and had himself, his wife and seven children all included in a family piece. "It was but one thing," said he, "and that is the portrait of my first wife—for this one is my second." "But," said the artist, "she is dead you know, sir; what can I do? she is only to be admitted as an angel." "Oh, no! not at all," answered the other; "she must come in as a woman—no angels for me." The portrait was added, but some time elapsed before the person came back; when he returned, he had a stranger lady on his arm, "I must have another cast of your hand, Copely," he said; "an accident befell my second wife; this lady is my third, and she is come to have her likeness included in the family picture." The painter complied—the likeness was introduced—and the husband looked with a glance of satisfaction on his three spouses. Not so the lady; she remonstrated; never was such a thing heard of—out her predecessors must go. The artist painted them out accordingly, and had to bring an action at law to obtain payment for the portraits which he had obliterated.—*Life of Copely, Family Library.*

GREAT IMPROVEMENT IN LITHOGRAPHIC PRINTING.—A very important improvement has been made in the lithographic printing machine by a young French engineer named Nicolle, by which the same precision and regularity of pressure is obtained as by the common hand-press. By the common lithographic process, not more than from 200 to 250 good impressions of designs, or about 1,000 copies of lithographic writing, can be obtained in twelve hours; by this new machine, which is also worked by hand, as many as 2,000 of the former, and 20,000 of the latter, can be obtained within the same period of time.

A SENSIBLE HORSE.—One of the truck horses of Mr. Hinds was unloosed for a minute or two, from the trucks, a few days since, in this city, when, on the driver looking around for him, behold he was missing. It was an hour or two, before the driver could discover his whereabout. It was very mysterious, he being a steady beast, and not subject to flights of fancy. However, he was at last found in the smith's shop, where he was wont to have his shoes repaired. The smith said the horse entered and took the usual stand for shoeing. Upon examining his feet he found one shoe off, which he supplied. That horse is a sensible beast.

THE PROPERTIES OF ZINC.—Professor Farraday, as we are informed in the London Athenæum, has made this metal the subject of many interesting experiments. He has discovered that it assumes new properties on being melted and poured into water, the metal becoming very malleable and soft, losing none of its tenacity, but still capable of being spun into the finest wire, pressed into any required form, or rolled into any thinness desired. This promises to be a very useful discovery.

A SPECIMEN OF VEGETABLE SILK, raised from seeds received from Italy, which came originally from Syria, has been presented to the National Institute. Some of the seeds have been forwarded to Florida to the Hon. D. Levy, for the purpose of being cultivated.

CAUSE OF SOUND IN THUNDER.—Thunder is one of the consequences resulting from lightning, and lightning appears to be occasioned by the combustion of some of the inflamable particles of air; or according to more recent opinions, of a condensation of aerial matter conducing to electricity, by which in either case, a vacum is created. The sorrounding atoms which remain uninfluenced by this change, being forced together by the whole weight of the atmosphere, greatly constrict each other; but their elastic nature causes them immediately to expand, and by this enlargement their sonorous property is acquired. A centrifugal force being thus established, it acts in all directions alike; but as the circle extends, its propulsive power becomes gradually diminished, till at last its pressure is no longer felt, nor sound created. The rumbling noise of thunder is produced by that portion of the sonorous circle which strikes upon the earth, whence it becomes condensed; and, being intercepted in its upward course by dense masses of vapor, it is again reflected, and this alternate motion and reverbration continue, until the interuption ceases, or the original force is exhausted. Echo is occasioned also by reverbration from one cloud to ahother.—*Webster's Principles of Sound.*

LIQUOR BURNT.—Among the property destroyed by the late fire, in this city, was a large quantity of intoxicating liquors, for which nobody ought to mourn. It is announced that 912 pipes of brandy, 200 pipes of gin, 100 puncheons of rum, 2000 pipes; half and quarter pipes of Madeira wine, 3000 casks of port wine, 1000 Malaga, 1500 Marseilles, 1000 claret, and 5000 baskets of Champaigne were consumed. How much more that is not told of, on account of the little sympathy the tale would excite, is not known. The operations of sundry large wine merchants are also rudely put a stop to.

N. Y. Evangelist.

CATALOGUE OF AMERICAN PATENTS

ISSUED IN 1844.

CLASS I.—*Agriculture, including Instruments and Operations.*

Bee Hives—Improvement in Bee Hives by Aaron E. James, Point Pleasant, Va., Jan. 6th.

Do. Samuel & J. D. Cope, Damascusville, Ohio, Feb. 8th.

Do. George B. West, Fairfield, Ohio, April 20th.

Do. James A. Cutting, Haverhill, N. H. June 24th.

Do. Jacob D. Fulkerson, Unity, Ohio, July 1st.

Do. Oliver Reynolds, Webster, N. Y., Dec. 4th.

Bee Palaces, Lemon Hamlin, Kirkersville, Ohio, July 13th.

Improvement in Churns—George W. Cook, St. Louis, Mo., Feb. 28th.

Do. Harmess Bently, Ballston, N. Y., April 20th.

Do. Jason B. Schermerhorn, New York, June 5th.

Do. Thomas Ling, Portland, Me., Aug. 21st.

Corn and Cane Cutters—Jacob Peck, Oakland, Penn., Aug. 28th.

Corn Fodder, Cutting and Crashing—Rudolph Miller, York, Penn., Oct. 3d.

Corn-Sheller—William McAll, Talladega, Indiana, April 13th.

Cultivator—Robert Nelson, West Point, Ia., Jan. 15th.

Cultivator—William Dyzert, Gettysburg, Penn., Aug. 16th.

Cultivator Teeth—James Birdsall, Hamorton, Penn., Nov. 9th.

Fruit-gatherer—Alexander McWilliams, Washington, D. C. March 13th.

Harrow, sward-cutting—Dennis Rice, Rowe, Mass., May 17th.

Hulling Clover Machines—A. B. Crawford, Wooster, Ohio, Dec. 31st.

Hulling and Pearling Rice—Jacob Groat, Troy, N. Y., July 11th.

Mowing, Grain Cradles—William A. Wood and John C. Loveland, Hoosick Falls, N. Y., Nov. 13th.

Mowing, Harvesting Machines—George Esterly, Heart Prairie, W. T., Oct. 22d.

Mowing, Hemp Cradles—Griffin Reynolds, jun. Washington, Ky., May 30th.

Mowing, Reaping Machines—William F. Ketchum, Buffalo, N. Y., Nov. 18th.

Improvement in Ploughs—John Thompson, Ripley, Ohio, April 17th.

Do. Aaron Smith, Bloomfield, Mich., May 6th.

Do. Jonathan Mooers, Hazelton, Penn, July 1st.

Do. Anthony Taylor, New Garden, Ohio, Dec. 19th.

Plough, adjusting—William R. Allan, Brownston, Ky., Jan. 31st.

Plough, combined—Harvey Crown, Payson, Ill., March 9th.

Plough, double—Aaron Smith, Bloomfield, Mich. May 10th.

Plough, excavating ditches—James Herbert, Lagrange, Ia., April 13th.

Plough, gathering weeds under the furrow slice—Dudley Hills, East Hartford, Ct. Oct. 7th.

Plough, wheel—Israel Long, Bucyrus, Ohio, March 9th.

Potato-Diggers—Archibald C. Ketchum, Schenectady, N. Y., Feb. 20th.

Rake, grain—Benoni F. Partridge, Onondaga, N. Y., March 13th.

Rattoon and Cane Cutters—Robert Lauve, Plaquemines, La., Sept. 17th.

Seeding, corn planters—Thomas H. Hoskings, Crawfordsville, Ia., Jan. 20th.

Seeding, planting machines—Dierck Brewer, Petersburg, Tenn., April 4th.

Seeding, seed planters—Lora Pratt, Amherst, N. H., April 25th, and Richard J. Gatling, Murfreesborough, N. C., May 10th.

Seeding, seed planters—U. Kilburn, Lawrenceville, Penn., and F. Haines, Marietta, Penn., Dec. 31st.

Seeding, sowing machines—Ezra Fisk, Fayette, Me., Nov. 18th.

Smut Machine—Meredith Mallory, Mount Morris, N. Y, Jan. 20th.

Smut Machine—Jacob W. Brown, Mount Airy, N. C. Feb. 28th.

Do. James M. Clarke, Strasburg, Penn., March 20th.

Do. Samuel Scammon and R. Nason, Waterville, Me., April 10th.

Do. Elisha S. Snyder, Charleston, Va., April 30th.

Do. Henry B. James, Mount Holly, N. J., May 17th.

Do. Abraham Straub, Milton, Penn., May 17th.

Do. Elisha W. Young, Parkman, Ohio, June 5th.

Do. Thomas H. Nelson, Harrisburg, Penn., June 5th.

Do. James W. Webster, Luray, Va., June 5th.

Do. John Pagin, Michigan City, Ia., Aug. 19th.

Do. Jacob Groat, Troy, N. Y., Nov. 9th.

Straw-Cutter—William Hovey, Worcester, Mass. Feb. 12th.

Do. Hiram M. Smith, Richmond, Va., Feb. 20th.

Do. Eliakim Taylor, Rochester, N. Y., Oct. 12th.

Do. Ezra Taylor, Monroe, N. Y., Nov. 6th.

Threshing Machine—Luther & Ezra Whitman, Winthrop, Me., March 20th.

Do. Charles W. Cathcart, New Durham, Ind., April 25th, and Frederick A. Stuart, Catharine, N. Y., June 5th.

Threshing and Winnowing Machine, and Grain Separaters—Jacob V. A. Wemple, Mohawk, and George Westinghouse, Schoharie, N. Y., July 13th.

Winnowing, Fanning Mill, for cleaning grain—Calvin O. Guernsey, Russia, N. Y., Oct. 12th.

Winnowing, separating grain from straw—Manning Packard and Christian B. Packard, Clarendon, N. Y., Nov. 8th.

people from various nations huddle together, without any other apparent occasion but to live on the breath of society; neither are they constituted by the proud mansions of retired aristocrats; but they are supported by cheerful and liberal industry, being constituted by the union of agriculture and manufacturing interests, concentrated by facilities of transportation, and cemented by education and temperance.

The well-cultivated fields and the hum of machinery in the mills, he adds, proclaim independence and plenty. Porter's verbal appreciation of the peace and plenty of the New England countryside is as advanced as are his frescoed records of their rural charm, which had been ignored as merely commonplace by all the fashionable painters of his day.

It is pertinent to note that the famous travel books of Porter's time commented either on the cosmopolitan social life of the metropolitan centers or on the "picturesque" qualities of rural scenery, while Porter described the peaceful routine of the ordinary New England village and painted the everyday aspects of the neat farmland he admired. He consistently expressed himself—in print and in paint—in the vernacular. The burgeoning literary growth of New England in this period (re-created by Van Wyck Brooks in *The Flowering of New England*) centered around the intellectual and cultural life of the century, with its bloodstream in aristocratic Boston. Porter's America, however, is that of the plain New England countryside peopled with farmers and small manufacturers; New York City bustling with commerce; Washington with its lively patent office and practical politics.

Creating the "century of the common man" has been the goal of major twentieth-century political movements. Rufus Porter, as editor of the most important scientific journals of his time was, through the new power of the press, helping to lay the foundations of this modern era in which the mechanic and farmer rival the prestige formerly accorded the wealthy landowner. As democracy developed, labor and the ordinary man began to assume an importance that challenged cultured leisure and the rich aristocratic classes. This tendency was noticeably accelerated in the nineteenth century, and Porter was in the vanguard of that active, progressive movement in the mid-1800s. Inherent in this movement was a strong element of romantic idealism in the attitude toward human rights and the equality of man—undoubtedly descended from Paine and Rousseau. Equally evident was a practical interpretation of the Declaration of Independence, and a profitable Yankee application of its principles. Porter's newspaper writings reveal all this, and a number of his editorials might be regarded as seeds of the American labor movement.

Porter's editorials in the *Scientific American* were frequently in verse. One poem is entitled "The Value of Labor"; another "To the Working Man." Still another, called "The Poor and the Rich" (April 2, 1845), points out the debilitating effect of inherited wealth in contrast to the vitalizing force of honest labor. The rich man's son, the verses tell, inherits lands and cares,

And piles of brick and stone and gold.

The poor man inherits stout muscles, a strong heart and a hardy frame, and his rank is adjusted by merit alone.

> King of two hands, he does his part
> In every useful toil and art;
> A heritage, it seems to me,
> A king might wish to hold in fee.

Much of Porter's editorial writing was designed to encourage and sustain two groups of Americans—farmers and mechanics. The former he considered the backbone of the nation, but he saw mechanical invention as the chief instrument to a glorious new future, and mechanics as the enviable agents who would usher in the new day.

In the August 6, 1846, issue, Porter discussed a couple of his own inventions which, he prophesied, would combine to make western farming a highly profitable large-scale industry. They are the "Field Engine," a machine for harrowing, sowing and rolling at the same time, and his earlier "Steam-Carriage," which could be used to pull the engine over fields and roads; this combination (see Figs. 15, 20) would save enough labor that "we may expect to see our western farmers thriving in the business of raising wheat at fifty cents per bushel." Porter visualized modern large-scale farming made possible by means of automatic farm machinery and new means of locomotion. Then market produce would be turned out in large quantities at so low a price that it would be readily accessible to all the people. This, too, was his ideal for art production!

One article (May 14, 1846) devoted to "The Effects of the Introduction of Mechanical Improvements" is an early and extremely progressive discussion of technological unemployment. Despite general public opinion that laborsaving machinery might become a disadvantage to the community at large by diminishing the demand for labor, Porter maintains that "invention of labor saving implements will increase the value of the labouring classes . . . opening new avenues of trade and new inducements of enterprise." The mechanic, as the man who will set in motion this chain of circumstances, assumes in Porter's eyes the greatest importance. He insists that the public regard him with the respect due his key place in the republic. In an article in the *Scientific American* entitled "The American Mechanic" (May 14, 1846) Porter states that the modern mechanic occupies a position of honor in the scale of man which has no parallel in the old world. As one who will have unprecedented influence he should read widely, and acquaint himself with the whole science of government and everything connected with the nature and affairs of his fellow-men. He, believes Porter, is the logical representative of the people. Rufus Porter speaks for the dignity of the mechanic who was considered a mere tool in the aristocratic society of the past century, and who is now heralded as a leader of men in the young Republic:

Among all the varieties that diversify the human race, there is no more honorable character than the American Mechanic—he sees himself a guardian of the institutions of his country and one of the governors of a mighty empire; he knows the common weal is committed partially to his care and must be influenced by his virtue and intelligence. He is in fact one of Nature's noblemen. We would have every American Mechanic feel the important influence which he must exercise upon the destinies of his race.

The *Scientific Mechanic,* the next weekly newspaper which Rufus Porter founded and edited, was published in New York and Washington in 1847 and 1848. It was much like Porter's other personalized scientific journals. The editor announced that the paper was intended "to instruct while it diverts," that it would omit "repulsive notices and details of crime" and "seldom notice casualties and calamities." Porter was a cheerful journalist, a philosopher and, since his boyhood, an amateur poet. All his newspapers carry his verses, which are brisk and frankly practical rather than flowing or "elevated." In one of his jingles, featured in the first issue of the *Scientific Mechanic,* Rufus Porter gives terse rhymed advice to his public, as follows:

> Be active—be active—
>   Find something to do
> In digging a clam-bank
>   Or tapping a shoe.
> Don't stop at the corners,
>   To drag out the day—
> Be active—be active—
>   And work while you may.

If you follow this advice, he ends,

> You'll live and be happy
>   And never complain
> Of the blues, or the dumps,
>   Or a dull heavy brain.

In 1847 the American Association for the Advancement of Science was organized in Boston. That same year the first issue of the *Scientific Mechanic* published a full prospectus for the "Inventors' Institute," which had been introduced in February and March 1847, in the *Scientific American* (Fig. 35), and for which a circular was subsequently published and circulated. The Institute was, we find, planned by Rufus Porter to "promote genius and enterprise by encouraging and aiding that useful class of men . . . inventors." The object was not to benefit a few wealthy stockholders at the expense of the inventors, but to put into practice the inventions of mechanics who needed financial support. This was to be done by one thousand or more practical mechanics forming a Joint Stock Association, each taking one or more shares, in one to ten lots, at $525 and then collectively planning and carrying out the promotion of promising inventions. This was really a combined mechanics' union and stock company. The Institute was very well received, according to editorial comment in

INVENTORS' INSTITUTE.

This is a brick building in the form of a hollow square. It was built in 1757, for barracks. and was occupied during the Revolutionary war by the British soldiers. That part of the building adjoining the Engine house has been torn down, but will be rebuilt.

A. Machine Shop.
B. Padlock Factory.
C. Keg Factory.
D. Engine House.
E. East wing, unoccupied and divided into eight distinct apartments for private workshops of inventors.
F. West wing, unfinished in the interior.
OFFICE.—16 by 36 feet.

The above is a correct representation of the buildings provided for the use and benefit of the Inventors Institute, or new association of American Inventors, to which we alluded in our last number. The object of the Institute is not to benefit a few aristocratic stockholders at the *expense* of inventors; nor the exclusive benefit of a few prime movers : but particularly to bring forward to perfection, and introduce to practical utility, the inventions of those whose circumstances are such that their inventions have hitherto been, and would otherwise continue to be dormant and obscure, for want of means and facilities to bring them into notice and practical use. The constitution of the Institute is not yet matured, but it is proposed to examine by appointed Committees, all new inventions, and plans of improvements that may be offered, and select those which are thought worthy of being constructed or manufactured ; to furnish pecuniary aid to inventors who require it, and facilities for perfecting their plans and inventions—procure patents and manufacture such newly invented articles as are suitable, and vend patent rights by territory or otherwise, of others, paying to inventors one half of the profits, or occasionally buying outright the inventions paying to inventors such prices as may be mutually agreed upon : and making an annual or semi-annual dividend of the profits arising from these operations to all the members of the Institute. Every inventor who produces an approved invention, or any other inventor or mechanic who may pay $50 at one time, may become a permanent member and stockholder ; and any inventor or mechanic who pays six dollars annually in advance, will be entitled to all the privileges and dividends of a stockholder during the year succeeding such payment. As before remarked, these are only proposed, and not the adopted features of the institute, which is not yet organized. But a charter on the most liberal terms has been obtained for fifty years under the title of the "Perth Amboy Manufacturing Company," and the buildings above represented, are already partly occupied by successful new inventions, and the manufacture of others : and it is contemplated to establish a ware house and Inventors Hall in the city of New York, where inventions will be deposited for examination, &c. We shall give further notice of the progress of the Institute occasionally, with extracts from the circular published and circulated. Those who are in favor of encouraging, and patronizing this institution are requested to signify the same by letter (postpaid) addressed to Dr. Solomon Andrews of Perth Amboy N. J. or to the editor of this paper.

Fig. 35. The Inventors' Institute, a cooperative association of American inventors, which Porter presented in the form of a detailed proposal in *Scientific American,* March 6, 1847. One Dr. Solomon Andrews of Perth Amboy, New Jersey, was evidently associated with Porter in this ambitious venture.

later issues of the paper. As in the case of many of Porter's enterprises, however, the idea was sound but the approach impractical, and the Institute was doomed to failure. The one characteristic Yankee trait that Porter entirely lacked was shrewdness about business and finance. According to an editorial announcement the plan was dropped because of some technicalities in partnership laws, and almost simultaneously the newspaper was discontinued. One cannot help suspecting that promotion of the Inventors' Institute was the chief *raison d'être* for the *Scientific Mechanic*.

When discussing Porter's airship we quoted from the *Aerial Reporter*, published bimonthly in Washington in 1852–1853, which was Rufus Porter's last newspaper (Fig. 36). The primary function of this short-lived journal was to promote Porter's Aerial Navigation Company by reporting on the progress of the aeroport which he was constructing.

In 1852 Porter published in Washington a tract entitled *Essential Truth* which expressed his personal thoughts on religion and supported them with voluminous biblical quotations (Fig. 37). The sixty-page pamphlets were for sale at five dollars a hundred, but only one copy survives today, in the Library of Congress. We quoted from Frank Rufus Porter's letter in which he mentions that in 1872 at Plantsville his father was engaged in writing "of a religious nature." In another letter he also states that Rufus Porter "published and circulated much literature on religious subjects." This material would have been published over a period of twenty to thirty years—between 1852 and 1882—but none has come to light. Porter's one known pamphlet ends with an original hymn entitled "Social Devotion," and it seems possible that he was also the author of other published hymns.

A frontier individualism in religion, exemplified by such men as William Miller, was symptomatic of the turbulent democracy of the times. Rufus Porter's active interest in religious questions was inspired by this fiery apostle; William Markoe, a friend of Porter's, mentions in a letter his "religious fanaticism." About 1843 he was struck by the religious mania of the Millerites, and was among the most ardent believers in Miller's prophecy of the impending Last Day and the Second Coming of Christ, scheduled for the year 1844. (His only surviving murals with religious subject matter, the biblical scenes in the Senigo house in East Weymouth, Massachusetts, were done in 1845.) In 1846, with the date for the millenium postponed, Porter published in the *Scientific American* a series of long articles on the history of the Millerites which discuss their beliefs as improbable but do not quite dismiss them. He seemed reluctant to leave the fold, and his articles on the sect read as if he wrote them to convince himself of the irrationality of their tenets.

A column on religion was an important feature in the early *Scientific American*. In the editorial introducing Volume 1, Number 1, Porter announces as one of the policies: "We shall advocate the pure Christian

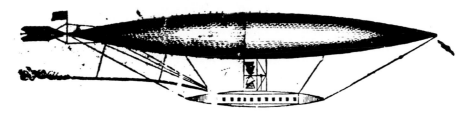

AERIAL REPORTER.

PUBLISHED SEMI-MONTHLY AT WASHINGTON, D. C., BY RUFUS PORTER.

VOL. I. SATURDAY, AUGUST 14, 1852. NO. 6.

Fig. 36. Masthead of Porter's *Aerial Reporter,* published in Washington, D.C., August 14, 1852; only one issue is extant, in the Library of Congress, Washington, D.C.

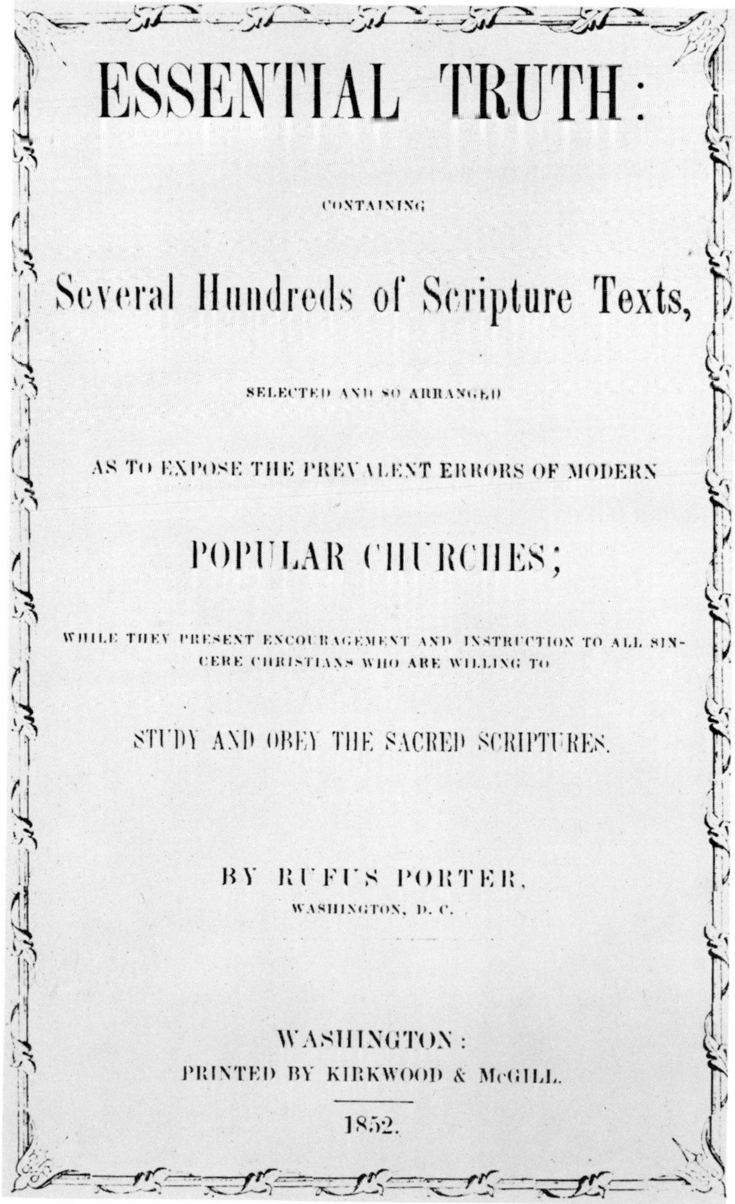

ESSENTIAL TRUTH:

CONTAINING

Several Hundreds of Scripture Texts,

SELECTED AND SO ARRANGED

AS TO EXPOSE THE PREVALENT ERRORS OF MODERN

POPULAR CHURCHES;

WHILE THEY PRESENT ENCOURAGEMENT AND INSTRUCTION TO ALL SIN-
CERE CHRISTIANS WHO ARE WILLING TO

STUDY AND OBEY THE SACRED SCRIPTURES.

BY RUFUS PORTER,
WASHINGTON, D. C.

WASHINGTON:
PRINTED BY KIRKWOOD & McGILL.

1852.

Fig. 37. Cover of *Essential Truth,* a tract Porter published in Washington, D.C., in 1852, to express his personal thoughts on religion. *Library of Congress, Washington, D.C.*

religion—shall make it a point to adhere to reason and common sense independently of the opinions of those whose interests and popularity depend on their rigid adherence to traditional doctrines and church creeds." Porter's ideal for religion was—as for art—personal freedom as against dogma. He was strongly against Roman Catholicism, which to him represented the opposite pole of liberal and independent religious thinking; while he consistently defended the Mormons' right to religious freedom and actively championed their cause. Porter's religious ideas had much in common with the philosophy of Thomas Paine. He was a freethinker, radically independent and, except for his brief orgy in Millerism, consistently for a "rational religion" which was the title of one of his articles in the *Scientific American.*

Essential Truth is closely related to Paine's *Age of Reason.* Paine had said "my own mind is my own church," and Porter might have taken that statement as the text for his tract. He affirms "that it is not profitable nor safe to be united to the popular churches, nor to follow the teachings of the popular clergy," that each man should study the Scriptures for himself, each find his own religious truths. He states flatly that "the principal tenets of all modern popular churches are mere fables—inventions of men." He stresses the spirit of Christianity as against the form, objecting to formalized churches and an ordained ministry. He advocates the teaching of religion by lay preachers who work "for love of God and of the truth" rather than for hire, without clerical degrees, or minister's dress or a church. "Professor Porter," dancing school master and aeronautical engineer, had become a self-appointed Doctor of Divinity. Rufus Porter clearly considered himself a lay preacher, expounding his tenets through the written word. In the realm of religion, tradition and formalized methods mean as little to him, a free approach as much, as in the practice of painting. Porter preaches the gospel of freedom, declaring that "salvation is free as air to all who are *free* to receive it."

Itinerant Limner

RUFUS PORTER HAD BEGUN PAINTING portraits when he moved from Portland to New Haven in 1816, and was active both as a portrait painter and dancing school master the following year. He painted in Hawaii about 1818, decorative and house painting perhaps, but almost certainly did portraits as well. About 1819 he returned from his voyage and continued his portrait painting in Boston. Later that year, he painted a pair of miniature water-color portraits in West Boxford (Figs. 38, 39), the only Porter portraits which, despite searching and advertising, I have been able to locate. An advertising flier (Fig. 40) owned by the American Antiquarian Society in Worcester, however, gives a clear picture of Porter's portrait style—both strong and decorative—and his price range, from silhouettes at twenty cents to ivory miniatures at eight dollars, "taken with elegance and despatch."

The portraits of Mehitable Tyler (Wood) and her brother John Tyler were, when I saw them some years ago, owned by Mrs. Clarence Bryant, granddaughter of Mehitable Tyler who married Captain Enoch Wood of Boxford. They are dated 1819 and were painted while the subjects, aged twenty-two and twenty-four, were still living in the old Tyler homestead in West Boxford. Though unsigned they have always been known in the family as the Rufus Porter portraits. The subjects were distant cousins of Rufus, both he and the Tylers having had a common great-great-grand-father, Moses Tyler; and the young Tylers' father, John, had captained the Boxford West Parish company in which Rufus served in 1812.

Records of two other sets of Porter portraits, owned by descendants, were brought to my attention soon after I saw the Tylers: one pair owned by the family of Mrs. Esther Doane Osman of West Newbury, Massachusetts, was destroyed in the 1938 hurricane, which blew off the roof of the house where the little portraits had been stored in the attic; a relative of Mrs. Sheldon B. Hickox, whose house in Groveland, Massachusetts, was deco-rated by Porter, burned the portraits Porter had painted of her grand-parents. The fact that he painted these portraits while he was frescoing walls in the house suggests the probability that he occasionally gained portrait commissions from the owners of the houses he decorated. Mrs. Hickox places these portraits, based on the ages of her grandparents, as about 1830, which coincides with the approximate date of the frescoes.

The serene little portraits of the Tylers reproduced here are the earliest examples found of Rufus Porter's work as a painter. They were executed when Porter, twenty-seven years old, had been painting portraits for four years. The oval setting for the portraits is related to the ivory miniatures, which Porter also painted on order, and the decorative details hark back to his ornamental painting. The glass covering the portrait of Mehitable (not shown in the large illustration and hardly visible in Fig. 39) is further embellished with a border consisting of an ornamental chain design outlined in gold leaf against the black, with clusters of stylized gold-leaf flowers in the corners.

Since the first publication of this book, dozens more Porter portraits have been attributed to him, based on close stylistic resemblance to the Tyler pair reproduced. These are all small watercolor profiles, several in the original gold-leafed frames with decorated glasses, like those made for the Tylers.

The flat profile poses and the fresh simplicity of treatment place these portraits on the modest level of primitive painting. There is nothing sophisticated or elaborate here, nothing suggesting academic training or artistic pretension of any sort. Rufus Porter painted the brother and sister with a keen feeling for characterization which is, however, subordinated to the design of the silhouettes. The handsome young people are immobilized and timeless in their neat oval frames. The drawing is firm, the coloring delicate and fresh. John wears a dark blue coat and pale ocher waistcoat; a transparent gray-blue dress and white ruff set off Mehitable's reddish hair and rosy complexion. It seems probable that Rufus Porter's portraits were all of the small watercolor profile type; it is certain that the subjects were simply portrayed rather than posed against imaginary velvet drapes or marble columns. It is also safe to assume that they were drawn, colored and composed with interest focused on the crisp design of the profile.

Mrs. Trollope, discussing in her *Domestic Manners of the Americans* a visit to the Pennsylvania Academy of Fine Arts in 1830, complained that she heard no word about drawing or composition used in any conversation on art, and that "the finish of drapery was considered as the highest excellence, and next to this, the resemblance in a portrait." These were not the criteria which Rufus set himself as a portrait painter. In his early years he casually ignored the goals of academic art, and later as an experienced self-taught artist he deliberately rejected the academic approach to painting.

Leaving Boxford in 1819, Rufus set out on foot with his paints and brushes to find customers for his portraits. His wife was still living in Port-

Fig. 38.   Watercolor portraits of Mehitable and John Tyler, painted in 1819 when Porter was 27. The subjects were distant cousins of his. Mehitable Tyler's granddaughter, Mrs. Clarence Bryant, was the last recorded owner of these portraits when they were photographed about 1950. Present owner, Mrs. Stuart C. Hurlbert.

Fig. 39.   Parlor-kitchen of the old Tyler homestead in West Boxford, Massachusetts. Porter's portraits of John and Mehitable Tyler hang over the mantel.

CORRECT LIKENESSES,

TAKEN WITH ELEGANCE AND DESPATCH BY

RUFUS PORTER.

Prices as follows—
Common Profile's cut double, - - $.0 20
Side views painted in full colours, - - 00
Front views, - - - - - - - 3 00
Miniatures painted on Ivory, - - - 8 00
☞ *Those who request it will be waited on, at their respective places of residence.*

Fig. 40. Rufus Porter's handbill when he worked as an itinerant portrait painter in the early 1800s. The blotted price for "Side views painted in full colours" can be assumed to be one dollar. *American Antiquarian Society, Worcester.*

land at this time and that he visited her on his return from sea is proven by the birth of a son in August of 1820. The visit must have been a brief one, however, for in 1819 and 1820 Rufus was walking southward peddling his portraits, from Massachusetts to New York, through New Jersey to Baltimore, and then on to Alexandria and Harrisonburg Hot Springs in Virginia. This was the first trip Porter had taken quite on his own and far from home ties. Since his Maine days he had led an independent life of course, but he was from time to time at least in contact with family and friends—Reverend Nathaniel Porter in Fryeburg, Dr. Aaron Porter in Portland, his uncle David Porter in Denmark, and his nephew Stephen Runnels at sea.

This trip south was the start of Porter's career as an itinerant, which he was to continue off and on for the rest of his life, traveling on foot or on horseback through the Atlantic and New England states as journeyman-painter and inventor. As a soldier in Portland Porter had seen the peddlers hawking their wares on regimental muster days, and he may have thought then that he would enjoy their wandering life. All of Rufus Porter's early years and careers seem to come to a logical focus in this life of professional itinerancy which he adopted in his late twenties, and his journeys in turn centered his attention as inventor on the everyday problems of travel, as artist on the possibility of beautifying the rural homes and wayside inns at which he stopped.

The Yankee peddler was a national figure in the nineteenth century, and seems somehow to symbolize one aspect of restless, adventuresome, young America. During this era hordes of daring lads took to the road, finding independence and excitement, seeing a bit of the world and tasting adventure before settling down to a family and a farm. The young Yankee's period of itinerancy was in a way like the more dignified Grand Tour of the young European. But the New Englander traveled with practical rather than cultural purposes, trying out his special talents and earning his way as he went. The Yankee peddlers were keen, reckless young fellows with plenty of grit and energy as their heritage, bent on getting a start in life and exploring their country, while the young European aristocrats were enjoying an expensive grand tour of picturesque scenery and historic landmarks.

When Rufus Porter took to the road in 1819 the Yankee peddlers were an established institution. They sold "Yankee notions"—combs, jewelry, buttons, pins, drugs, soap, candles, tinware, woodenware, cloth, books, clocks—and wooden nutmegs, too, we are told. Rufus' traveling companions were itinerant peddlers, doctors, lawyers, painters, preachers, teachers, circus masters and puppeteers. An entire cross section of American life was on the move in the early years of the nineteenth century, literally carrying to every outpost the newest manufactures, literature, art, religion, law, medicine and entertainment. Every man was being offered an equal share in the products of the new American democracy, and the itinerants knocking on the door were its personal representatives. They established an all-inclusive network of service and communication long before the days of railway express and telephones and daily newspapers.

The motley company journeyed at times by stagecoach and sleigh and canal boat with goods stored 'in carpetbags or packed in small wooden trunks covered with deer's hide or pigskin. More often they traveled on foot pushing two-wheel handcarts or on horseback with huge saddlebags.

The highways the travelers followed, well described in *From Here to Yender* by Marion Nicholl Rawson, were as varied as the wares and services they peddled. Some roads were made by laying the heavy branches of cut trees across the roadbed and covering them with earth. There were "corduroys" made of logs laid transversely one after the other on the road. The beaver dams in marshy spots, three or four feet wide and often very long, were always incorporated into these roads when possible. The smoothest highways of all were the "sleigh roads," for in winter when mud froze and hollows filled with snow the roads were generally at their best. Winter travel was therefore popular, and the itinerants were often accompanied by a long line of farmers' sleighs carrying food and homespuns to market. The winter roads were kept in good shape after snowstorms by the simple process of "kittlin' out": a pair of oxen dragged a bobsled that had two large brass kettles fastened to the end of the runners.

The early road-makers were practical and ingenious. Horse troughs made of hollowed logs were placed at convenient intervals, and halfway up steep hilly ways there would be built a raised ledge or "thank-you-marm" where the wheels of a cart or wagon could rest while the horse caught his second wind. The bridges were of various kinds, and some were quite elaborate. There were foot bridges, horse bridges made of planks and long covered bridges for heavier traffic. Then there were the rafts made of tree trunks lashed together and poled back and forth across a small river; and the more complicated "wire ferry," a scow in which a ferryman pulled the traveler and his burdens across a stream by catching with a hooked pole at an overhead cable fastened to tall poles on either shore. There were also ferries run by horsepower, in which one or more horses propelled the boat by walking a treadmill which moved a large underwater wheel. (See Fig. 19, the horsepower boat Porter designed and presented to the public in 1842.) All these roadway conveniences involved expenses which were covered by the revenue from numerous tollgates. Even foot travelers had to pay, and besides paying they might be obliged to wait for an hour while dozens of turkeys and hundreds of sheep were counted and checked through the gate.

Toward the end of each day the itinerants would all begin to look for the friendly tavern sign that would mean shelter for the night and food and drink. Tavern life was high life in the early days. It represented good living, good company and plentiful entertainment. Thomas Hamilton records (in *Men and Manners in America*) a supper served at a wayside inn in 1833, consisting of dishes of beefsteaks, broiled fowl, ham, cold turkey, toast broiled in melted butter, waffles, tea, coffee, etc.—the etc., of course, included rum. At dinner, and afterward sitting by the fire, travelers from all parts of the country met, discussed politics, religion and trade, passed on news and gossip, and regaled the company with stories of their travels, freely spiced with tall tales that were not always believed but always told again. It has been said that to sit by a tavern hearth in those days was to have an ear to the world.

Rufus Porter must have been a welcome addition to any tavern gathering for he could play his fiddle by the fireside or, if the tavern had a ballroom, for a lively country dance. While games of pitching pennies went on in taproom corners he undoubtedly told many an exciting tale of his recent years at sea, of savage Indian fights off the Northwest Coast and of the strange life in Hawaii. On his portrait painting trips he probably ended the day with orders for likenesses of the tavern keeper and his family, and some of the guests as well. He may often have spent several cozy days at a time off the road doing portraits from tavern headquarters, and perhaps repainting the tavern sign before he left. Later, when he became a fresco painter, we know that he painted the rooms and ballrooms in a number of New England taverns, earning his fee with board and lodging while he worked.

On his portrait painting expedition into the South Porter seems to have headed for the cities, rather than small towns as he did when painting frescoes in New England. The reason for this is obvious. Portraits were in demand in the urban centers, and Porter followed his market. Baltimore, like Boston, New York and Philadelphia, was an important center for artists and Porter undoubtedly secured a number of portrait commissions when he arrived. Here, too, he must certainly have visited the new Natural History Museum which had been founded in 1818 by Rembrandt Peale as a branch of Charles Willson Peale's museum in Philadelphia. Among the prime exhibits at this time were the portrait gallery, the "Great Sea-Serpent" and the "Pandean Band" consisting of a single Italian named Signor Helene who played on five different instruments at the same time.

From Baltimore Porter went on to Alexandria where in 1820 he made a camera obscura to enable him to paint portraits in fifteen minutes and bought a handcart to facilitate traveling with his extra equipment. He was now ready for quantity production of likenesses costing one dollar each. He adorned his camera box with brilliant colors, set the whole on the handcart, which was further decorated with a flag, and started out with his gallery-on-wheels for Harrisonburg Hot Springs. According to the 1884 account in the *Scientific American* he was welcomed in every village, his little show attracted constant attention, and as his fifteen-minute portraits were greatly in demand he collected lots of dollars.

Porter's use of a camera obscura as a mechanical aid to portraiture, like his use of stencils in landscape painting, was symptomatic of the changing times. Art in the eighteenth century was a high-priced luxury for the aristocratic leaders of society. In the flourishing democracy of the nineteenth century art became a product wanted by all, and so axiomatically to be made available to all. The same problem was being posed in all fields: how to make desirable products and services available to the masses of people who now considered it part of their proclaimed birthright of equality to have them. The answer to this problem promoted an important new group of Americans—the inventors.

It is interesting to note that many representatives of the most purely creative field of endeavor—art—now developed a practical bent. Their fertile imaginations, formerly directed to mainly esthetic ends, became increasingly applied to utilitarian tasks. This explains the early-nineteenth-century connection between art and invention. The fact that a number of nineteenth-century inventors were also painters—Fulton, Morse and Rufus Porter are prime examples—is not a coincidence. Biographies have spoken of the versatility of the great inventor-painters, but that isn't the basic point. There was a fundamental connection between pictorial inventiveness and practical invention in the early nineteenth century, and there was a logical development from the one to the other. The latter explains the transitional stage of inventive, partly mechanical painting, such as Porter's camera portraits and stencil and cork-work frescoes, which evolved in response to the new democratic desire for "cheap-and-easy" art.

Rufus Porter is a striking representative of nineteenth-century artists whose original creative ability developed along practical, inventive lines. During his first itinerant trip we find him devising a useful laborsaving device for portraiture and expanding an art to an industry. At the same time he became an active inventor, originating mechanisms of various sorts as he traveled from town to town painting portraits. He practiced this dual itinerant career of artist and inventor for the greater part of his life.

The use of a camera for quantity production of portraits was the first major instance of Rufus Porter's anticipation of the practical demands of his times. A precedent for painters' experiments with the camera obscura had been established in another age of scientific pioneering by the greatest of all artist-inventors, Leonardo da Vinci. Of this Rufus Porter was probably unaware. It is possible, however, that he knew of the description of a portable tent camera for sketching published in the first art instruction book generally known in New England, *Graphics, or the Most Ancient and Excellent Art of Limning* by Henry Peachem of London. First printed in 1612, this was the ancestor of a long line of such books, of which Porter's *Curious Arts* was a descendant. In *Curious Arts*, published in 1825, Rufus Porter gives a working description of the camera obscura which he first constructed in Alexandria in 1820:

A very convenient camera obscura, for drawing landscapes, or even portraits, may be constructed as follows: Make a box of boards, in the form of a regular cube, being one foot in length, breadth and height; bore a hole of one inch diameter, through the centre of the top; and on this, fix a double convex lens, the focus of which must reach the bottom of the box. Make an aperture of about six inches in length, and one in breadth, through one side of the box at the top, by shaving off, or holding the edge in such manner that when you put your face to the aperture to look into the box, it will exclude all the light except what falls through the lens. Make a hole through each end of the box, near the bottom, large enough to put in the hands, with paper and pencil. On the top of the box, on the right and left sides of the lens, fix two pieces of boards, which may be about four inches high, eight inches long, and three inches distant from each other. Between these boards, fix a piece of looking glass, three inches square, and facing from you; the lower edge of the glass, being near the lens, on the side towards you; and the upper edge inclining towards you about thirty degrees from a perpendicular. Directly over, and nearly four inches above the lens, place another mirror, the centre of which must face directly towards the lower edge of the first—cover the glass-box so as to exclude all the light from the glasses except what falls on them horizontally from objects directly in front of you, and place a sheet of paper on the bottom of the box inside. The rays of light, passing from objects in front, will be reflected from the first mirror to the second, and from the second, through the lens to the paper, where you will have a perfect similitude of the objects in view, in full colours, and true perspective, and may trace them on the paper, with a pencil or pen.

By the first years of the eighteenth century the camera obscura was in common use as a sketching instrument (young Benjamin West had employed one) and by the middle of the nineteenth century it was already being successfully applied to photography by Daguerre. Porter's contribution was to construct and popularize in the first quarter of the nineteenth century a practical easy-to-make portable camera—one that could be made and used by anyone for amateur or professional portrait painting.

Carl Drepperd describes in his *American Pioneer Arts and Artists* an early Philadelphia amateur "who gave the Daguerrists a run for some of the trade." This anonymous portrait painter posed his subjects before a camera obscura, "a fearful contraption" according to one sitter. Working in the dark in the camera he outlined the features on tracing paper and from this made a faint positive print on the final sheet. He then drew over the faint lines and colored the portrait. These "quick-painted" miniatures were sold for ten dollars a dozen. Mr. Drepperd comments that this painter may have drawn his technique from Porter's *Curious Arts*.

Simple mechanical aids to painting such as Porter's primitive camera did not in this early period achieve anything like a photographic effect. In fact, the paintings made in this way are strikingly unnaturalistic. This is probably the result of the necessity for the two-part method in which a simplified outline drawing was first made of the reflected image, and this outline subsequently colored in. Thus, paradoxically, instead of achieving optical realism the camera technique tended to sharpen the painter's interest in linear design and flat color patterns.

Rufus Porter's rapid-style portrait and fresco painting was developed to meet a growing desire for inexpensive original art. As we will find to be the case in all his major activities, Porter pioneered in the field of popular portrait painting. Starting a kind of primitive portrait factory in 1820, he led the field by a full decade. It was not until the thirties and forties that itinerant portrait painting entered the large scale production phase. We find many enterprises similar to Porter's portrait-for-a-dollar cart—but always ten to twenty years later. That Rufus Porter had correctly gauged the growing popular art market is evident from the thousands of portraits by talented itinerants in the second quarter of the nineteenth century.

We left Rufus Porter wending his way toward Harrisonburg Hot Springs, doing a booming portrait business from his handcart headquarters. As he neared the area of the hot springs he became obsessed with the idea of discovering the substance that was capable of yielding perpetual heat. After he had arrived some time in 1820 he optimistically began to bore deep into the earth near the springs with a five-foot auger in search of this hot substance which could make a fortune for the discoverer. But he found nothing more remarkable than a hydrate of lime and so abandoned the project and started northward with his cart, again painting portraits along the way.

About this time he thought of the practical possibilities of a power-driven airship and began inventing mechanisms of all kinds. On his trip north in 1821 and 1822 his profession of itinerant painter alternated with that of inventor. Between 1822 and 1825 he became involved in several quite ambitious projects: inventing and introducing a revolving almanac, a twin boat propelled by horsepower, a horse flatboat, and a cord-making machine.

Rufus Porter's trip south to Virginia and then back north, painting and inventing all along the way, had taken several years—from 1819 to 1822. In 1823 he could have been found walking with his cart and camera through New England. He was then accompanied, according to our much-quoted *Scientific American* account, by a lad "Joe," a relative. This boy was probably Rufus' nephew Jonathan D. Poor (1807–1845), the son of his sister Ruth Porter and Jonathan Poor of Sebago, Maine. A search of the Porter genealogy does not uncover any young relative of Rufus' named Joseph; but the Joe of the *Scientific American* might certainly have been "Joe" or "Jo" for Jonathan. Jonathan D. Poor was, in the thirties, the most productive member of Rufus Porter's school of mural painters. It seems reasonable to assume that in 1823 the sixteen-year-old lad started his itinerant career as an apprentice-assistant with Porter's traveling portrait shop. The portrait business, it is clear from Porter's advertising leaflet, had evolved from the dollar-a-likeness handcart to a more ambitious enterprise, with a larger range of products and prices—and now an assistant.

An example of a printed and hand-colored family register, with an 1820 marriage and an 1823 birth date entered, suggests that designing and selling these popular items was a sideline to the portrait painting business. One example (Fig. 41) is inscribed "Published by Rufus Porter" and the printer's name seems to be Henry Bowen of Boston. These registers wanderings in 1823 they spent some time in New York City, painting portraits as usual. Here is an amusing incident which the obituary article were undoubtedly printed in large quantities and colored by Porter and Joe en route as needed for sales. During the course of Rufus' and Joe's

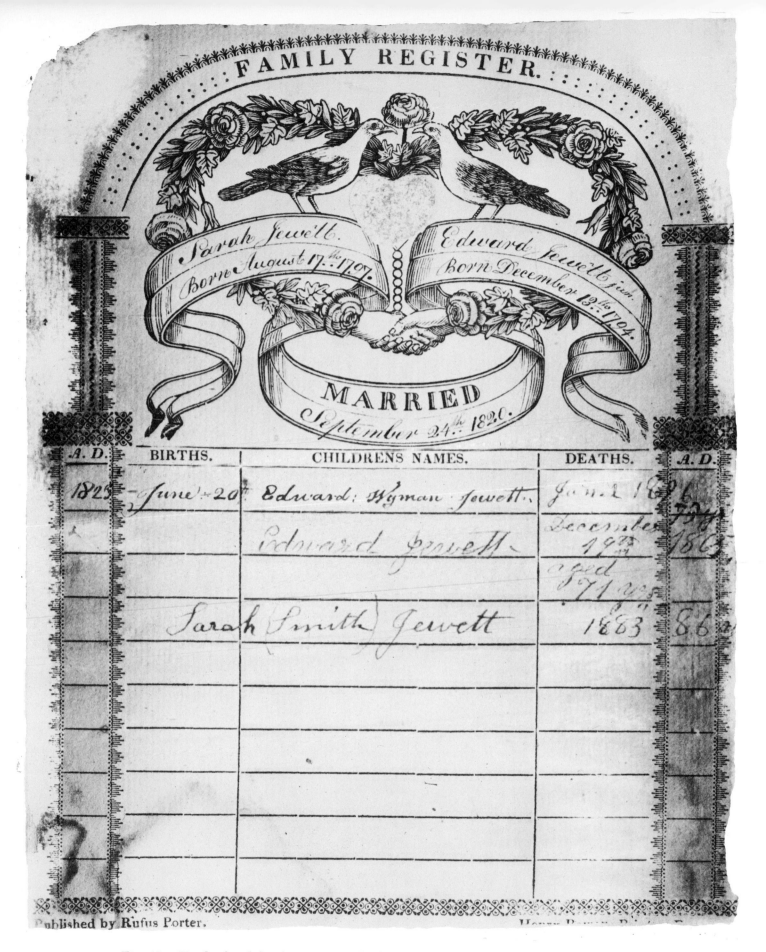

FAMILY REGISTER.

Sarah Jewett. Born August 17th 1707.

Edward Jewett jun. Born December 13th 1704.

MARRIED September 24th 1820.

A.D.	BIRTHS.	CHILDRENS NAMES.	DEATHS.	A.D.
1825	June 20	Edward Wyman Jewett	Jan 2 1826	
		Edward Jewett	December 19th aged 71 yrs	1863
		Sarah (Smith) Jewett	1863	86

Published by Rufus Porter.   Henry Bowen, Printer, Boston

Fig. 41. Hand-colored family register, published by Rufus Porter, probably c. 1820. Lettering at right reads "Henry Bowen, Printer, Boston," according to the owner of this Porter item, Nina Fletcher Little.

in the *Scientific American*, our basic source for Porter biography, records:

> One morning he was out strolling with Joe, when he saw some people about to start in the stage for Philadelphia. An impulse instantly seized him to go along. So he joined the party, directing Joe to get the camera and send it by the next stage. But the box failed to come, and he was obliged to foot it back to New York, earning his meals by cutting people's portraits out of paper with scissors.

These few sentences tell the whole story of Rufus Porter's temperament—impulsive, ignoring minor practical considerations, and cheerfully getting out of any fix with never-failing ingenuity.

On his brief visit to Philadelphia Rufus undoubtedly visited the Pennsylvania Academy of Art and Charles Willson Peale's Natural History Museum. This museum was considered a "world in miniature" and, like Rufus Porter's *Curious Arts* (a sort of literary parallel), was almost all-inclusive. There were curiosities of all kinds—natural, historical and artistic. Franklin had contributed a stuffed French angora cat, Jefferson a collection of Indian tomahawks, scalps and wampum belts. Exhibits included a live baboon, a lady's shoe from Canton, feathers from the South Seas, a portrait gallery, and the mastodon bones which Peale had dug out of a peat bog in 1801. This excavation project might be seen as a sign of the new interest in natural science and of the large optimistic approach to the subject.

Charles Willson Peale, soldier, scientist and painter, must have been a man temperamentally much like Porter. In 1823, the year of his visit to Philadelphia, Porter could have listened to a lecture on natural history which Peale delivered at the museum. It is tempting to wonder whether Charles Willson Peale and Rufus Porter may have met as Peale was nearing the end of his long career as a painter and a scientist and Porter was just embarking on his.

Sometime after Peale's death, on July 4, 1838, his museum was renamed the Philadelphia Museum and opened to the public in a building at the corner of Ninth and Sansom Streets. Here, besides the portrait collection, there was in the north gallery a profile department set up for taking silhouettes on the spot. This would have especially interested Rufus Porter, whom we may assume visited Philadelphia more than once. In an early description of the old Philadelphia Museum, which burned in 1854, there is mention (Scharf & Westcott, *History of Philadelphia*) of a "fine landscape scene" which filled up the extreme end of the hall from gallery to ceiling. This sounds as if it could only have been a wall painting, and as most of the large-scale mural landscapes painted about that time have turned out to be Porter's it would not be surprising to learn that he had indeed contributed to as well as visited the Philadelphia Museum.

Some time between 1823 and 1824 Rufus Porter's interest shifted from portrait to landscape painting. There is a tradition, recorded by A. J. Philpott in one of his *Boston Globe* articles, that Porter sold his camera to another itinerant limner and began painting landscapes, but found no market for them and so turned to mural painting. Recently, a pair of oil landscapes, one signed *R. Porter 18—Portland*, was brought to my attention. It now seems likely that this prolific artist painted many more landscapes, to be rediscovered in the future, it is hoped. In 1824 we know that he began traveling about New England painting mural landscapes for houses and taverns.

His portraits, which date from 1816 to his late years, and his silhouettes were probably never signed. The silhouettes would be almost impossible to identify now, and we have no idea how many he may have cut—at twenty cents apiece probably a large number. An estimate of the production of small portraits painted over a period of more than fifty years must lead to the conclusion that probably well over a thousand were made by Rufus Porter during the first three quarters of the century. This is a startling figure for nineteenth-century portrait painting. But when one recalls that during the years 1815, 1816, 1818 and 1819–1823 portrait painting was a chief activity of Porter's, it does not seem extravagant. Let us just consider the four years of concentrated portrait painting in 1820, 1821, 1822 and 1823, when the camera obscura made possible quantity production of the popular portraits. If during those years Porter had averaged just one fifteen-minute portrait every other day the total for the four years would come to 730 likenesses. Adding his earlier and later years of portrait painting to this nucleus, the estimate of upwards of a thousand portraits seems quite conservative. And only one pair has been found! Yet family portraits are the category of early American art that was most carefully preserved in the past and is most eagerly purchased in modern times. Where are all the Porter portraits?

Judging from the one identified pair and his advertising leaflet, they would have unusual charm and a distinctive style. In Porter's *Scientific American* article of January 22, 1846, on "Miniature Painting" he describes exactly how small watercolor portraits are to be executed, and this article should help in identifying some of his own portraits. He tells his pupils to draw the outline in pencil, then retrace in diluted colors with a fine camel's hair brush. "The outlines of the features may be traced with lake; those of the hair, with burnt umber, and the drapery with blue and black." The lead pencil lines are then rubbed off, and the main color applied. The face is washed with diluted Venetian red, laid on smoothly and uniformly. The cheeks of "beautiful faces" are colored a light carmine. The hair is painted with a mixture of black and burnt umber, with additions of red if the hair is sandy or reddish. Yellow ocher is used if the subject is young and the hair very light. The coat is painted black, blue or green, the color mixed with white so as to be opaque. For all other parts the colors are worked transparently. The face and the white part of the drapery are shaded with a neutral tint. White is used only for small specks representing the reflection of light from the eyes, or from jewelry. Porter's miniature portraits were undoubtedly painted in just this manner. They are probably all small bust or three-quarter-length profile portraits, precisely executed in watercolor on paper as described, with delicate "hair pencil" outlining. Certainly a good number of them must be extant; and perhaps the fine pair here reproduced will serve as a core around which the body of Rufus Porter's work as a portrait painter will eventually be assembled.

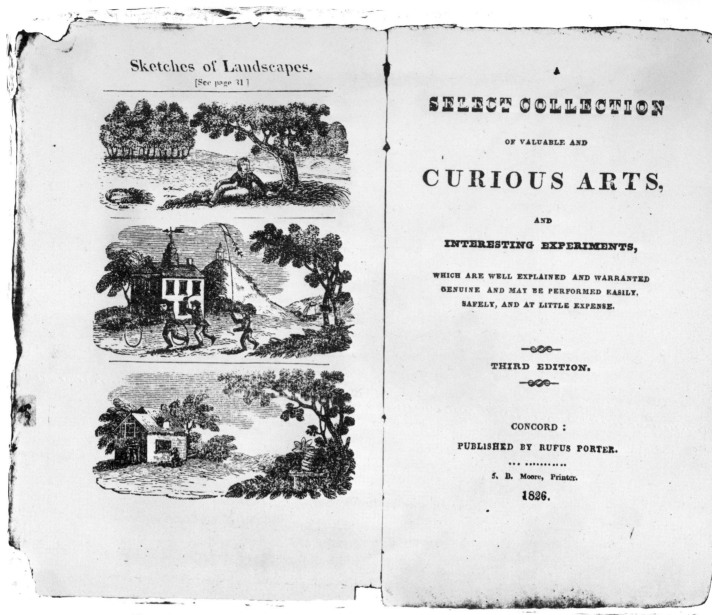

Fig. 42.   Frontispiece and title page of *Curious Arts,* third edition, Porter's best-seller art instruction book which went into four editions in 1825 and 1826.

Fig. 43.   "The Amateur Painter" engraved by Rufus Porter for an article on landscape painting in *Scientific American,* December 11, 1845.

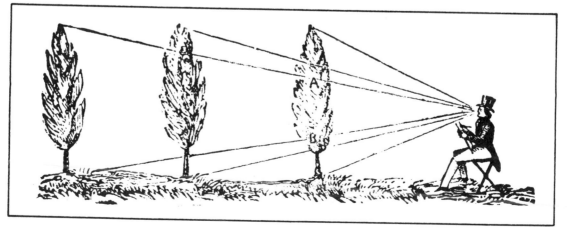

Art Instructor to the People

IN 1825 RUFUS PORTER WROTE—AND PUBLISHED at Concord, New Hampshire —a book titled *A Select Collection of Valuable and Curious Arts, and Interesting Experiments* (Fig. 42), one of the many popular art instruction books which were printed in America from the end of the eighteenth century well into the second half of the nineteenth. (A slightly different and undated *Collection*, about half the length of *Curious Arts*, was published by Porter, in Concord, Massachusetts, probably shortly before the first edition of *Curious Arts*—see Bibliography. The single surviving copy known to this author is in the collection of Old Sturbridge Village in Sturbridge, Massachusetts.) Hundreds of these little art instructors survive to show, in one field, the spirit that motivated early America and produced our nineeenth-century Americana. These books were written for the numerous individuals who were eager to become amateur artists. Around the middle of the century itinerant art teachers traveled about transforming farmers and housewives into artists quite literally overnight. The art instruction books, which found their way into every corner of the countryside and were passed along from hand to hand, were earlier itinerant instructors, in print.

An unprecedented creative urge coupled with a willingness to try any experiment resulted in a surge of popular self-expression in the early years of the nineteenth century unique in American history. The Declaration of Independence had found its personal echo in the minds of the people. Their dependence on Europe was over, and they were happily confident that they could do anything and everything themselves. They were enterprising, eager to learn and entirely willing to teach themselves.

This was the era of the Jack-of-all-trades, and painting was just one more promising activity that might be added to the versatile American's repertory of accomplishments. The Russian diplomat Paul Svinin, who visited America in the beginning of the nineteenth century, had expected art to become a "universal accomplishment." It did. In the early years of American independence dozens of popular art instruction books were published and thousands of laymen became pioneer artists. This pioneer art was a spontaneous outgrowth of the new spirit of American democracy and as such is especially significant in the history of American art.

The preface to the first American edition of *One Thousand Valuable Secrets in the Elegant and Useful Arts,* one of the ancestors of *Curious Arts,* points out that in 1795 America was still indebted to the workshops of other nations for most of its finer articles, and proclaims the belief that "it will be sound policy, as well as good oeconomy [sic] to produce all that we can among ourselves, and no longer remain tributary to foreign markets. This will be the surest means of establishing our independence on the firmest basis." There was one all-embracing Declaration of Independence but there were subordinate ones in every field, and the lines quoted above speak for American arts and crafts. It was this nationalistic attitude that eventually produced an American tradition in art and kept it free from continental influence; and it is a striking fact that the modest little art instruction books rather than the formal art academies originally sponsored this indigenous approach to the arts. According to the American editor of *One Thousand Valuable Secrets* the book was planned for "common readers" and intended to "open an extensive field for the exercise of American ingenuity and improvement." The academies were planned for a select group of professional artists, and both the schools themselves and the art they taught were based entirely on English and European models.

Rufus Porter's popular *Curious Arts* was an example of the early instruction books which represented native as against continental traditions in the arts and crafts. The arts it taught were founded on craft techniques and these arts were to be practiced by the layman as simply and directly as a wheelwright would make a wheel or a cobbler a shoe. The instruction is of the most elementary kind, and the preface makes it clear that the book was intended for the "profit or amusement" of amateurs.

Curious Arts is a personally selected compendium of practical art recipes, simple experiments in general science and the tricks of a number of trades. The chances are that most of the arts described in 102 pages—from glass painting and etching to painting carpets and wallpapers—were at some time attempted by the author, and a number of them Porter had practiced professionally. He had done ornamental painting in Portland, and in several New Hampshire houses he had decorated the woodwork as well as stenciled walls and painted murals by this time. He was, in fact, working in New Hampshire as a mural painter at the time *Curious Arts* was published. A longish section details the method for "Landscape Painting on Walls of Rooms." Among the 115 other items contained in this little book are:

> To paint in figures for carpets or borders; to paint in imitation of mahogany and maple; to change wood apparently to stone; copper plate etching and engraving; mezzotint engraving; etching in aqua-tints; ornamental gilding; to make sympathetic ink for secret correspondence; luminous ink that will shine in the dark; painting on glass; best method of tracing or copying a picture; the construction and use of a copying machine; to kindle a fire under water; to produce detonating balloons; construction of a galvanic pile or battery; to freeze water in warm weather; the art of manufacturing paper hangings; to change the colours of animals.

Then there are formulas for making various paints, inks, glues, varnishes, crayons, and a final item entitled "Sundry Experiments." An appendix prints a "catalogue of the various articles mentioned in the preceding pages, with the prices, explanations, etc"; and following a marginal cut of a pointing index finger is a note stating that "The articles which have this mark * prefixed may be procured at 135, Washington-street, Boston." As only seven out of seventy-five items do *not* boast the asterisk, it seems reasonable to assume that as usual Rufus had several irons in the fire and to suspect that his business connections with an artists' supply shop at 135 Washington Street had something to do with the writing of this book. Porter may have been a shopkeeper for a brief while, though most probably the shop belonged to a more static businessman who sponsored or contributed to the publication of *Curious Arts*.

The amateurs who learned how to paint from art instruction books like *Curious Arts* proceeded in a way that was entirely different from the manner in which, in their time or today, a "finished" academic painter would work. The art instructors gave concentrated short-cut lessons, and the things they did not teach are as important in the final result as the things they did. The one all-important factor in the development of a professional academician was the training of his eye; and the capability of the artist was measured by the skill with which, after many exercises and long practice, he was able to approximate in paint the exact visual appearance of things. Thus sketching from models and drawing from nature were the basic first steps in formal art schools. Not so with the printed art instructors. Their simple lessons could not aim at sophisticated illusionistic painting, and the works produced under their tutelage came closer to abstract than to realistic art. The art instruction booklets could not provide their students with plaster casts or masterpiece models to look at, but they could and did give concrete directions for every part of a painting which were as clear and specific as for dyeing silk or making ink. Stencils and other mechanical aids to painting were freely advocated by the instruction books; never, of course, by the academies.

If we look at a few of the art instruction books we will understand their practical approach to the art of painting, which in turn explains the stylized, unillusionistic and unromanticized art which the amateurs produced. All of these books considered painting primarily as a craft. They stressed the materials used in painting and the process of using them. In the academies the basic point of departure for the artist was not the tools of his craft but his noble function as the exalted representative of the Fine Arts, which alone could stir and "elevate" the emotions. There was nothing grandiose in the vocabulary of the instruction books, and they left the emotions out of the picture entirely. They considered and addressed the prospective painter as a simple workman learning a new technique. Having given detailed directions for grinding and mixing the colors and making or selecting the brushes, they proceeded to the methods of painting the specific items which make up a picture, in just the way carpenters' manuals explained the construction of the parts that would be put together to build a coach or a house. In *The School of Wisdom* (1787) we read in a few lines just how to draw "Eyes, Ears, Legs, Arms, Hands, Feet, etc." In the "Rules for Drawing Beasts" one is told to begin at the forehead, draw downward into the nose, mouth, and upper and nether chop, and end the lines at the throat. Another item on "The Method of Colouring Beasts" prescribes specified color mixtures for sheep, hogs, mice, a bear, a wolf, a gray wolf, the elephant and the unicorn. *One Thousand Valuable Secrets* contains an item on "the choice of colors fit for expressing the various complexions" which reads, partially, as follows:

1. For women and children; mix a little white and a little turnfel.
2. For men; a mixture of white and vermillion is proper.
3. For old folks; you may use some white and ochre.
4. For horses; you must choose bistre, ochre, and white.

In *Curious Arts,* Section 32 on "Landscape Painting on Walls of Rooms" tells exactly how to compose the design; how (to the inch) to space the various parts; how (with paint formulas) to color the sky, clouds, mountains and trees; how to use the brushes. The account begins, not with a discussion of the beauties of mountain or ocean scenery, but with the direction to "dissolve half a pound of glue in a gallon of water, and with this sizing mix whatever colors may be required for the work."

It is clear that the primitive painter—of which Porter was a prime example—worked as a craftsman. He did not think of himself as an artist recording in paint a visualized object or scene. He was a workman building his picture, bit by bit, and could best do so by proceeding logically from one part to the next. This additive approach is largely responsible for the abstract style of amateur art, and it made the use of stencils a normal procedure for constructing a picture. In Matthew Finn's instruction book, *Theoremetical System of Painting*—a significant title—the fact that the primitive artist thought of his picture in terms of separate parts rather than the whole is strikingly apparent. In a section on landscapes the author of this book remarks that "the component parts of landscape are the sky, trees, rocks, water, buildings, &c. All of these, it is evident, require distinct and careful study." It is obvious that in primitive paintings the separate parts of a picture were not unified by means of an optically consistent perspective or enveloping atmosphere, both of which are notably missing in typical primitives. The binding agent in primitive painting was design, and this largely explains their abstract rather than illusionistic appearance. The primitive painter did not attempt to re-create any specific moment of actual reality but instead painted a timeless, composite scene. In these paintings anything could be omitted or anything included. The seemingly contradictory fact that some primitive paintings are overcrowded while others are almost empty as compared with true-to-life paintings results from a selection and addition of the typical elements in any typical situation. Whether the artist chose to include more or less than would appear in real life is immaterial; both choices exclude that which was outside the pale of the primitive painter—an accurate representation of normal, visible reality.

Curious Arts is representative of the instruction books which fostered our early American arts and crafts and which lent a helping hand to primitive painters. Neither the approach nor the plan of Porter's book was original, deriving both specifically and generally from earlier instructors such as *The School of Wisdom* (1787), *The Artist's Assistant* (1794), *One Thousand Valuable Secrets* (1795) and *The Artist's Companion* (1814). *Curious Arts* was one of the most widely read of all the early instruction books because it was brief and simply written and its wide variety of contents was carefully selected for general use. Porter's special contribution in the field of early art-and-experiment books was to produce a practical and popular anthology. In just this way he had popularized the well-known but slightly used camera obscura as a practical means for speeding up portrait painting.

Porter was in his early years a sort of natural sponge for the curious arts of his time, which he enthusiastically absorbed and then gave back to the public in tested ready-to-use recipes. In his later years he became more originally constructive, striking out in new directions rather than developing and popularizing the existing trends of his time. Except for the original discussion of mural painting, his *Curious Arts* is a prime example of his early attitude; and it is interesting to note that it was by his youthful and only moderately progressive efforts that he achieved his measure of popular success. The early camera obscura portraits were greatly in demand and Porter made a good deal of money painting them; his early cord machine and other prosaic inventions were very successful; *Curious Arts* was read all through New England. His later and more ambitious projects were not so well received. The *Scientific American,* originated under Porter's advanced editorship, prospered only when it passed to conservative management. Porter's automobile was entirely ignored and the "aeroport" abandoned through lack of public support. Rufus Porter's prophetic *Aerial Navigation,* which detailed in 1849 the possibilities of a transcontinental passenger airship, was openly ridiculed; but old-fashioned *Curious Arts* had gone into five editions within a year of publication. Porter's contributions were favored or slighted in his time in inverse proportion to their long-term significance, and a twentieth-century re-evaluation is very much in order.

Rufus Porter's *Curious Arts* was a best seller, and when he began his newspaper career he drew upon this earlier publication and reprinted most of its contents in two serial columns titled "Curious Arts" and "Interesting Experiments." These appeared in the *New York Mechanic* in 1841–1842 and again in the *Scientific American* in 1845. In the latter he added a third feature called "The Art of Painting." The articles in this series, though based on a number of items in *Curious Arts* and on a few new articles published in the *New York Mechanic*, were entirely rewritten and substantially improved. The articles, published in the *Scientific American* between September 11, 1845, and April 9, 1846, when Porter was editor-publisher, were all headed "The Art of Painting" with subheads specifying the content. The how-to-do-it subjects included house, sign and carriage painting, ornamental gilding and bronzing, painting on glass and on cambric for screens and window shades, landscape and portrait painting, miniature painting, "Imitation Painting," "Chrystaline Changeable Painting," and, most important of all, nine articles on "Landscape Painting on Walls of Rooms." (See Porter's "Amateur Painter" in Fig. 43.) In the first issue, the editor stated: "Being practically acquainted with every branch of painting, from the plainest house and shipwork, to the finest miniature portraits, we propose to give in a series of numbers complete instructions in every branch."

These articles make up a complete art instruction serial which represents Porter's mature approach to the problems of painting. In *Curious Arts* an experienced self-taught painter gives specific instruction to amateurs. In the newspaper articles, written twenty years later, this is done too; but Porter in his editorial capacity now adds significant critical comment on the character and aims of his unacademic art instruction, and on the approach, subject matter and achievements of the self-taught painter.

Rufus Porter was the first American to deliberately formulate, practice and promote the "natural" as against the academic approach to painting; the first to point to the rich possibilities of design as opposed to academic realism; the first to see the homely beauty of rural American farms and villages as unparalleled subject matter for American landscape painting. Porter was not only an art teacher but an active crusader for an honest American tradition in painting. To say that he was the first artist to appreciate and depict the plain New England countryside does not adequately define his unique position in the history of American landscape painting. Before the middle of the nineteenth century he was teaching and preaching the beauties of American farm scenery, and painting it in simple, lucid scenes on the walls of hundreds of New Engand homes and inns, while all the famous contemporary artists were painting in the manner of the Old World masters.

Porter's appeal for an everyday American art was a voice crying in the wilderness in his time, and created scarcely a ripple in the tide of academic eclecticism. It was not until the surge of nationalism following World War I that an indigenous tradition flourished. Painting in America had evolved in a melting-pot manner, with a native American approach a minor tendency until the twentieth century. Under the influence of Dutch and English painting in the seventeenth century, American art was dominated in the eighteenth by English style under the leadership of Gilbert Stuart and Benjamin West. During the nineteenth century, Homer, Ryder, Eakins and the folk painters represented the native minority. In the continental tradition were the artists of the Hudson River School who painted in the manner of the Düsseldorf masters; the genre painters influenced by the realism of the Dutch school; the landscape group inspired by Salvator Rosa and the French romanticists; the expatriates who worked abroad; the American painters who looked to the French Impressionists. This foreign tradition was broken in the years following World War I by a group of regional artists who claimed their admiration for the American scene and their freedom from foreign influence. This is what Rufus Porter had done nearly a hundred years before. Generations ahead of his time, he advocated and practiced a type of robust, unacademic American painting that was popularized in the twentieth century by Grant Wood, John Steuart Curry, Thomas Benton, Peter Hurd, Marsden Hartley and a whole school of painters of the American scene.

A natural originality of style allied with strong convictions as to personal freedom explain Rufus Porter's dislike for hidebound academic precepts. His artistic aims were diametrically opposed to those of the academicians of his time. It is interesting to juxtapose Porter's art instruction, as presented in his unpretentious newspaper series on the art of painting, with that of the imposing academies that dominated taste in the nineteenth century.

In 1805 the Pennsylvania Academy of Art was founded in Philadelphia. The seventy founders of this first American art academy, Charles Willson Peale among them, met in Independence Hall and pledged the new association "to promote the cultivation of the Fine Arts in the United States of America, by introducing correct and elegant copies from works of the first masters in Sculpture and Painting." The key words "Fine Arts," "correct," "elegant," "copies" and "masters" foretell the history of academic art in America.

During the next half century, academic painting flourished. Its sponsors were advanced professional painters whose patrons were wealthy connoiseurs. Headquarters were the large urban centers. The education of the academicians was based on foreign masterpieces and study abroad. They taught their pupils to choose exalted subject matter, to achieve a sophisticated refinement of finish, and above all to arrive at accurate visual correctness in the representation.

This was the art that Rufus Porter disclaimed; its exact opposite was the art he preached. The pupils he sought were laymen who might learn their art at home and practice it in the parlor or on the highway, for the enjoyment of their fellows. Their source of inspiration and subject matter for painting was to be the American scene, their technique based simply on sound craftsmanship. Their style would be their own affair, for they were free to experiment at will with design and color. Rufus Porter preached the modern gospel of painting for pleasure. In his articles on the art of painting his credo is made clear. His direct approach to his amateur public is summarized in the introduction to the article on landscape painting in the *Scientific American* for December 11, 1845: "We shall not, in this place, give the theoretic and systematic rules of perspective drawing, as usually taught in the schools, and which tends, invariably, to check, if not destroy a natural taste for drawing and painting; but arrange our instruction in such a manner that the learner will be amused with the task and encouraged to proceed."

The academies had more ambitious aims for painting, and looked to Greece, Italy, France and England for inspiration.

Benjamin West, the lion of the Pennsylvania Academy, accepted the honorary membership to the Academy with a speech in which he expressed the hope that Philadelphia would become "the Athens of the Western World." It did its best. The Academy building, built in 1806, was a magnificent Roman affair complete with rotunda. By March enough European canvases and plaster casts of classical sculpture had been acquired to warrant an exhibition. West contributed two Shakespearean paintings. In 1809 an ancient mosaic from Florence was added, then more antique casts, and soon the Academy boasted a large collection of foreign antiquities and art works of all kinds. By 1830 the antique statue gallery was one of the sights of the town. Mrs. Trollope describes the alternate groups of male and female visitors sneaking in and delightedly allowing their delicacy to be shocked by the plaster casts. In 1812 and 1814 there had been two exhibits which were later described in *Lippincott's Magazine* (February 1872) as showing how American work was coming to the fore in the early years of the century. To prove his point the anonymous critic describes Rembrandt Peale's contribution, "The Roman Daughter," as a composition good enough to have earned the accusation of having been copied from the French painter Gérard! For the 1814 exhibition the *pièce de résistance* was evidently Sully's "excellent copy" of Rubens' "Tribute Money." Both the early exhibitors and the late critic had the same academic attitude, and saw nothing incongruous in an American art based on a combination of classical subject matter and continental style.

The American Academy of the Arts, chartered in New York in 1808, opened its first exhibition in 1816. In 1817 an official account of its collection lists a number of classical sculptures; paintings by Salvator Rosa, Teniers and others; copies of paintings by Veronese, Titian, Rubens, etc. The few contemporary American portraits must have seemed almost an anachronism. In the list of busts there are nineteen classical subjects—Euripides, Pythagoras, Plato, Juno, Mercury, Bacchus, Nero, Seneca and so on—and then, at the end, we find Washington, Hamilton, Napoleon—and Benjamin West!

The primers for the early academies were the casts of classical sculpture and copies and engravings from the great works of European master painters. Study and practice taught the young American artists how to go about copying and assimilating these models. Annual exhibitions of contemporary academic art further stimulated their efforts, and the most promising pupils were sent to European cultural centers to study masterpieces at first hand. Benjamin West, the closest link between American and English art, had drawn two generations of American students to his London studio. With the rise of the American academies scores of budding artists were sent to Italy to study.

It is significant to note that Samuel F. B. Morse, the first president of the National Academy of Design, organized in New York in 1826, boasted that our National Academy was firmly founded on a great English model, the Royal Academy of Arts. In this same tradition is the remark of an unnamed art critic who in an 1828 issue of the *North American Review* states that "no artist can expect here the highest rewards of his art. He must seek them if he is entitled to them, in the great capitals of Europe."

Rufus Porter, campaigning for an American art, was the first critic to speak for the desirability of seeking inspiration for our art without depending on European tradition. Having sampled the academicians' attitude, let us examine Porter's as expressed in his articles on the art of painting.

"In coloring a picture," he states in an 1845 issue of the *Scientific American,* "it is better to endeavor to imitate the natural appearance of natural objects, than to imitate the paintings of even celebrated artists. On this account it is not infrequently the case that the productions of self-taught artists, far surpass in excellence those of regular bred artists who have studied with the most popular Italian masters."

And then, in an 1846 issue, he expressed the crux of his belief in home-grown inspiration for American painting: "There can be no scenery found in the world which presents a more gay and lively appearance in a painting, than an American farm, on a swell of land, and with various colored fields well arranged." Earlier, in 1841, Porter had described in the *New York Mechanic* the best possible subject matter for American landscape painting —an American farm "presenting the appearance of thrift and life," with everything giving an idea of the life of a happy and prosperous farmer. Another scene he suggests as particularly appropriate is a waterfall, and on the banks of the stream "a factory of some kind, and one or two mechanical shops, showing the water wheels, by which machinery may be supposed to move in the shops." The artist was to depict with patriotic pride the peace, prosperity and industry of the fine farms and villages of his countryside. Porter suggested painting, and himself painted, not only the appearance but the very spirit of rural New England in his time. This, as the expressed aim of a mid-nineteenth-century painter, was entirely unprecedented.

A totally different sort of landscape painting was produced by academic artists like Bierstadt and Cole. They, too, saw in American scenery a fit subject matter for painting, but they saw it as if through the eyes of Delacroix or Salvator Rosa. They painted the dramatic and romantic aspects of American scenery and entirely overlooked the neat, cultivated American scene in which Porter in the nineteenth century and painters like Grant Wood in the twentieth found their inspiration.

In literature, Cooper, Washington Irving and Hawthorne were writing of the American environment but they, like the academic landscape painters, were concerned with the romantic and picturesque rather than the simple and commonplace aspects of American life. Porter's interest in the homely, rural American life and scene was far ahead of that expressed in contemporary art and literature.

Governor DeWitt Clinton, president of the American Academy, delivered an address in 1816 which expresses the typical academician's attitude toward American landscape painting. He lauds the "sublime grandeur" of American scenery as fit inspiration for American artists. He speaks of the elevated mountains, prodigious rivers, cataracts, boundless forests filled with wild beasts and savage men. He concludes that "this wild, romantic, and awful scenery is calculated to produce a correspondent impression in the imagination—to elevate all the faculties of the mind, and to exalt all the feelings of the heart." This attitude is responsible for the predominantly grandiose character of American landscape painting throughout the century.

In 1825 an address was delivered by G. C. Verplanck on the occasion of the tenth exhibition of the American Academy. The speaker decries the "defects of our rural architecture" and advocates introducing classical elements, colonnades, porticoes and towers, which would endow the ugly countryside with grace and majesty when seen through the foliage "bosomed high in tufted trees."

Thomas Hamilton in his *Men and Manners in America* comments on the New England countryside in 1833 and summarizes the academic-romantic attitude toward scenery painting. "The country," he states, "is too new for a landscape painter . . . the worm fences, and the freshness and regularity of the houses, are sadly destructive of the picturesque." Porter was able to evaluate the "freshness and regularity" of the American scene positively rather than negatively. He emphasized those very characteristics which Hamilton disparaged and deliberately evolved in the second quarter of the nineteenth century an original kind of clean-cut, stylized landscape. Except for isolated primitive examples this sort of painting was unique until the advent of the twentieth-century scene painters.

Rufus Porter had developed his art instruction from the factual recipes of *Curious Arts* into a well-formulated critical approach to the art of painting. In one important way, however, the newspaper articles and *Curious*

Arts upheld exactly the same point of view—that art was a craft and the art of painting should be based on simple, native craft techniques. Unlike the academicians Porter did not consider the "useful" and "elegant" arts in separate categories. His *Scientific American* articles on the art of painting include: house painting, sign painting, ornamental gilding and bronzing, painting on glass, painting screens and window shades, landscape painting, crystalline painting for boxes or trays, imitation painting (graining and marbleizing), portrait painting, miniature painting, and landscape painting on walls of rooms. There is no differentiation between the practical and fine arts. All painting was a simple, practical undertaking, whether it concerned a house, window shade, portrait or landscape. Porter consistently stresses sound craftsmanship and a matter-of-fact approach. He states in his articles on landscape painting that with a small quantity of paint and two or three brushes an amateur can produce a very fair picture. He recommends that the artist grind and compound his own colors, tells him how to keep the brushes in good order, and how, very simply, to plan and execute a portrait or a landscape. The amateur is given the rudiments of drawing and painting, with exact workmanship directions for each part. He is then expected to develop his art at home, in his own way, with models for portraiture and landscape found at hand—his family, his home and his farmlands. The academic painters on the other hand were expected to attain, from long practice and the study of exhibited masterpieces, a high degree of technical proficiency. Mrs. Trollope discusses a portrait by a Mr. Ingham as the painting most admired at the annual exhibition of the Pennsylvania Academy in 1830. This she describes as of meticulous finish, even to the pile of the velvet in the drapery. Verisimilitude, achieved through drawing, perspective, chiaroscuro, and even the reproduction of textures, was the chief aim of the academicians.

The desire for visual correctness resulted in the disciplined realism of academic painting, while Porter's freedom from this goal of precise fidelity to visual fact left him free to explore his personal inclinations in design. It is interesting to note that in discussing landscape painting he always speaks of "the design" rather than "the scene." In his articles on painting he emphatically preaches the freedom of the artist, who is assumed to be painting primarily for pleasure. Porter says specifically, and in many different ways, that the artist need not adhere to exact realism but may depart from any rules, and should consult his individual taste in planning the composition, content and color of his painting.

At the end of the first academic season of the National Academy of Design, President Morse in his address to the students tells them that "Correctness is the first requisite in Drawing. Your great object should be to imitate the model before you precisely as it appears." Rufus Porter tells his newspaper audience that "the learner, for the purpose of acquiring the art of designing, should . . . imagine various scenes in his mind, diverse from anything he has seen." Morse states that "it is a mistake which young artists are apt to commit, to suppose they must improve upon their model." Porter tells his students that in painting landscapes "the taste of the artist can be displayed in shaping and finishing the trees"; that fields may be painted according to "the fancy of the artist" in diverse colors "to add a pleasing variety to the scenery"; that buildings may be painted "in any color to please the taste." "Seek accuracy," says Morse, "and style will follow without your being conscious of it." "There are," says Porter, "a great variety of beautiful designs, which are easily and quickly produced with the brush, and which excel nature itself in picturesque brilliancy, and richly embellish the work though not in perfect imitation of anything."

In 1846, when Porter was formulating this significant critical idea which implies a marked tendency toward formalized design (amazingly close to twentieth-century abstraction) as opposed to visual realism in painting, the Cummings School of Design was established as one of the branches of the National Academy. The course of study was announced in the prospectus as "the General Education of the Eye, in its appreciation of form, light, shade and color; *Elementary Drawing* in lead pencil and crayon from 'examples,' from the 'round,' from 'nature,' and the *'living models'*; Painting in oil and watercolors, and the general principles of Composition, with lectures on Anatomy, Perspective, and other subjects connected with art, by competent professors."

This was the typical academic approach to painting which Porter opposed in theory and practice, because he thought it tended to "check if not destroy" natural talent. Porter believed that the layman, given an honest craft approach to his art and clear working directions, could paint pretty much as he pleased and, if talented and left to his own devices, would produce sound work. He believed that with the thriving American countryside as his theme and a few brushes and paints for his equipment, any American could pioneer in painting. Rufus Porter proved his point in his vivid New England murals which are among the most interesting examples of the native tradition in American art.

Painter of the American Scene

THE HISTORY OF AMERICAN WALL PAINTING prior to 1850 is—with an occasional minor exception—the history of foreign styles. Like the imported scenic wallpapers, these murals were considered desirable decorations for the homes of the wealthy merchants and landowners. Typical examples are the anonymous Empire-Pompeiian frescoes in the Alsop house in Middletown, Connecticut, and Corné's romantic foreign landscapes in the Oak Hill Mansion in Peabody, Massachusetts (Fig. 44), and in the Sullivan Dorr house in Providence, Rhode Island. The group of murals published by E. B. Allen in his definitive book on *Early American Wall Paintings 1710–1850* (in the chapter titled "American Landscape Group") are a striking exception. These are simple country scenes painted on the plaster walls of New England farmhouses (see Fig. 45). Allen discusses them with great enthusiasm as the remarkable product of a number of anonymous New England painters. The entire group is the work of Rufus Porter and his assistants.

These early murals impressed me as among the most original and interesting pieces of work in the field of American painting; and this was the beginning (about 1940) of the search for all the missing pieces of an intriguing biographical puzzle which resulted in the publication of this book.

The puzzle began with the homogeneous group of nineteenth-century landscape frescoes which Allen had located and which he considered "veritable painted pages of history." He first published examples of these frescoes in *Art in America* in 1922. In a later article in *House Beautiful* he said that nothing was known about the artists who painted these scenes except a few vague traditions: one was believed to have been a British spy in the War of 1812, another a wandering sailor, while another was a painter

Figs. 44, 45. M. F. Corné's foreign genre scene over an elaborately carved mantel in the Oak Hill Mansion in Peabody, Massachusetts (c. 1815) makes a striking contrast with Porter's overmantel (right), with its spare New England landscape, in the Wagner house in Lyme, New Hampshire (c. 1825–1830).

who came from Boston on horseback. In his book Allen recorded the fact that an elderly resident of Westwood, Massachusetts, had heard the artist of the frescoes mentioned in her childhood; according to her he worked freehand and very rapidly, often finishing a room in two or three days. The painter is reported to have spent a winter in Westwood and to have decorated houses in nearby towns as well. Other residents of Westwood recalled that the frescoes were supposed to have been the work of two men. Nancy McClelland in her *Historic Wall Papers* quoted a letter from the sister of Kate Douglas Wiggin about the frescoes in Quillcote, her house in Hollis Center, Maine. They were done, according to this letter, by a painter who came from Boston and who mixed his paints with skim milk. Allen had found the signature "R. Porter—1838" on a Westwood fresco and concluded that this was the name of one of the itinerant painters. Then in an article on "Old Westwood Murals" in *Antiques* Louise Karr mentioned this signature and above it on the wall the signature of one S. T. Porter. Janet Waring, in her *Early American Stencils,* reproduced landscape paintings from two New Hampshire houses which clearly belong with Allen's series. Janet Waring and Esther Stevens Brazer, in *Early American Decoration,* quoted from Rufus Porter's *Curious Arts* discussion of wall painting but did not connect him with any known frescoes.

It was obvious that the "R. Porter" of the Massachusetts frescoes was no other than Rufus Porter, nineteenth-century inventor, editor, writer and painter. It seemed evident that the stories about the British spy, wandering sailor and itinerant on horseback all referred to Rufus Porter too, and S. T. Porter proved to be his son Stephen Twombly. With the murals as a point of departure I investigated the details of Rufus Porter's life, and found him not only the creator of our most important early American frescoes—among which are those in famous Quillcote—but one of the most remarkable personalities in the history of nineteenth-century America.

A number of Rufus Porter's paintings had been well known and well published though not under his name. In an article for July 5, 1936, the *Boston Globe*'s art editor, A. J. Philpott, definitively ascribed a number of frescoes to Porter (finding the article was a gratifying corroboration of my conclusions), but this newspaper attribution evidently was ignored. Though Porter's name is again mentioned in connection with the murals in a couple of Massachusetts newspapers in 1937 and 1938, his frescoes were, until my publication of the wall paintings, described by their owners and by art historians as anonymous works. Although Porter painted his way all through New England, only a few Massachusetts murals were—as anonymous works by the same painter—credited to him. We have mentioned that E. B. Allen, Louise Karr and Janet Waring reproduced and discussed the frescoes as important early American paintings, but they did not connect them with Rufus Porter—who had signed a fresco in a Westwood house "R. Porter" and had inscribed his name on two other frescoes. Frances Parkinson Keyes chose one of Porter's murals for the endpapers of her 1943 novel *Also the*

Hills, and referred to the frescoes as great—but anonymous—art. A 1940 W.P.A. publication called *Hands that Built New Hampshire* discussed the Porter frescoes in Lyme and East Jaffrey, but did not name the hands responsible for the art. Kenneth Roberts, in *Rabble in Arms* (1933), described a frescoed hunting scene in a Maine house—clearly a Porter mural—as done by "a painter from the German settlement at Dresden on the Kennebec."

Several New England newspapers have proudly published the locally famous wall paintings but, undoubtedly associating them with imported scenic wallpapers, have been almost unanimous in ascribing the murals done by Porter and his New England pupils to French or English artists. An Augusta, Maine, newspaper (June 22, 1924) headlined an illustrated account of the Hanson house frescoes in Winthrop, "Marvels of Art on Walls of Old Maine Mansions"; the journalist stated that "the general landscape gives the appearance of English design," and spoke of the unknown author as "evidently a man of genius." An item in the *Lewiston Journal* (October 31–November 4, 1908) told how the frescoes in the old Stanley house in Fairbanks, Maine, were done by "a foreigner who chanced along who professed great skill as a painter of landscapes and waterscapes." The frescoes in the old Cushman Tavern in Webster Corner, Maine, were recorded twenty years later in the *Lewiston Journal* (January 22, 1927) as painted by a stranger from England. The decorations in the Mague house (old Squire Flint Mansion) in North Reading, Massachusetts, were described (*Boston Globe,* September 27, 1925) as having been done by one of the "roving English artists" who, possessing "a good appetite as well as ability to use the brushes . . . became one of America's first interior decorators in exchange for his board and lodging." Marion Nicholl Rawson discussed Porter's New Hampshire frescoes in *Candle Days,* and imagined an "unfortunate Frenchman" as their author who, poor in money ways, used his wealth of artistic ability to get a night's or a week's lodging as he traveled. A pictorial calendar published in 1925 by Sprague Brothers of Boston reproduced Porter's frescoes in the Coburn Tavern in East Pepperell, Massachusetts, and stated that "the old dance hall at the top of the tavern is well worth a visit for the remarkable fact that crayon sketches on its walls, which are still in a state of perfect preservation, were drawn by French soldiers, who were held in confinement by the English." Museum photographs of Rufus Porter's frescoes are still similarly annotated, and most of the owners of the frescoed houses still speak glibly of some unknown foreign artist who long ago traveled about New England decorating walls with scenic designs.

Rufus Porter's homely, unpretentious New England scenes are at the opposite pole of continental style, and an account of what they are and what they represent in American painting is long overdue. This account must begin with a close look at Porter's own writings, which we have already scanned in connection with his art instruction. From 1826 to 1846 he published a voluminous serial on "Landscape Painting on Walls of Rooms" the subject is introduced in 1825 in *Curious Arts,* reappears in 1841 in a series of illustrated articles in the pages of the *New York Mechanic* and is presented in final form in 1846 in the *Scientific American.*

The item in *Curious Arts* concisely describes the fundamentals of Porter's fresco technique and reveals his approach to mural painting in 1825. It is here reprinted in full:

Dissolve half a pound of glue in a gallon of water, and with this sizing, mix whatever colours may be required for the work. Strike a line round the room, nearly breast high; this is called the horizon line; paint the walls from the top to within six inches of the horizon line, with sky blue, (composed of refined whiting and indigo, or a slip blue,) and at the same time, paint the space from the horizon line to the blue, with horizon red, (whiting, coloured a little with orange lead and yellow ochre,) and while the two colours are wet, incorporate them partially, with a brush. Rising clouds may be represented by striking the horizon red colour upon the blue, before it is dry, with a large brush. Change some sky about two shades with slip blue and paint your design for rivers, lakes or the ocean. Change some sky blue one shade with forest green, (slip blue and chrome yellow,) and paint the most distant mountains and highlands; shade them while wet, with blue, and heighten them with white; observing always to heighten the side that is towards the principal light of the room. The upper surface of the ocean must be painted as high as the horizon line, and the distant highlands must rise from ten to twenty inches above it.—Paint the highlands, islands, &c. of the second distance, which should appear from four to six miles distant, with mountain green, (two parts sky blue with one of forest green,) heighten them, while wet, with sulphur yellow (three parts whiting with one of chrome yellow,) and shade with blue-black, (slip blue and lamp black equal.) Paint the lands of the first distance, such as should appear within a mile or two, with forest green; heighten with chrome yellow and shade with black; occasionally incorporating red ochre, french green or whiting. The nearest part, or fore ground, however, should be painted very bold with yellow ochre, stone brown (red and yellow ochre and lamp black equal,) and black. Paint the shores and rocks of the first distance with stone brown; heighten with horizon red, shade with black. For those of the second distance, each colour must be mixed with sky blue.—The wood lands, hedges and trees of the second distance are formed by striking a small flat stiff brush endwise, (which operation is called bushing, and is applied to the heightening and shading all trees and shrubbery of any distance,) with mountain green deepened a little with slip blue; with which also the ground work for trees of the first distance is painted; and with this colour the water may be shaded a little under the capes and islands, thus representing the reflection of the land in the water. Trees of the first distances are heightened with sulphur yellow or french green; and shaded with blue-black. Every object must be painted larger or smaller, according to the distance at which it is represented; thus the proper height of trees in the second distance, is from one to two inches, and other objects in proportion. Those in the first distance from six to ten inches generally; but those in the fore ground, which are nearest, are frequently painted as large as the walls will admit. The colours also for distant objects, houses, ships, &c., must be varied, being mixed with more or less sky blue, according to the distance of the object. By these means the view will apparently recede from the eye, and will have a very striking effect.

From the 1841 articles in the *New York Mechanic* we realize how the artist has, fifteen years later, formulated his approach to the art of fresco painting. His attitude remains entirely practical. The articles proceed in logical sequence to give directions for preparing the colors and brushes, planning the design, mixing and applying the paints. The chief advantage claimed for wall painting is that painted walls are more practical than wallpaper which "is apt to get torn off, and often affords behind it a resting place for various kinds of house insects."

The actual procedure of painting is not very complex; any layman can rapidly acquire the art. By giving "a tremulous motion to the brush" when shading the trunks of trees "a very good representation of bark can be formed." A "bushing" stroke will produce presentable foliage, the brush being merely held differently for different kinds of foliage. To shade trees or the shores of islands one need only bear down hard on the outside of the brush when drawing the outline.

The method of designing and executing a landscape fresco is exactly described, point for point. Everything is reduced to a logical and exact scheme of design, space and color. First sky and clouds are painted. Next the rivers, lakes and mountains should be designed. Each distance must be colored and shaded differently, and paint-mixing directions are given for each part of the composition. Inch by inch specifications are given for objects in the various distances. "The trees on the second distance, should be from eight to twelve inches high; those on the third distance, about three or four, and on the fourth distance, they should not be more than from one, to one and a half inches high." Cities and villages are seen to best advantage in the fourth distance, animals and boats in the second or third.

Color, too, is arbitrarily simplified. "For the leaves of small shrubs two colors only need be used, one for the light, and one for the dark side." Rushes should be heightened with green, the leaves of ferns with lemon yellow, the stalks drawn with vermilion. Farm fields may be painted in any pleasing variety of greens and yellows, and buildings in any color the artist fancies. Stencils are recommended for the latter.

The landscapes were to be composed by the artist of pleasant rural ingredients—water, houses, animals, villages, trees—selected and combined in a design and colored so as to make up an attractive whole. Porter ends his series of *New York Mechanic* articles by remarking that everything that is pleasing—nature, farm life, hunters, woodcutters at work—can be painted on walls at little expense in colors that will be permanent. The four walls of a parlor can be completely painted in watercolors in less than five hours, and at a total cost of ten dollars. The editor hopes that "this kind of work will come into general use."

The *Scientific American* series continues the campaign for landscape painting in place of paper hangings, aiming to build up "a competent supply of artists who could accommodate the public with this kind of painting." In these 1846–1847 illustrated fresco lessons we see most clearly how Porter's admiration for the New England countryside and his feeling for design had crystallized to create a unique style in American landscape painting. And no one could doubt the attribution for Porter's *oeuvre* after seeing these illustrations (Fig. 46).

The editor introduces his articles on mural painting with the remark that about twenty different colors, twenty small tin cups and a dozen com-

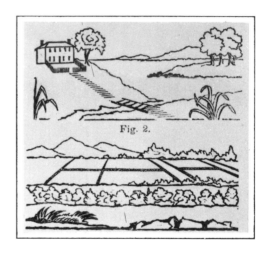

Fig. 2.

Fig. 46. Porter's illustrations for his serial on "Landscape Painting on Walls of Rooms," published in 1846–1847 issues of *Scientific American*.

mon paintbrushes of different sizes are all the essential materials. He then describes the medium—colors ground and mixed with water (lampblack with rum and water) and tempered with alum and glue. Such opaque watercolors will, he says, create an extremely brilliant effect and be most durable. This was no idle boast. Now, after more than a century has passed, many of Porter's frescoes are amazingly well preserved and the forms and colors remain clear and bright.

The lessons begin with instructions for mixing and applying the colors and suggestions for laying out the design:

Make a *sky-blue* by adding celestial blue to whiting . . . also make a *horizon red* by mixing together ten parts in bulk of whiting with two of orange red and one of chrome yellow. Then make a *cloud color* by mixing an indefinite small quantity of horizon red with whiting. . . . The sky-blue may be applied by a large common paint brush, either new or worn; but a brush for the application of the cloud color should be large and short. . . . As a general rule, a water scene,—a view of the ocean or a lake,—should occupy some part of the walls. . . . Other parts, especially over a fireplace, will require more elevated scenes, high swells of land, with villages or prominent and elegant buildings. On the more obscure sections of the walls, especially such as are expected to be obscured by furniture, high mountains with cascades or farm hills may be represented. Small spaces between the windows and the corners, may be generally occupied by trees and shrubbery rising from the foreground, and without much regard to the distance.

Porter goes on to tell in detail how the design should be arranged and the colors properly applied. Then practical instructions are given for the use of stencils in landscape paintings:

In painting the pictures of steamboats, ships, and other vessels, it is convenient to have a variety of outline drawings of vessels of various kinds, sizes and positions, on paper: the back sides of these papers are to be brushed over with dry venetian red; then by placing one of the papers against the wall, and tracing the outlines with a pointed piece of iron, bone, or wood, a copy thereof is transferred to the wall ready for coloring . . . the painting of houses, arbors, villages, &c., is greatly facilitated by means of stencils . . . for this purpose several stencils must be made to match each other; for example, one piece may have the form of the front of a dwelling house . . . another the form of the end of the same house . . . a third cut to represent the roof; and a fourth may be perforated for the windows. Then, by placing these successively on the wall, and painting the ground through the aperture with a large brush . . . the appearance of a house is readily produced, in a nearly finished state. . . . Trees and hedge-fences . . . are formed by means of the flat bushing-brush. . . . This is dipped in the required color, and struck end-wise upon the wall, in a manner to produce . . . a cluster of small prints or spots thus. . . .

In two other articles the author considers the problem of how to acquire the art of designing landscapes:

This branch of painting admits of such an endless variety of designs, that it would be vain to attempt to give even a tolerable assortment for the use of the practitioner. . . . Some of the most prominent objects and scenes which may be often repeated, though under different arrangements, are farms, fields, forests, farmhouses, palaces, arbors, wind-mills, observatories, villages, high rocks, ships, steamboats, sail-boats, islands, hunting scenes, carriages, cattle feeding or watering, children at play, military parades, water-falls, flower gardens, flocks of birds, baloons, canals, water-mills, railroads, bridges, &c. There must be a general consistency observed, and one scene made to connect with another, even although the different scenes should represent different seasons of the year. . . . The learner, for the purpose of acquiring the art of designing, should habituate himself to making close observations of objects, and scenery, and to imagine various scenes in his mind, diverse from anything he has seen, and practice sketching such designs when his mind is most free from other cares.

The design, Porter says, must be carefully planned in the artist's mind, but in executing it "if there appears any break, or imperfect match between the sections, he has only to build a tree or bush over it." The teacher suggests that a consistent season of the year should be maintained within one painting, but various seasons may be represented in different parts of the room. Shrubbery, tall ferns and flag irises, he advises, may be placed near doors and windows as a sort of border for other scenes, and rough ledges of rock are often placed in the immediate foreground to give variety to the first distance. We have already quoted Porter's surprisingly modern advice on finishing a landscape painting with original designs which "richly embellish the work though not in perfect imitation of anything." "This remark," he states, "is particularly applicable to various wild shrubbery suitable for filling up the foreground, and usually based on the bottom of the first distance."

It seems extraordinary to find that a provincial nineteenth-century painter thought it neither necessary nor expedient to imitate nature when more attractive designs might be conceived by the artist. Rufus Porter's desire to "excel nature itself" in the interest, clarity and brilliance of design and color largely accounts for the contemporary look of his deliberately stylized landscapes. His non-illusionistic approach must be stressed in considering the style of his painting, for it is this which most fundamentally determines its character. Rufus Porter painted the New England scenery he knew, but he did not copy it. He recorded it from a clarified, composite picture in his mind's eye, using personal formulas for the perspective and the design. The content of the painting, the drawing and coloring, are reduced to the simplest terms. The artist speaks in his articles of "cloud color," "stone-brown," "mountain green"; and we find in his frescoes that his fences are generally black and white, his boats red and yellow—which he may have decided on as "fence color" and "boat color." Elements of one scene, and whole scenes, are repeated in the various frescoes; and many of the details, radically simplified, are executed with stencils. A number of the frescoes are painted in monochrome (Porter called it "Claro Obscuro"), which technique he discusses in an 1847 article on "Light and Shade painting on walls." These murals, done in neutral tones of umber, gray, gray-green or plum color and accented with white, are the simplest and most perfectly architectonic of the murals, and perhaps the most beautiful. Porter always thought of his landscapes as simple wall decorations, architecturally related

Fig. 47. The Porter-school mural art was closely related to the decorative painting of the time—which Porter himself had practiced. This New England chest, owned by Stephen Score, is painted in ocher on gray-green; it is clearly related to Porter frescoes. It does not seem dangerous to risk a firm attribution; compare the rows of trees with those on the walls of the Coburn Tavern in Fig. 51.

Figs. 48, 49.   Jonathan D. Poor, Porter's nephew and assistant, signed and dated this fireboard in 1831; it is now in the Shelburne Museum, Shelburne, Vermont. As evidenced also by Porter's sponge-decorated fireboard recently removed from the Joshua Eaton house in Bradford, New Hampshire (now in the author's collection), ornamenting fireboards as well as graining woodwork, stenciling floors and frescoing walls was part of the old-time decorator's job. Recently, several fireboards, overmantel panels, and a landscape mantel have been discovered that can be variously attributed to the Porter school and Porter himself.

to the space they were to ornament; these monochrome murals most perfectly exemplify this idea.

The relationship between Rufus Porter's early paintings and the crafts which he had practiced in Maine is quite apparent. Certainly the delicate, decorative drawing of his portraits is related to the ornamental painting of the time, and the stencil motifs which he introduced into his landscapes reflect his early interest in decorative painting. In comparing Rufus Porter's highly stylized frescoes with Corné's illusionistic murals on one hand and with decorated contemporary furniture and accessories on the other (see Figs. 47–49), we again see how Porter's art developed from native American craft techniques rather than from academic and continental traditions.

By comparing the early with the late frescoes it will be possible to attempt to trace in detail the evolution of Porter's style. His changing aims and methods in the instruction series we have just examined of course parallel exactly the changes in the style of the murals, and this helped to check our approximate dating where no documentation or actual dating was to be found. In the early paintings the drawing is tighter and the shading sharper and more arbitrary. The stippled or sponged foliage, the limited color range and the naïveté of many of the details is primitive, close to craft work. The later paintings show a looser and larger handling and a greater variety of designs with more genre incidents animating the scene. The perspective is sophisticated. The color is bold and varied, and in the monochrome frescoes the tonal range is rich and full. The stylized foreground plants are a late invention, and add greatly to the now deliberate formalizing of the design. In contrasting the early paintings with the late ones we realize, as we do if we compare Porter's early writings on wall painting with those of a later period, that his murals evolved in two decades from a spontaneous and ingenuous kind of primitive decoration to a highly stylized formal art.

Internal stylistic evidence and corroborating data make it possible to divide Porter's frescoes roughly into five periods.

The frescoes in East Pepperell, Massachusetts, Bradford, East Jaffrey, Langdon and Greenfield, New Hampshire, and Sebec, Maine, are examples of his very earliest murals, most closely connected with his former career as house, sign, sleigh and drum painter. The 1884 *Scientific American* obituary states that Porter started mural painting in 1824, probably about the time he published his undated *Select Collection of Approved, Genuine, Secret and Modern Receipts*. That same year he constructed a horsepowered flatboat—thirty-five feet long, with a cabin—and worked it on the Connecticut River for a short time before selling it. This boat was undoubtedly his first headquarters when, about 1824–1825, he began to decorate a large number of New Hampshire houses along the Connecticut River.

In 1825 he published *Curious Arts* in Concord, New Hampshire, and evidently painted murals in a good many houses in New Hampshire and in

Fig. 50.   The Coburn Tavern, East Pepperell, Massachusetts, where Porter frescoed the ballroom c. 1824, the year he began his career as itinerant mural painter, was photographed in the 1940s; it looks the same today.

Fig. 51.   Ballroom frescoes in the Coburn Tavern, photographed in the 1940s, are still extremely well preserved.

several towns in Maine during the next five years. He seems to have worked a bit later, roughly 1830–1835, in Massachusetts, Maine and Vermont. In the late thirties he apparently decorated a large number of houses in eastern Massachusetts. By 1840 Porter's interests had shifted from mural painting to journalism, and the 1845 frescoes in East Weymouth, Massachusetts, the latest in the series and the least primitive in style, probably represent one of the few mural commissions which he executed during his years of active editorship.

The old Coburn Tavern in East Pepperell, Massachusetts, on the road from Groton to Townsend (Fig. 50), was probably one of the first places that Porter decorated with his painted landscapes. On a stylistic basis it seems reasonable to date these murals (with a few in New Hampshire and one in Maine) about 1824, the year he started wall painting. The three-story brick tavern was a landmark in the Massachusetts countryside. The gambrel-roofed ballroom occupying the entire third story is large enough to accommodate a hundred dancing couples, and the decoration of such a vast area of wall space was a courageous undertaking for an inexperienced young landscape painter. The former owner of the tavern, Mr. Thomas Hayes, stated that the nameless artist's daily schedule was said to have been painting in the daytime, visiting the taproom in the evening and fiddling for dances in the ballroom all night. Perhaps Porter, discouraged by his unsuccessful attempt to sell small landscape paintings about this time, had gone back to his old profession of playing for dances, and had then thought of decorating the dance halls with large mural landscapes to add to his fiddler's fee. And the style of Porter's painting—bright, gay, rhythmical—certainly relates to his liking for lively martial and dance music. (A decade later he decorated a similar ballroom in the old Damon Tavern in North Reading, Massachusetts, a stagecoach stop between Boston and Haverhill and Salem and Lowell.) In the Coburn Tavern he painted all the walls of the huge ballroom, even decorating the fiddler's stand with a landscape; and he also painted the entire second story hall and the stairway walls leading up to the ballroom. These frescoes (Fig. 51) are rather haphazardly planned and crudely colored, mostly in greens and yellows. The trees are painted with half of the foliage yellow ocher, half black, in a naïve, stylized interpretation of the lighted and shaded sides of a tree—a characteristic of the earliest murals.

The Beale house in Orford, New Hampshire, decorated by Porter just after it was completed by Dyar T. Hinckley in 1824, is one of a group of fine hip-roofed houses on a ridge of rolling land with fences, trees and grassy slopes, overlooking the Connecticut River. The Orford ridge houses still look so much like a Porter scene that I made a memo of "Orford—Porter-like scenery" ten years before it came to my attention that Porter had worked in this town (see Fig. 52). A painting of Orford in 1831 (Fig. 53), attributed to Henry Cheever Pratt, a native Orford artist, shows the Academy building with cupola and the Howard hat factory, both built in

Figs. 52, 53.   The Ridge in Orford, New Hampshire, where Porter decorated the old Hinckley house about 1824, still looks like a Porter landscape. Below, a view of Orford painted in 1831, attributed to Henry Cheever Pratt of Orford, owned by A. Wheeler.

the 1790s and burned about 1850, and the original church built in 1797—all the kind of rural ingredients that Porter favored for his scenery.

It is tempting to suppose that Porter, who was beginning his career as an inventor as well as a painter at this time, met in Orford the older inventor Samuel Morey (1762–1843), whose career, original personality and versatile interests as a practical visionary seem extraordinarily similar to Porter's. (Morey's life and career are recounted in Alice Doan Hodgson's story of Orford, *Thanks to the Past*.) It would have been most unlikely in a town as small as Orford was about 1825 that Porter and Morey would *not* have met. Furthermore, in one of the Beale house frescoes there is a steamboat that, according to Mrs. Beale, closely resembles the drawings of Morey's steamboat which he had constructed about 1820. Similar steamboats are featured in many of the later Porter frescoes as well.

The old red brick Prescott Tavern, torn down about 1950, was located in East Jaffrey on the third New Hampshire turnpike between Boston and northern Vermont (Fig. 54). (The frescoes were removed to the Goyette Museum in Peterborough, New Hampshire, which is now closed; the frescoes are stored in the building.) Here, after passing the tollgate in East Jaffrey village, Porter arrived one day, very possibly in 1824, the year he is reported to have started wall painting. He stayed to paint on the walls of the large tavern taproom—in payment for his board, it is said—a remarkable variety of landscape scenes (Figs. 55, 56, Color Plates, 1, 2). The floor of the frescoed room was stenciled—most likely by Porter too, who was, as we know, a house painter before his wall-painting years. We should notice that Porter's tavern murals are characteristically more animated and more varied in subject matter than those done for private dwellings. In the Prescott Tavern the parlor contained a harbor scene locally thought to be Boston harbor (Portland more likely); an overmantel featuring buildings executed with stencils, probably representing Dartmouth College—very much stylized, as seen in comparison with an early print (Fig. 57) and repeated almost exactly in the Solomon Russell house and the Gardner Davis house (Figs. 58, 59) in New Ipswich and in the Beale house in Orford; a woodland hunting scene including a large man and a horse-sized dog; and a section of farm countryside backed by a Vesuvius-like mountain. The latter may have been suggested by the view of Mount Monadnock which could be seen from the tavern on a clear day, with the erupting smoke a recollection of a Hawaiian volcanic mountain. Porter's early combination of naïve theme and crisp, primitive design is strikingly illustrated in the stream of black smoke coming from this mountain, with two isolated puffs which drift beyond a doorway but are moored to the main stream by a bold stroke of rust-colored paint. All this scenery is topped with a stenciled black, orange and yellow frieze. The overmantel is framed with woodwork marbleized in gray, rust and black, and the baseboards are similarly painted. The chief colors of the frescoes are yellow, rust, black and white, with yellow ocher dominating. The parlor faced south and east, and seeing these brilliant

Fig. 54. The old red brick Prescott Tavern in East Jaffrey, New Hampshire, which Porter decorated c. 1824, is seen in this photograph taken when it was offered for sale about 1945. It was demolished about 1950, sold for its bricks and woodwork. The Porter murals were removed to the Goyette Museum in Peterborough, New Hampshire; when it closed they were stored by the owner, Mrs. Hazel Goyette. Restoration instead of demolition would have been costly—but this was a great and marvelously decorated old stagecoach tavern.

Fig. 55. One of the painted walls of the Prescott Tavern, featuring a volcanic mountain (see Color Plates, 1, 2).

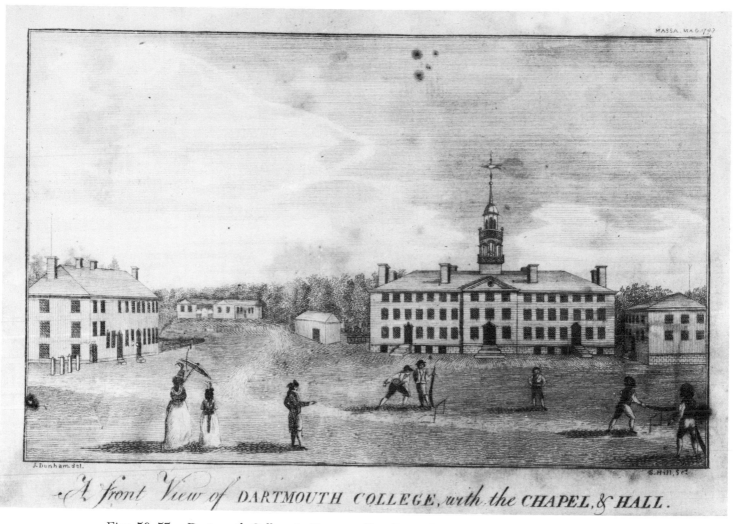

A front View of DARTMOUTH COLLEGE, with the CHAPEL, & HALL.

Figs. 56, 57.   Dartmouth College in Hanover, New Hampshire, as it looked to an early printmaker, and (left) as Porter painted it—with more leeway for imagination—over the mantel of the central fireplace in the Prescott Tavern, East Jaffrey, New Hampshire, c. 1824. Note the marbleized framing.

110

Figs. 58, 59.   The Porter frescoes in the Gardner Davis house in New Ipswich, New
Hampshire, c. 1825, were photographed about 1950, shortly before they were destroyed, for Nina Fletcher Little's *American Decorative Wall Painting*. Note the stenciled frieze and Dartmouth College overmantel, very similar to those in the Prescott
Tavern (Figs. 55, 56).

decorations as the shadow cast by the midday sun reached the notched noonmark on the floor of the front hall was a breathtaking experience.

Porter was frankly experimental in coloring and designing these early tavern frescoes. In one scene there are three houses in a row, each one treated somewhat differently. Five varieties of trees are painted, and the foliage seems to have been done with sponges, corks and brushes in a technique quite similar to that used for decorating furniture at that time. Porter was experimenting with stencils, too, and in one tree we find half a dozen squirrels, three black and three brown, all done with the same stencil but each one placed in a different position. A balanced group of huge stenciled stars, a rising sun with a very human face in the overmantel, a waning moon smiling from the opposite wall, and elongated trees whose branches grow into a stylized vine frieze over the windows are details which make these early paintings seem closer to pure decoration than to ordinary landscape painting.

In the decoration of the Joshua Eaton house in Bradford, New Hampshire (Fig. 60, Color Plates 3–5)—as in the Ellerton Jetté house in Sebec, Maine (Figs. 61, 62)—stenciled walls attributed to Moses Eaton, Jr., and Porter murals are attractively combined. In the Joshua Eaton house Porter's frieze design and the leafing of the trees are done using the very same technique; his ornamental and landscape painting are closely connected. The frescoes in this house represent some of the earliest of Porter's murals, and in them we see in embryo the elements of his later landscapes. The large trees, the foreground plants, the house with steps, sailboat, clouds, islands, even the reflections in the water are typical of his work. But the execution and the manner in which these things are combined are clearly immature as compared with the frescoes in the Massachusetts towns; and Porter's interest in perspective, almost as a featured design within a painting, has not yet appeared.

In the Bidwell Tavern frescoes in Langdon (Figs. 63, 64), as in those in the Prescott Tavern, we see how the top branches of the trees are turned into a kind of border vine motif which is as frankly ornamental as the all-over spongework design covering the ceiling. This room, said to have been decorated as a bridal chamber for the tavern keeper's young wife, is described by Marion Rawson in *Candle Days*. She calls attention to an interesting detail, the pink painted sunset glow in the western corner of the room where the actual sunlight fell, a characteristic frequently found in Porter's New Hampshire frescoes. Mrs. Rawson senses exactly the primitive naïveté of these paintings, and comments on the then anonymous frescoes as "so full of the grotesque yet so overflowing with desire to express the beauty that appealed to the artist." Mrs. Rawson writes of the tavern fresco reproduced in Fig. 64:

The eye is led past an island or two; and there, as large as a nearby house, graze black cows, with great white African horns and white tails; compact groups of trees are constrained from going to sea, by snugly-fitting split-rail fences; a row-

Fig. 60. Bedroom stenciling in the Joshua Eaton house in Bradford, New Hampshire, c. 1824. The stenciling is attributed to Moses Eaton, Jr., the fireboard and the murals to Porter (see Fig. 49, Color Plates 3, 4, 5).

Figs. 61, 62.   The house in Sebec, Maine, owned by Mr. and Mrs. Ellerton Jetté, at one time had every wall covered with freehand or stenciled decoration; the work is attributed to Porter working with the stenciler Moses Eaton, Jr., c. 1824. The photographs, taken in 1967, show the remarkable quality and condition of these designs.

Figs. 63, 64. In the Bidwell Tavern in Langdon, New Hampshire, there was a so-called bridal chamber which Porter decorated with frescoes c. 1824. The dado was gray monochrome, the rest in color; note the walls in another room decorated with spongework. The photographs were taken in 1925, a few years before the tavern burned.

Figs. 65, 66. The Squire Craigin house in Greenfield, New Hampshire, was decorated by Porter c. 1825. This photograph was taken before the frescoes were restored in 1941; they were subsequently papered over; the paper was recently removed. Note the Old Man of the Mountain, a New Hampshire landmark.

Figs. 67, 68.   The Porter frescoes in the Daniel Carr house in North Haverhill, New Hampshire, datable c. 1825–1830, were woven into the story of Frances Parkinson Keyes' *Also the Hills* and reproduced as endpapers. These photographs, taken in the 1940s, show the excellent state of preservation in which they remain today.

boat is tethered by a rope, a good quarter of a mile long; and a slender light-house waves three flags, thus guiding to land some distant caravels, whose keels ride gaily the tops of the waves.

The Squire Craigin house frescoes in Greenfield, New Hampshire, which Porter did about this time, are also filled with intriguing scenery which includes an odd cliff-top town on a river and Franconia Notch's famous Old Man of the Mountain (Figs. 65, 66).

In Frances Parkinson Keyes' *Also the Hills* the frescoes in the Carr house in North Haverhill (Figs. 67, 68) are woven into the story. The following excerpts from the novel are interesting bits of analytical comment on these early New Hampshire works:

He saw, for instance, that in the fresco on the nearest wall, the flags on the sailboats were blowing in one direction and the smoke from steamboats in another, that the island lay on top of the water like a platter, and that the crude execution of the grass and houses was completely at variance with the graceful design of the great central tree.

"Well now, I don't know," Daniel said doubtfully. "You mustn't get your hopes up about those frescoes. They're sort of crude, when you come right down to it. I don't suppose they were made by a professional. I suppose they were done by some fellow living around here, who'd never had any lessons. Or maybe by one of those itinerant artists who went from place to place on horseback and painted to pay for their board and lodging, the same as the itinerant cobblers made shoes and the itinerant tailors made coats."

"But, Father Farnam, Tante Odilisse always says that rugmaking is in some ways the most remarkable of all the arts, because rugs are made by uneducated persons and yet these people have such a great feeling for symbolism and beauty that they reveal it. I think the man who painted the frescoes may have had the same kind of a feeling. If he did, and could show it, then wasn't he a great artist whether he'd ever had any lessons or not?"

The qualities of Porter's earliest frescoes should certainly be viewed in a positive manner. The early murals were painted with a simplicity and a sharp, vivid style that was necessarily lost in the ampler rhythms of the mature designs. The incisive drawing of the early New Hampshire frescoes such as those in the Squire Craigin house in Greenfield is unique in Porter's work. In the early frescoes, too, well exemplified by those in the Wagner house in Lyme (Figs. 45, 69) and in the Holsaert house in Hancock (Color Plates 6, 7), the limited range of color and the serene, open design are especially effective for mural painting. The color scheme of the Holsaert house paintings is an almost neutral background of light gray for sky and water, pale yellow ocher for the foreground and light green for the middle distance, with small accenting bits of vivid color and black shading. None of the later frescoes, except those done in monochrome, quite equal the perfect appropriateness of these early paintings as wall decorations for the spare New England houses they adorn.

The Maine and Massachusetts frescoes which Porter painted around 1830 show more robust handling with fuller designs and richer color. These traits can be seen in the Fryeburg, Maine, frescoes (Color Plates 14, 15) which, according to tradition, also date from 1830. In this period the trees

Fig. 69. The Wagner house in Lyme, New Hampshire, was frescoed by Porter c. 1825–1830. These photographs, taken in the late 1940s, show how closely the foliage of the trees is related to the contemporary spongework decoration for furniture, woodwork and walls. The murals are in remarkably fine condition today.

Figs. 70, 71 (opposite). The Porter landscapes in Quillcote, home of Kate Douglas Wiggin in Hollis Center, Maine, were probably painted c. 1830, restored in 1910, and are still in good condition. These photographs were taken for picture post cards about 25 years ago. In connection with the fireboard decorated by Porter in the Joshua Eaton house in Bradford, New Hampshire, and one by Jonathan D. Poor (Figs. 48, 49), it is interesting to find that Louise Karr mentions (in *Antiques,* see Bibliography) that a fireboard in one of the frescoed New Hampshire houses is "identical with the overmantel in the Quillcote house." The whereabouts of this fireboard is now unknown.

Fig. 72. The Ingalls-Colby house in East Haverhill, Massachusetts, was decorated by Porter c. 1830–1835, during the ownership of Dr. Timothy Kennison, who bought the house in 1824. This is a gray-green monochrome mural like the one shown in Color Plate 8. The photograph was made about 1940; these frescoes remain in fine condition.

Figs. 73–75. The fine murals in the Bartlett house in Amesbury, Massachusetts, were
done by Porter c. 1830–1835; these photographs were taken about 1940; the frescoes
have been damaged since then.

Fig. 76. Porter frescoed this room in the Faith Gardner house in Lunenburg, Massachusetts, c. 1830–1835. The paintings, found under wallpaper almost 100 years ago,
were photographed about 1945; they have deteriorated since then.

are the all-important feature and they occupy most of the landscape space. It was interesting to find owners of frescoed houses in three different Maine towns referring to their "tree room," one of which is the bedroom in Quillcote in Hollis Center (Figs. 70, 71).

About this time Porter seems to have decorated a number of Massachusetts houses—in Georgetown, Groveland, East Haverhill, Lunenburg, Amesbury and Harvard (Figs. 72–76, Color Plate 8)—and one in Topsham, Vermont (Color Plate 10). The frescoes in the Elwin Chase house in Topsham seemed most logically dated about 1831–1834, due to the depiction of the frigate *Potomac* (identified by pennants bearing the name of the ship and of Commodore Downes, her commander) whose voyage around the world in those years was prominent news. It is remembered in Georgetown that the local murals were done in 1832 by a "tramp painter" who went about like a modern hitchhiker, getting his board for work along the way. So we can establish approximate dates for this stylistically homogeneous group.

The gray-green monochrome panel removed from the former Whitney house in Harvard and now preserved in the Fruitlands Museums there (Color Plate 8) is a good example of the monochrome murals that Porter specialized in at this time and in this area. The mossy color somehow suggests at the same time a neutral gray wall and the green tones of the scenery. Mr. Carlton Moore, a former owner of the Pingree house in Georgetown which contains splendid examples of Porter's "stone green" murals (now papered over), said that he was told the painter got his green coloring matter from the mud banks of Georgetown. Pigment was often derived from natural clays, and the rosy plum monochrome frescoes in the Savery homestead in Groveland look as if a clay pigment was used. There is such a plum-colored clay; and gray-green and plum clay-base stones in exactly the colors of Porter's monochrome pigments can be found washed up all along the Massachusetts beaches. About fifteen years after the group of eastern Massachusetts houses were decorated, Porter, in an 1847 issue of the *Scientific American*, tells how to make a "plumb" color by mixing black with red, a "stone green" by mixing black with chrome yellow; but it is quite likely that the earlier colors were made directly, and very economically, from the local clays and shaded with black and white. Other colors recommended in this article on monochrome painting were Prussian blue, burnt umber and chrome yellow—these to be employed for variety's sake when many rooms were to be painted in the same house—but Porter adds that in most cases green or purple are preferable. No monochrome frescoes in blue or yellow have been found, but there are two in umber and many in gray, which Porter does not mention.

In these Massachusetts frescoes we begin to be aware of greater interest in perspective, larger handling, and more deliberate development of formal design. The stylized foreground shrubs become prominent at this time and from now on are a trademark of Porter's frescoes, like the large

Figs. 77–80.   Porter's frescoes in a group of Westwood, Massachusetts, houses, c. 1838, photographed about 1925, show his peopled landscapes at their best. The murals in the Storer Ware house (*left*) and the West house (*center two*) were subsequently papered over, then stripped and restored; the Guild house (*right*) was demolished. Porter's son, Stephen Twombly, probably assisted in these Westwood murals.

foreground elms. We might note here that the motif of a stenciled sailboat with a man at the tiller is ànother Porter signature, which he used in his murals during two decades.

The late Massachusetts frescoes, dating from the general period of the 1838 Westwood murals (Figs. 77–84), exemplify Rufus Porter's mature landscape art. The first sight of these frescoes is an exciting experience. One is struck by the ample and yet compact design of a whole wall painting, and then by such details as fields checkered in emerald, ocher and brown, with pink and lemon-yellow houses set against a clear blue sky; the strong outline of a lake; the staccato rhythm of receding fences; the sweep of sails; the fine design of stylized plants and shrubbery. One is impressed with the fact that, despite their primarily decorative nature, nothing is haphazard or flimsy in these frescoes. The designs are as structurally conceived as an architect's blueprint. A shoreline is a half-inch border of solid brown, the houses are sturdy four-square structures, and all the colors are full-bodied and clear.

Rufus Porter's late frescoes are brimming with gay, lively action; especially through the genre elements we become acquainted with our itinerant painter, and sense the flavor of the vigorous, free life he led and the cheerful person he was. In the best of the scenes in the recently demolished Dr. Howe house (Figs. 81–84) a steamboat—painted in brilliant flat red, yellow, turquoise, black and white—churned its brisk way across a bright blue bay. An entertaining painting (Color Plate 16) could be seen as just two trees, or as the figure of a man—said to be Napoleon. In this same house there was a mountain-climbing scene—the one signed by R. Porter and S. T. Porter in 1838—which most appropriately ran up the stairway wall; here we could follow some frisky mountain goats and at the head of the stairs meet a man who looked over the precipice while a timid lad drew back from the dizzy height. In the sunny upstairs hall a painting of a peaceful farm setting with a herd of cows struck a relaxing note after the energetic climbing scene. The staircase in the old Guild house (also torn down) in this same town contained a similar craggy landscape, with hunters chasing a deer which, at stairhead climax, leapt off the edge of the cliff. At the foot of the steps there was a pair of cats hissing at each other from two trees, and at the top a quiet village scene complete with neat houses, well sweep, and a couple holding hands in a hammock. A unique signature for Porter, musician-painter, was the fiddle crossed by a bow found at the foot of a

Figs. 81–84 (see following pages). The Porter murals in the Dr. Francis Howe house in Westwood, Massachusetts, built 1818, demolished 1965, were first photographed about 1925, as reproduced here (see also Color Plate 16). These walls, of key importance because they are the only ones found that were both signed and dated by Porter, were purchased by Benjamin M. Hildebrant, removed intact, and remain in perfect, unrestored condition. The stairway mural is signed "R. Porter, 1838" on a rock halfway up the stairs. Above it, not legible in the photograph, is the signature "S. T. Porter"— Stephen Twombly Porter, Rufus Porter's son. These murals were exhibited at the Whitney Museum of American Art in 1968 on the occasion of first publication of this book.

Fig. 81

Fig. 82

Fig. 83

Fig. 84

Figs. 85, 86. The old Damon Tavern in North Reading, Massachusetts, is now the Weeks Memorial Library. The foreground elms are prominent in the recent photograph, as well as in the tavern ballroom which Porter decorated c. 1835–1840. The ballroom was photographed in 1967 before restoration was begun.

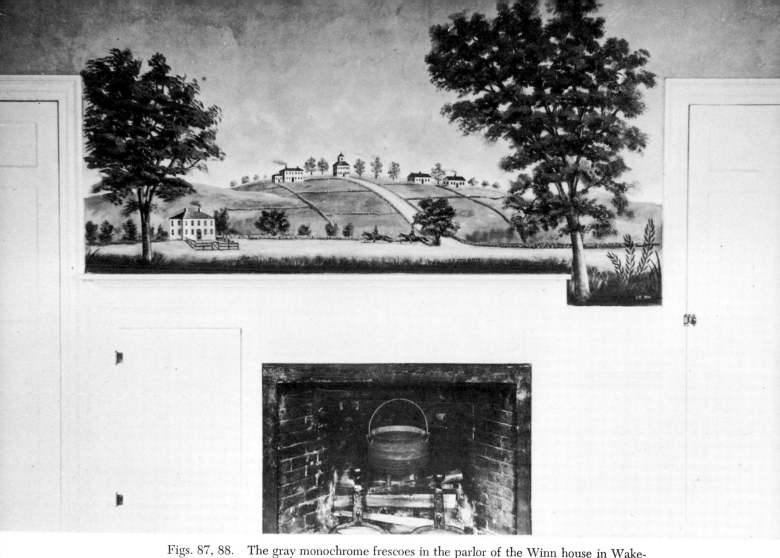

Figs. 87, 88.   The gray monochrome frescoes in the parlor of the Winn house in Wake-field, Massachusetts, are an example of excellent early restoration—done in 1910, photo-graphed about 1940. Porter painted them c. 1835–1840; they are still in fine shape.

row of elms in one of these murals. In the old Ware house, also in West-wood, the downstairs hall is decorated with an attractive panorama of houses, fences and trees, cows, and a lake with a sailboat; while up the stairway we find accelerated action in another animated mountain-climbing scene. In the Andrew house in West Boxford the harbor scene is typically serene (Color Plate 12); the stairway hunt ends at the bottom with a water-fall, dramatically following the incline of the stairs.

As we travel from house to house we are especially impressed with Porter's method of coordinating the design and tempo of his frescoes with the shape and function of the walls on which they are painted. The frescoes in the old Damon Tavern in North Reading (see Figs. 85, 86) are perfectly suited for the ballroom walls. In some of Porter's landscaped rooms, stiff, vertical trees stop the eye at doorways, and sharpen corners; in others a large, branching tree is painted over two sides of a corner to minimize the break in the walls and suggest a continuous panorama; on some of the walls a Jack-and-the-beanstalk sort of tree connects the upper and lower halls. The reproductions of the smoke-gray monochrome decoration in the Winn house in Wakefield (Figs. 87, 88) give a good idea of the architectonic plan for Porter's frescoes. Especially worth noting is the vertical emphasis of the paintings on the side walls and the horizontal sweep of the roadside over-mantel scene, with the two stenciled horsemen scooting along over the exact center of the mantel.

Rufus Porter's late overmantels are among his most important wall paintings, and in these the deliberately balanced rhythmic design is most apparent. The umber monochrome overmantel in the Van Heusen Seven-teenth-Century Farms in North Reading (Color Plate 9) is a typical exam-ple as is the one in full color in the Emerson house in Wakefield (Color Plate 11). Of special importance in this house is the waterfall scene with Porter's signature on the rock to the right of the waterfall (Figs. 89, 90).

Under sixteen layers of wallpaper, gray monochrome frescoes were re-cently found in every room and hall of a Beacon Hill, Boston, boarding-house. These murals, most similar in style to those in the Winn house in Wakefield, can be dated c. 1835–1840—or possibly 1843 when Porter was working in Boston as an electroplater.

The biblical scenes in the Senigo house in East Weymouth—unique in theme and Porter's latest datable frescoes (dated 1845)—are most highly stylized. The decorative tropical landscape reflects Porter's youthful voyage to the Hawaiian Islands. The subject matter of these frescoes, however, is specifically connected with his mature interest in religion. His concern with the Millerites, the religious column in the *Scientific American,* and his re-ligious pamphlet *Essential Truth* all date from the same period as these late biblical paintings. In the sacrifice of Isaac (Fig. 91) the compact honey-comb of spectators in the right foreground is an interesting detail, as are the mottled columns of billowing smoke which are strongly reminiscent of marbleized woodwork. In the scene depicting Moses striking the rock (Fig.

Figs. 89, 90. A Porter mural in the Emerson house in Wakefield, Massachusetts, c. 1835–1840, was signed by the artist, who also identified himself as "painter." The signature is on the middle of the rock to the right of the waterfall.

Figs. 91, 92. The biblical scenes in the Senigo house, East Weymouth, Massachusetts, are the latest of Porter's murals to be found; they are dated 1845. The two scenes represent the sacrifice of Isaac and Moses striking the rock. Porter's painting is bolder and more accomplished than in the earlier murals, but decorative details such as the billow of smoke are not unlike those in scenes done 20 years earlier (see Color Plate 2). These photographs were taken about 1940; the murals have not deteriorated since then.

141

92) the jagged rocks and a waterfall form a stagelike setting for the action which builds up to a crescendo in the figures of Moses and the high priest. In these richly designed biblical scenes, and in the conscious simplicity of the late monochrome landscapes, it is clear that Porter's wall painting had undergone an amazing evolution since the days of the primitive Coburn, Bidwell and Prescott tavern decoration.

A good many of Porter's frescoes, from the earliest to the latest, seem to have been executed with the help of assistants; in Maine most of the frescoed houses were executed by or with assistants. The early decorations of the Joshua Eaton house in Bradford, New Hampshire, are recorded in Janet Waring's *Early American Decoration* as the work of "two young men," and a late mural in the Howe house in Westwood, Massachusetts, was signed by Rufus Porter and his son Stephen Twombly. There is verbal information about another painter named Swift who also worked on some of the Westwood murals and of a Paine who painted around Parsonfield, Maine. According to tradition Orison Wood executed the Porter-like murals in and about Lewiston, Maine. There are signatures of "E. J. Gilbert" and "E. V. Bennett" on Porter-style frescoes in two houses in Winthrop, Maine, and of a "J. D. Poor" in the Priest house in Groton, Massachusetts. Poor was also remembered in a number of towns in the vicinity of Vienna, Maine; on investigation he turned out to be Rufus' nephew, Jonathan D. Poor.

Rufus Porter had from his early twenties been actively interested in teaching. By 1815 he had been a teacher of drumming and drum painting and master of two district schools and a dancing school; by 1825 he had published detailed instructions for mural landscape painting, and in 1841 and 1846 these lessons were printed in revised form. It seems reasonable to suppose that from about 1824 to 1846 he was not only practicing but also teaching the art of wall painting—in fact as well as in print—and that his son Stephen Twombly, Messrs. Gilbert and Bennett, Swift, Paine, Poor and Orison Wood were among his students. Rufus Porter, a modest itinerant painter, evidently had a sizable following in his day. He was quite literally a "master" of mural painting with a "school" of pupils—which is unique in the annuals of American provincial painting.

It is interesting to note that, despite the detailed instructions for wall painting published in the *Scientific American* as late as 1846, this activity seems to have virtually ceased when, after 1840, Porter devoted his time to his newspapers rather than to painting. The Porter "school" flourished while the master was at work, but we can only assume that the how-to-do-it instruction did not succeed without a practicing supervisor since there seem to have been no close followers after Porter's period of activity.

One exception may be Granville Fernald, who is reported by a Bridgton, Maine, historian, Katharine M. Rolfe, to have "aided Mr. Rufus Porter in his efforts." A *Centennial History of Harrison, Maine* records that in 1851 Granville Fernald (1828–1908) took up carriage painting and house painting, which he carried on until 1854 in Harrison, Bridgton, Otisfield and adjoining towns (an area in which Porter and his school had been active). The murals in the Fox house in Gorham and the Pride house in Westbrook are related to Porter's but not attributable to any of his other followers in Maine: Poor, Paine, Wood, Bennett or Gilbert; they may possibly be Fernald's work. While he was working as a house painter in the early 1850s, however, Porter—whose similar work in Gorham, Westbrook and neighboring Maine towns would likely have come to Fernald's attention—was occupied in Washington, D.C., with the promotion of his aeroport. Mrs. Rolfe's word-of-mouth information about Fernald aiding Porter connects the two, though "aided" would have to be reinterpreted as having worked as a house decorator in the manner which Porter had practiced and taught.

Orison Wood (1811–1842) of Auburn, Maine, was Porter's outstanding follower. He is listed in the Wood genealogy as "a painter by trade" who was also a schoolteacher. His father, Solomon, had gone to Boston as a young man to seek his fortune, and had found employment with an Italian who made, painted and peddled decorative plaster ornaments. Orison evidently learned the plaster painting technique from his father, using it to decorate plaster walls instead of figurines. About 1830 he frescoed at least four houses in West Auburn, Lewiston and Webster Corner, Maine, with landscapes clearly planned after Porter designs. These were executed in Porter's recommended technique, perhaps actually under his supervision. Wood was, however, no mere assistant; his animated murals have, within the Porter formula, a distinctive gracile style of their own (Figs. 93, 94). We get a firsthand glimpse of the painter's sales technique from an old issue of the *Lewiston Journal* (January 22, 1927) where we can read the story—recorded by Captain Cushman's daughter—of how a stranger came to the door of the Cushman Tavern in Webster Corner soon after it was built in 1826, said he was an artist, and could paint the walls with marvelous decorations which would help to advertise the Cushman House far and wide and make its name notable on the lips of the traveling public. Wood's frescoes must have brought travelers to the Cushman Tavern in his day. Perhaps now, after these works have been ignored for over a century, some people will once more come to the former tavern on the old stage road from Portland to Bangor just to see the frescoes. Certainly these landscape designs in which willowy trees fill the space in a bold pattern are outstanding examples of early American art.

Orison Wood's interpretation of Rufus Porter's murals carries the master's feeling for abstract design and decorative color to a dramatic culmination. His highly stylized versions of Porter's murals are actually more interesting, as pure design, than the original models, but as wall decorations they fail to achieve the fine functional relationship to the wall itself which characterizes Porter's frescoes. Rufus Porter's landscapes seem to open out the space on all sides, to make of the wall a gentle transition between outdoors and in. The painted perspective amplifies the room and

Fig. 93. About 1830 Orison Wood painted the walls of the old Cushman Tavern, which stands at a crossroads of Webster Corner, Maine. These frescoes are outstanding examples of highly stylized primitive painting. The photograph was taken about 1940; the murals are in fine shape today.

144

Fig. 94. The Otis B. Tibbets house in West Auburn, Maine, was frescoed by Orison Wood c. 1830. The photograph was taken about 1940; the murals are still in exceptionally good condition.

Fig. 95. One of the murals in the Priest house in Croton, Massachusetts, is signed "J. D. Poor." Jonathan D. Poor, Porter's nephew and the most prolific member of his "school," did these paintings c. 1835–1840. The photograph of this wall was taken about 1940; it looks the same today.

the color lightens it, and still the decoration emphasizes the structural lines of the walls. Wood's robust colors and vivid designs, quite differently, project themselves into the room and crowd the space with their strong, staccato rhythms.

Jonathan D. Poor, who lettered "J. D. Poor" on a paddle-wheel steamboat in a fresco in Groton, Massachusetts (Fig. 95), and signed or initialed a number of frescoes in the vicinity of Vienna and Parsonfield, Maine, was the son of Rufus' sister Ruth Porter Poor. She had married Jonathan Poor of Baldwin (later Sebago), Maine, shortly after the Porter family moved from Boxford to Baldwin in 1801. Their son Jonathan D., presumably the lad "Joe" who traveled with Rufus in 1823 as a portrait painting assistant, evidently spent ten years—from about 1830 to 1840—as an active member of the Porter landscape school. In 1831 he signed and dated a fireboard, painted on wood (Fig. 48). It is now owned by the Shelburne Museum in Shelburne, Vermont. More than thirty houses that he frescoed in a dozen Maine towns are recorded in the appended Checklist, and local residents remember that there were many more long since burned or destroyed. He most likely also worked in a number of Massachusetts towns besides Groton; he was by far the most prolific of Porter's wall-painting pupils.

Poor stuck exactly to Porter's designs and coloring, so that the difference is hard to describe. It is solely a difference of artistic personality and artistic power. Poor's coloring is a bit more haphazard, his content a bit more repetitive—and that is about all. Also, most probably, Porter and Poor often worked together—in Maine especially—which makes it even harder to attribute the Maine murals; many of those listed as by Poor may have been done jointly. This is borne out in a letter from a great-granddaughter of Benjamin Porter, Edith R. King, who lives in Mt. Vernon, Maine: "Jonathan and Rufus visited relatives in Vienna and Mt. Vernon while they painted, as they had plenty of them to stay with as they worked."

Jonathan D. Poor was living in Vienna about 1833, according to family records, and at that time decorated at least two houses there. (Vienna was the home of his wife, Caroline M. Porter, the daughter of Benjamin Porter, Rufus' uncle who had moved there from Winthrop in 1788.) In 1834 Poor signed and dated a fresco in the old Benjamin Bachellor house in South Chesterville. This date may be considered approximate for his work in Chesterville, Farmington and the neighboring Maine towns in which he worked (Color Plates 17–22). The only Massachusetts murals by Poor are those in the Priest house in Groton mentioned before. Porter may have had more commissions in Massachusetts towns than he could execute, and perhaps asked Poor to come down and work on the Groton frescoes in his place. These frescoes were probably painted at about the same time as those around Farmington and may be dated about 1835–1840. In 1840 Poor, back in Maine, signed and dated a fresco in the Norton house in East Baldwin. He died in 1845, and the 1840 frescoes done near his birthplace are the last evidence of his work as a mural painter.

An account in the *Franklin Journal* (Franklin, Maine, September 15, 1944) describes the frescoes in the old Russ house in Farmington Falls, Maine, built in 1795, which was first a store, then a tavern and then a dwelling house. The *Journal* reports that the colors were very distinct, the landscapes being painted in brilliant pigments that remained remarkably well preserved after almost a hundred years, even after the roof came off and they were exposed to the elements with no protection whatsoever. Porter's claim that his recommended paints were durable was a modest understatement. "The man who did the painting in this house," continues the account, "was named Poor and he did many other houses in the vicinity . . . one . . . is the Stanley house in Fairbanks. This house has two remarkably fine rooms on the second floor and these are well preserved. Mr. Poor went about the country painting rooms and he lived with the family whose house he was decorating and received about $10.00 for each room." Porter, in one of the *New York Mechanic* articles, mentions ten dollars as the estimated cost for painting a room with landscape frescoes. It seems likely that this was the standard fee for Porter and his group of wall painters, just as it was their convenient custom to live with their clients while at work.

In the vicinity of Standish and Parsonfield, Maine, a number of houses were decorated by two painters who may have worked either with Porter or under his tutelage. One was Jonathan D. Poor, and the other identified only as Paine. Paine, probably not coincidentally, is the name of one of the early Boxford families. There is a section of Standish at Watchic Lake known as the Paine neighborhood, where four Paine brothers built homes about 1800. The "Paine" who decorated houses with murals a generation later probably can be credited with those in the Barbara E. Parker house in Standish, said to have been built by one of the older-generation Paines, and with work in Fairbanks, Farmington, Farmington Falls, Limerick, North Parsonfield and Parsonfield.

The frescoes attributed to Paine have the same content, designs and technique as Porter's, but a less meticulous brushwork and looser composition are immediately apparent. There are also trunks of trees scarcely related to the superimposed foliage; enormous, clumsy, elm-sized cedars; and details executed in a careless way in which Porter never worked. Paine's signature seems to have been an uprooted dead tree which falls between the crotched branches of another. This trademark tree is to be found in all of the frescoes ascribed to him; but in the Curtis M. Sweat house in North Parsonfield (Color Plates 19, 20), the signature "J. D. P." under a fallen limb proves that Jonathan D. Poor painted that wall at least. He and Paine probably worked together in this area.

Examination of some of the Maine murals near Farmington, traditionally ascribed to Poor, reveal the Paine dead tree as part of the composition, suggesting that Paine and Poor collaborated on some of the wall paintings here, too. This was the case in the old Russ house frescoes in Farmington Falls and those in the Milton Gay house in Fairbanks (Figs. 96, 97), whereas the Benjamin Stanley house in Fairbanks was probably decorated by Poor alone (Figs. 98, 99). East Baldwin, where Poor signed a fresco in 1840, was very near Parsonfield and Limerick where Paine had worked. It looks as if Poor worked a bit in the vicinity of Parsonfield with Paine, and as if Paine collaborated with Poor in and around Farmington, while Porter was possibly designing and directing the work in both areas.

E. J. Gilbert and E. V. Bennett, who signed frescoes in Winthrop, were two more pupils who worked—with Porter or under his direction—in Maine. The frescoes Bennett signed are not very different from Porter's. In these and the unsigned murals in the old Benjamin house, probably by Porter and a helper (Color Plate 13), the coloring is slightly muddy and parts of the drawing seem a bit heavy-handed, indicating the work of an assistant who did not have Porter's sure touch. The Knowlton house frescoes containing two stenciled signatures of "E. J. Gilbert" (Fig. 100) are stylistically quite different from Porter's though the designs are essentially similar. These frescoes also show definite connections with certain details of the Paine, Poor and Wood murals, which strengthens the supposition that a number of Porter's pupils did collaborate and work as a "school."

The chevron-striped cedars and the birds perched on the trees in Gilbert's paintings are identical with those found in the Poor-Paine Farmington frescoes and in Orison Wood's. Like Wood, Gilbert colored the ground in oddly mingled stripes of ocher, rust and green. Both pupils misunderstood Porter's use of yellow ocher for the foreground, green for the middle ground and "horizon red" in the far distance; it was typical of copyist work to combine the colors in an arbitrary arrangement as Wood and Gilbert did. In the foliage of the trees in the Paine frescoes yellow and green are casually mingled, while Porter always painted the foliage yellow on one side of the tree and green on the other to indicate the lighted and shaded sides. Porter had a painting shorthand vocabulary which his pupils generally misread; and this helps to identify Porter's original frescoes.

"Swift" of Westwood, Massachusetts, was reported in the town to have been another of Rufus Porter's assistants, and Porter's son Stephen Twombly, who signed one of the Westwood murals, was undoubtedly a partner in the wall-painting business as he was in the publication of the *American Mechanic*.

There are anonymous landscape frescoes in various New England towns such as those in the old Captain Dan Mather house in Marlboro, Vermont, and some murals executed by a John Avery in half a dozen houses in Wolfeboro and Middleton, New Hampshire, all of which look as if relatively inexperienced painters had been inspired by Porter's murals to try some of their own. These, however, cannot be listed with those of Porter's imme-

Fig. 96. The Russ house in Farmington Falls, Maine, was photographed by Ben Stinchfield during demolition in 1914; it had once been the Jeremiah Stinchfield store. The stylized elms in the ruined room and those outside make a striking, though unplanned, surreal scene. The frescoes are attributed to Jonathan D. Poor, working with a painter identified only as "Paine," c. 1830.

Fig. 97. The detail of a mural in the Milton Gay house in Fairbanks, Maine (now papered over), shows the dead tree in the crotch of another which was a kind of signature for the painter known as "Paine." Stylistic evidence suggests that he worked in this house, formerly a tavern, as well as in a number of others in Maine, with Jonathan D. Poor, c. 1835–1840.

Figs. 98–99.   The delightful frescoes in the Benjamin Stanley house in Fairbanks, Maine—attributed to Jonathan D. Poor, c. 1835–1840—were photographed before they were papered over, prior to 1950. A similar overmantel with soldiers was painted by Poor for the ballroom of the Milton Gay house in Fairbanks.

Fig. 100. The old Knowlton house in Winthrop, Maine, was decorated c. 1830–1835 by E. J. Gilbert, who signed two walls. The photograph was taken about 1940; the frescoes are still in very good condition.

diate school. One Nathan Thayer of Hollis, Massachusetts, is credited by family tradition with having painted the walls of the Priest house in Groton and the Coburn Tavern in East Pepperell, but this has not been substantiated adequately enough even to suggest that Thayer may have been a Porter assistant—especially as the Priest house frescoes are signed by Jonathan D. Poor and differ drastically in style from those in the Coburn Tavern.

It is worth noticing that in a large proportion of the frescoed houses in which Porter assistants or pupils worked, marbleized or grained woodwork and stenciled wall decorations are also found. There is decorative painting, however, in only a few houses apparently frescoed by Porter alone. We know that Porter had done house painting in Portland. He had discussed in *Curious Arts* and the painting articles the techniques of marbleizing and graining of woodwork, painting in figures for carpets and borders, and painting walls "plain or figured." There is little question that Rufus Porter had done some woodwork painting and possibly he also did wall stenciling before starting on his fresco painting career. It seems probable that he did a bit of this decorating at the same time that he painted the landscape frescoes, in which indeed he made liberal use of stencils. It seems likely, however, that he delegated most of this routine decoration to assistants, a number of whom may have been itinerant house decorators who were learning from him the art of mural landscape painting.

In the Bidwell and Prescott taverns, in the Solomon Russell and Gardner Davis houses, and in Quillcote there is no evidence of any work by an assistant, and the stenciled designs, different from any used by other stencilers, may be assumed to be Porter's. In the Joshua Eaton house both the landscape paintings and the stenciled walls are definitely recorded as the work of the two young men who also marbleized the woodwork and ornamented the parlor mantel. E. J. Gilbert stenciled a border in the Knowlton house, and he did some woodwork graining similar to that executed by Orison Wood in the Cushman Tavern. In the Parsonfield houses frescoed by Paine and Poor there is the same type of grained woodwork, and in the McDonald Inn in Limerick which Paine frescoed there is a room with a frieze of ropes and tassels stenciled in rust and yellow. J. D. Poor stenciled a frieze of brown, black and blue on a light rose ground in an upstairs room of the Priest house; and in the old Russ house in Farmington Falls he (or Paine) decorated the large ground floor room and stairway with stenciled designs in yellow, pink, red and black. In several towns in which Poor painted landscape murals—Groton, Massachusetts, and Readfield and Mt. Vernon, Maine—the walls of a number of other houses were decorated with stenciled designs. This suggests that he either did landscapes or stenciling, or both, as preferred by the house owners. On the basis of the stenciling in all these houses it is obvious that Rufus Porter and his school were responsible for a number of the early stenciled wall decorations which have recently been so much admired.

An interesting possibility is that, just about the time Porter began painting murals (about 1824–1825), he also learned the latest methods of wall stenciling from the two Moses Eatons, father and son, and later passed these techniques and designs on to his assistants. The Eatons were the best known stencil artists of the time, and they were living and working in the tiny village of Hancock, New Hampshire, while Porter was there painting mural landscapes; quite a number of houses stenciled by the Eatons and frescoed by Porter remain in good condition today. In the Holsaert house in Hancock which Porter frescoed, there was a stenciled room, now replastered, which is said to have been done by Moses Eaton, Jr. It seems likely that he and Rufus Porter, who were almost the same age, collaborated for a while, Porter doing the landscapes and Eaton the stenciling. It is probably that Moses Eaton, Jr., was the other of the "two young men" who decorated the Joshua Eaton house in Bradford; Joshua Eaton was, of course, related to Moses. The stencil decoration in this house (Fig. 60) and in the Ellerton Jetté house in Sebec, Maine (Figs. 61, 62), is certainly identical with the Eatons' known work, and the patterns correspond exactly with the Eaton stencils found in an old kit that is now in the collection of the Society for the Preservation of New England Antiquities. In the Jetté house every one of the stencils in the Eaton kit was used on the walls. Mr. Jetté says that he thinks "Moses Eaton must have got marooned here for the winter as every room, every hallway, every inch of space in the house was stenciled." It is said that the freehand decoration in this house was done by an "assistant"—who was, I believe, young Rufus Porter. The spongework trees on these walls are closely related in technique and style to those in the Porter landscapes in the Joshua Eaton house, and the repeat pattern of the stenciled man with horse is the sort of thing Porter did frequently in his early frescoes. It seems most reasonable to assume that Rufus Porter and Moses Eaton, Jr., were the two young men who decorated both the Joshua Eaton house and the Jetté house— Eaton doing the stenciling, Porter the freehand decoration. The stenciling was certainly the major project in the Jetté house, so Porter could well have been considered the assistant on that job. It is worth remarking that the stencil decorations found with Porter frescoes are limited to the early period in New Hampshire, when Rufus Porter may well have worked with or been inspired by the Eatons. No stencil decorations are found with his later Massachusetts frescoes.

The Porter or Porter-school wall stencils, unlike the frescoes, would be impossible to attribute without external evidence. It is only safe to assume that the stenciled borders found in houses which Porter alone frescoed are his; perhaps at some later date more examples of his work as a stencil decorator and facts about when and where he worked will come to light.

Attributing the frescoes, fortunately, presents few difficulties. The Porter and Porter-school murals are distinguished by a typical style and content which makes them easy for anyone to identify. Their most obvious characteristics are their large scale, clear, bright colors, and bold design and execution. The three most frequently recurring scenes are harbor views much like Portland harbor as seen from Munjoy Hill with houses, ships and islands, mountains in the distance, and large "feather-duster" elm trees and small shrubs in the immediate foreground; mountain-climbing or hunting scenes used for stairway decorations; and farm-village scenes, most often used for the overmantel fresco, with buildings, fields, fences, roads, and again the large elms and small stylized shrubs in the foreground. The large trees invariably occupy almost the entire height of the painted wall and establish the first plane of the picture in a manner which was Porter's special invention and which he consistently used. Other earmarks of his murals include the use of stencils for many details such as houses and boats, the billowing round clouds, the clear reflections of objects in water, and the sharp shading of the darkened sides of houses and trees. Occasional exotic details such as tropical trees and vines, based on recollections of Hawaiian scenery, are also characteristic of the frescoes.

In the Checklist which follows this chapter well over a hundred early New England houses are listed as decorated by Rufus Porter and his assistants or close followers. Many others must have been redecorated, rebuilt or destroyed since Porter's time, and quite a number have undoubtedly escaped my attention. In 1841 Porter stated in the *New York Mechanic* that "hundreds of rooms and entries have been painted in New England scenery." It seems certain that he decorated many hundreds of rooms during his twenty years of fresco painting.

These paintings do not strike one as dull antiquities today but seem fresh and vital and modern. Although the Porter frescoes are still generally considered the efforts of isolated anonymous painters (relatively few people have read my small monograph published in 1950), they have in the last decades been increasingly appreciated. Mrs. Hickox of Groveland, Massachusetts, had cuts of three of her frescoes printed on her personal stationery. Frances Parkinson Keyes reproduced one of the New Hampshire frescoes as endpapers for *Also the Hills,* and the painted rooms are the most prominent piece of stage setting for this best-selling novel of New England life in the twentieth century. In the Howe house in Westwood the tenant brought one frescoe up to date during the last World War by chalking on the wall next to the steamship *Victory* a large V with three dots and a dash! A small number of owners of Porter-painted houses have, it is pleasant to record, read my earlier account of Porter's murals and decided they were worth preserving and restoring. Several present owners of frescoed houses bought them primarily because of the murals. A few people who owned frescoed houses, not wishing to undertake restoration, have covered the murals with removable wallpaper or wallboard—a procedure most highly recommended.

The other side of the picture is that dozens of fine Porter frescoes have been carelessly neglected, papered over, repainted or destroyed. One owner said frankly that he couldn't bear to live with the paintings and so had them wallpapered, the fate of almost half of the recorded Porter murals.

In concluding the discussion of Rufus Porter's frescoes I wish to make a strenuous plea for their preservation. The highest hope for this book is that it may result in sufficient interest in the frescoes for more of them to come to light, and for more museums and historical societies to take the best of them into safekeeping, either by removing the frescoes or preserving the houses that contain them, so that at least a few typical samples of Porter's art may be saved for posterity. When one considers all the elegant nineteenth-century interiors that have been set up in our great museums, it seems reasonable to hope that examples of these wonderfully fresh and vital painted rooms which Rufus Porter created in the simple New England homes and inns of his day might be included as well. Before the middle of this century, the late Clara Endicott Sears had one of the local murals moved to her Fruitlands Museums at Harvard, Massachusetts; a house in Sturbridge, Massachusetts, containing Porter murals was bought by Messrs. A.B. and J.C. Wells, of the American Optical Company, for Old Sturbridge Village which they founded to display and teach early New England arts and crafts; the late Major Goyette salvaged some of the frescoes from the old Prescott Tavern for his museum at Peterborough, New Hampshire; and just as this book went to press the good news came that the Maine State Museum had removed the murals from the Captain Samuel Benjamin house in Winthrop before it was demolished (See Fig. 101) and added them to its collection, to be exhibited in its new museum in Augusta which will open in 1970. May these be good examples to our other museums!

It seems amazing that any of the frescoes have escaped such pernicious enemies as leaks, cracks, mildews, dirt, wallpaper and repaint to survive in excellent condition for over a century. A few of them have indeed led a charmed life and appear today almost as bright and perfect as they did when they were painted, but more have suffered the expected fates.

On one field trip (in 1944) I visited the four Massachusetts towns of Westwood, Wakefield, West Boxford and North Reading to investigate a dozen houses believed to have Porter landscape frescoes on their walls. Of these, one house had burned to the ground. In one the frescoes were, according to the owner, "so far gone that we did away with them and replastered." Who can tell now what competent restoration might have achieved? In one house the frescoes had been so repainted as to be caricatures of the originals. In another they were thickly varnished over. One of the frescoed rooms in this house had been papered a generation ago and the paper had not been removed. In another house most of the frescoes which were "faded" had been wallpapered. In one a door had been cut through the hallway fresco leaving only three grazing cows to represent the former farm scene. In one house the painted walls were scrubbed with

Fig. 101. The frescoed walls in the Captain Samuel Benjamin house, probably by Porter and an assistant, c. 1830–1835, were removed in 1968 by the Maine State Commission for preservation in the Maine State Museum in Augusta.

Fig. 102. Caution! Murals are being painted in old taverns and houses "in the manner of Rufus Porter." This is one by Adele E. Ells, done in 1944 for Jefferds' Tavern in York Harbor, Maine.

soap powder on cleaning day. In another the rust-red baseboard strip—part of the mural design—had been enameled dark green. Of all these painted rooms only two had escaped real injury. One had been well restored in 1910 and was lovingly cared for at this time by the owner; another had, in an unkempt house teeming with children, miraculously escaped with only a few scratches and scribbles on the painted walls. Here, however, the tenants were definitely uncomfortable about living in a house so "strangely" decorated, and were asking the owner for permission to paper over the murals.

A sad postscript to this 1944 report is that in 1980 the Porter-decorated houses in this area (as everywhere else) are rapidly vanishing. In Westwood, the key town in which Porter decorated five houses including the only one where he signed and dated a mural, the record is now as follows: one burned; two torn down, including the one with the signed fresco; two remaining—in one all but one wall are papered over, and in the other the wallpaper has been removed and the frescoes, in fair condition, restored.

Since my research on the murals, however, a number of owners of Porter-painted houses have been impressed with the value (historical and financial) of their possessions and have rushed to restore them, in many cases carrying out the job in a less than professional manner and doing irreparable damage to the paintings. One professional restorer added Porter-style scenes to two other walls in the room in which he restored the old Porter mural; this could certainly confuse future art historians. Going a step beyond this, there is a strong possibility that in years to come twentieth-century Porter murals may drastically complicate the picture. The old Jefferds' Tavern in York Harbor, Maine, was decorated in 1944 with landscapes painted in close reproduction of some of Porter's Maine frescoes (Fig. 102). Mrs. Esther Doane Osman of West Newbury, Massachusetts, painted a Porter-type scene in her front hall; and then Alvah Hayes, in a report on Porter murals (see Bibliography), added West Newbury to the towns I had recorded as on Porter's painting itinerary. Some time ago a Mrs. William P. Elliott wrote to report that she had painted an umber monochrome mural "in the manner of Rufus Porter" for her Stage Coach Inn (an old inn built in 1737) in Scotch Plains, New Jersey. By now a number of visitors to the Stage Coach Inn may have thought it a fine idea to paint murals instead of papering walls in their old houses, and it would not be surprising to find future accounts mentioning Porter's New Jersey period.

Rufus Porter's mural paintings, like his inventions and his scientific journals, were pioneer products, far ahead of their time. They represent our first native landscape school, and are among the most original and important artistic achievements of nineteenth-century America. It is imperative to save them from destruction now and to insure their future preservation.

A. J. Philpott remarked in an article written for the *Boston Globe* (July 5, 1936) that Porter was "a Yankee genius, if ever there was one," and that "Rufus Porter was probably the kind of 'Connecticut Yankee' that Mark Twain wrote about." He went on to point out that Mark Twain lived in Hartford for many years and knew all about the "characters" in that part of Connecticut, implying that Porter, who in his late years resided in Hartford and New Haven counties, and who—known as an eccentric inventor, painter, writer, and most certainly a "character"—would not have escaped Mark Twain's notice. The Connecticut Yankee's personality and interests do seem sufficiently akin to Porter's to lend some credence to Philpott's interesting hypothesis. Mark Twain's hero, after having practiced several other trades, had gone to work in the great Colt arms factory in Hartford where he began his real career of learning to make all kinds of laborsaving machinery. "Why," says he, "I could make anything in the world, it didn't make any difference what; and if there wasn't any quick new-fangled way to make a thing, I could invent one—and do it as easy as rolling off a log." In King Arthur's court he realizes that he is just another Robinson Crusoe, who, "to make life bearable must . . . invent, contrive, create, reorganize things; set brain and hand to work, and keep them busy." He does just this, modernizing everything in the realm from education to industry, introducing large-scale advertising and the telephone, starting the *Camelot Weekly* as the first newspaper. The Connecticut Yankee, that democratic, wide-awake adventurer romping through the sixth century promoting and prophesying, inventing and improving, might well have been in part inspired by the life of our bold pioneer, Rufus Porter.

More significant is that Mark Twain's Connecticut Yankee was a great novelist's personification of the tough, free, creative Yankee spirit—while Rufus Porter was a living representative, a living symbol, of that spirit.

Plates 1, 2.   The Prescott Tavern in East Jaffrey, New Hampshire, built 1803, demolished about 1950, was decorated by Porter with frescoed walls with stenciled borders and a stenciled floor—all in the main ground-floor room. These perfectly preserved examples of his early work (c. 1824) are now stored in the former Coyette Museum in Peterborough, New Hampshire. The black-and-white photographs (Figs. 55, 56) were taken in the tavern about 1935, the color photographs after removal of the walls about 1945.

Plates 3, 4, 5. The Joshua Eaton house in Bradford, New Hampshire, was built in 1814 and was a Masonic meeting place for a number of years after 1818 (note Masonic emblem in overmantel decoration). It was recorded as decorated by "two young men," probably Rufus Porter and Moses Eaton, Jr. working together, c. 1824. The stencil designs are attributed to Eaton, the freehand frescoes and borders and the fireboard to Porter. The color photographs were taken in 1967, the photograph showing the fireboard (Fig. 60) before 1940. The murals are in exceptional condition.

Plates 6, 7.   The Holsaert house in Hancock, New Hampshire, was decorated by Porter c. 1825–1830. These murals are a splendid example of Porter's work at its simplest and best—and they are almost as fresh today as when he painted them. The room was photographed in 1967.

Plate 8.   Porter's gray-green monochrome mural, c. 1830–1835, was moved a generation ago from the Whitney house in Harvard, Massachusetts, to the Trustees Room of the Fruitlands Museums in Harvard. It is a fine example of the technique he called "Clara Obscuro," in his "stone green" color. This piece was photographed at the museum in 1967.

Plate 9.   The umber monochrome frescoes in the Van Heusen Seventeenth-Century Farms in North Reading, Massachusetts, were executed by Porter c. 1835–1840, photographed about 1940; though varnish has darkened the tone they are still in fine condition.

Plate 10. The Elwin Chase house in Topsham is the only one in Vermont found with Porter frescoes. The murals include the frigate *Potomac*, identified by one banner lettered "Potomac" and one "Com. Downes," under whose command the *Potomac* circumnavigated the globe during the years 1831–1834—which establishes approximate dates for these frescoes. The photographs were taken about 1965.

Plate 11. The parlor of the Emerson house in Wakefield, Massachusetts, was decorated by Porter c. 1835–1840, and he signed one of the murals "R. Porter, painter." The wall shown in this recent photograph is in fine condition; the owners, Mr. and Mrs. Robert N. Duffie, covered two damaged walls with wallboard to preserve what remained of the frescoes—an admirable procedure.

Plate 12.   West Boxford, Massachusetts, was Porter's birthplace; he came back c. 1838 to decorate a number of houses, among them the Andrew house. The mural shown is in the downstairs hall, photographed about 1940, and is still in good condition.

Plate 13.   The house built by Captain Samuel Benjamin in Winthrop, Maine, in 1819, probably frescoed by Porter and an assistant c. 1830–1835, was scheduled for demolition in 1967. In the nick of time, spurred by Porter enthusiasts, the Maine State Commission voted funds to remove the murals, still in good shape, for preservation. The photograph was taken about 25 years ago by Bartley A. Jackson, one of the people involved in the Commission's decision to save the murals; they are now in the collection of the new Maine State Museum in Augusta, which will open in 1970.

Plates 14, 15.   The Barrows homestead is in Fryeburg, Maine, where Porter had attended the Academy in 1804. Tradition records a date of 1830 for these frescoes, which may have been executed with the assistance of Jonathan D. Poor. The photographs were taken more than 25 years ago; the frescoes are in splendid condition.

Plate 16. A panel from the Dr. Francis Howe house in Westwood, Massachusetts, was painted by Porter in 1838. It was photographed in 1967 by Benjamin M. Hildebrant, who removed the murals from this house when it was demolished. Note the figure, supposedly Napoleon, formed by the space between the trees. Other walls of this house, before demolition, are reproduced in Figs. 81–84.

Plate 17. The old Pederson house in Standish, Maine, formerly a tavern, had the usual upstairs ballroom, now divided into two rooms. It is said to have been decorated by Jonathan D. Poor, datable c. 1830–1835. The photograph was taken about 20 years ago; the frescoes are still in excellent condition.

Plate 18. The front hall murals in the Dr. Moses Mason house in Bethel, Maine, are in an exceptionally fine state of preservation. They are attributed to Jonathan D. Poor, c. 1835–1840. The photographs were taken about 25 years ago.

Plates 19, 20. The Curtis M. Sweat house in North Parsonfield, Maine, has a wall signed "J. D. P." This and three other frescoed houses in North Parsonfield are all attributed to Jonathan D. Poor working with one Paine, whose first name is not known, c. 1830–1835; this is the only one in good condition. The photograph was taken about 25 years ago.

Plates 21, 22.   The murals in the old Captain Dudley Haines house in Readfield, Maine, are attributed to Jonathan D. Poor, who signed a mural in another house in Readfield. Both are datable c. 1835–1840. The photographs were taken about 25 years ago; the frescoes are in an especially fine state of preservation.

Appendixes

Checklist of Murals
by Rufus Porter and His School

UNLESS OTHERWISE INDICATED the murals are in full color. Names of owners and condition of murals are recorded as of the time I visited or investigated them, from about 1940 through the 1960s, a recheck questionnaire having been sent to town clerks and house owners in 1967; each house is listed beginning with the name by which it is best known in the town. Approximate dating of murals is based on stylistic relationships to datable ones. Exact or approximate dates for construction of houses is given when known; others can be dated as prior to approximate dates given for murals. Except for the houses printed in italics—where murals are attributed to assistants or close followers of Rufus Porter—all are attributed to Porter, or, as specified, to Porter with another painter; it should be noted, however, that in many of the Maine murals attributed to Porter assistants, Porter probably directed or worked with them.

The houses are listed in text and captions by the names under which they have been previously identified. This checklist has been revised to bring the names of the owners up to date, based on new information sent to the author.

MASSACHUSETTS

AMESBURY
> Bartlett house (old Captain Samuel Smith Colby house). Owned by Mr. and Mrs. Arthur L. Bartlett, Jr., built 1809. Frescoes, c. 1830–1835, in an exceptionally fine state of preservation until 1950; since then damages to the plaster and attempts at washing the painted walls have injured them. (Figs. 73–75).

ANDOVER
> Poor-Perry house. Owned by Mr. and Mrs. William T. Bride, Jr., built 1763 by Deacon Daniel Poor. Frescoes in northwest bedroom, c. 1835–1840, restored in 1916 by a local artist, H. Winthrop Pierce; now in fair condition.

BEDFORD
> *Frescoes, all c. 1830–1835.*
> Penniman-Stearns house. Owned by E. C. Tillson, built c. 1771 by Reverend Joseph Penniman. Frescoes faded; wallpapered before 1950 by a previous owner (Owens) in a way that paper could be removed without harming murals.
> Jonas Monroe house. Built c. 1823, owned by and until recently the restaurant of the Bedford Motel, now threatened with demolition. Frescoes "touched up" by daughter of previous owner and drastically damaged in the process.
> Dutton house. Owned by Mrs. Eva Browman, built by George Dutton c. 1828. Frescoes papered over, paper steamed off in late 1940s, now in poor condition with the exception of a portion of a harbor scene which is in quite good shape.
> Carroll Dunham house. Frescoes papered over before 1950, since then paper removed, paintings in fair condition.
> Job Lane house. Bedford Historical Society, built in 1664 by Job Lane. Gray monochrome frescoes, papered over.

BILLERICA

Frescoes, all c. 1830–1835.

Donald Schult house (formerly Bartlett). Built 1822. Frescoes papered over before 1950.

Lyons house (formerly Colonel Baldwin). Owned by Agnes and Mary Lyons, built c. 1810. Frescoes papered over before 1950.

Dyer house (old Parker Winning house). Built c. 1820. Front hall frescoes whitewashed and papered over before 1950, upstairs room frescoes in excellent condition when house burned recently.

Manning Manse. Owned by Mr. and Mrs. Ralph Stoker. Frescoes papered over before 1950.

BOSTON

Beacon Hill boarding house. Owned by Nancy Casey and Mary Cocuzzo. Gray monochrome frescoes, discovered under 16 layers of wallpaper, in every room and hall in the house; murals in poor condition, now papered over. Datable c. 1835–1840 or possibly 1843 when Porter worked as an electroplater in Boston.

CHARLESTOWN

Frescoes, c. 1835–1840.

Levi Prosser house. Built c. 1810. Frescoes papered over before 1950.

Several other unidentified houses mentioned by A. J. Philpott, *Boston Globe,* July 5, 1936.

DEDHAM AND DOVER

E. B. Allen mentions in *Early American Wall Painting* that a number of houses in the vicinity of Dedham and Dover were decorated in the late 1830s by the same artist who signed a Westwood mural "R. Porter"; Elwin I. Purrington of Wakefield stated that he heard of but never saw two frescoed houses in Dedham. I have been unable to find any trace of these houses, nor has the Dover Historical Society. The Dedham Historical Society reports several old houses with handpainted wallpaper that may have been erroneously described as frescoed.

EAST HAVERHILL

Frescoes, c. 1830–1835.

Ingalls-Colby house. Owned by Dr. Sherwood B. Lee, built c. 1700. Frescoes in an addition built 1800, painted during ownership of Dr. Timothy Kennison who bought house in 1824. Upstairs frescoes gray-green monochrome, downstairs in color, all in an exceptionally fine state of preservation (Fig. 72). Wood graining on three doors opening from upstairs hall.

Enoch Foote house. Torn down about 1940.

EAST PEPPERELL

Coburn Tavern. Owned by George G. Hayes, built c. 1800. Frescoes c. 1824, in good condition (Fig. 51).

EAST WEYMOUTH

Senigo house. Owned by Joseph A. DuBois. Frescoes, dated 1845, papered over before 1950 (Figs. 91, 92).

GEORGETOWN

Frescoes, all c. 1832.

G. Arthur Merrill house. Gray-green monochrome frescoes, recorded as done in 1832, in good condition.

Pingree house. Owned by Dr. Kenneth Field, formerly owned by Carlton Moore. Gray-green monochrome frescoes, in good condition; well restored in 1937, during ownership of Dr. Carlton W. Moore, by Mr. William Ilsley; now painted and papered over.

Peirce house. Owned by Mr. and Mrs. C. H. Judge. Living room frescoes in fair condition, with large damaged areas repainted by an artist; hall frescoes damaged by alterations, not restored.

Ethel M. Fredrick house. Frescoes in living room papered over before 1950; paper removed in 1967 and frescoes in fair condition, restored with little damage to original paint surface.

John C. Wilkins house. Murals covered with wallpaper.

GROTON
Frescoes, attributed to Jonathan D. Poor, c. 1835–1840.
Donald L. Priest house. Built 1793 by Oliver Prescott, Jr., Mural signed "J. D. Poor." Hallway fresco papered over before 1950, paper since removed; paintings in fair condition upstairs, good downstairs; parlor frescoes in excellent condition (Fig. 95).
Dr. Harold Ayres house. Owned by Forge Realty Trust Co., built 1803 by Martin Jennison. Frescoes in old ballroom (house formerly a tavern). Most of murals repainted about 35 years ago by Mrs. Ayres; overmantel in fair condition, untouched.

GROVELAND
Frescoes, all c. 1830–1835.
Harold Stacy house. Frescoes in an exceptionally fine state of preservation.
Savery homestead. Owned by Mrs. Sheldon B. Hickox, built 1825. Plum monochrome frescoes in good condition (endpapers).
Spofford house. Plum monochrome frescoes, papered over before 1950.
Edna Worthing cottage. Frescoes papered over before 1950.

HARVARD
Frescoes, all c. 1830–1835.
Joseph E. Lamborghini house (formerly William A. Potter). Built c. 1823. Gray-green monochrome frescoes papered over; wallpaper removed and frescoes restored about 1948 by Robert Atkins, who added Porter-style murals to two other walls of the frescoed room.
R. Raymond Warren Apartments (formerly Harvard Inn). Built c. 1790–1795. Frescoes in center hall plum monochrome, in south hall gray-green monochrome, all papered over. Wallpaper removed in late 1940s, frescoes in damaged condition; those in center hall repaired and in south hall restored by Robert Atkins.
Wallace F. Bryant Estate Apartments (formerly Whitney house). Gray-green monochrome frescoes plastered over or may have been removed.
Fruitlands Museums. One gray-green monochrome mural from the Whitney house (above) in excellent condition, removed to Trustees Room (Color Plate 8).

LEXINGTON
Joshua Simons house. Owned by Mrs. Otto E. Wolff, built 1720. Frescoes in two rooms and hall, c. 1830–1835, recently restored by Mrs. Estelle Weir.

LUNENBURG
Faith Gardner house (old Emery house). Built in early 1800s. Frescoes, c. 1830–1835, found under wallpaper almost 100 years ago; in good condition until about 1945, deteriorated since then (Fig. 76).

MERRIMAC
Sargent homestead. Owned by Mrs. Albert B. Smith, built 1728. Frescoes, probably c. 1830–1835, papered over; paper removed in 1965 and frescoes repainted in oils by owner and her daughter.

MERRIMACPORT
Ronald Shaw house (formerly Edward Gibbons). Built c. 1820. Gray-green monochrome frescoes, c. 1830–1835, discovered on stair wall when a hall wall was removed to enlarge living room; in fair condition.

NORTH READING
Frescoes, all c. 1835–1840.
Van Heusen Seventeenth-Century Farms (old Colonial Inn). Owned by Mr. and Mrs. Frederick Zarick. Umber monochrome frescoes in upstairs room varnished, darkening the color, but painting remarkably clear and well preserved; colored frescoes in downstairs room papered over before 1950 (Color Plate 9).
Frances Shay Mague house (old Squire Flint Mansion). Built 1713. Umber monochrome frescoes in hallway in good condition. Colored frescoes in front parlor faded.

Weeks Memorial Library (old Damon Tavern). Built 1812. Ballroom frescoes papered over, paper partially removed about 1962; in poor to fair condition—plaster cracked and in places had been worked over with crayon and oil paint; overmantel completely gone. Rest of paper removed and in process of restoration by Mrs. Barbara Blanchard; overmantel to be copied from the Van Heusen Seventeenth-Century Farms, above (Fig. 86).

Unidentified house on Route 28 near flying field. Frescoes, papered over, described by Elwin I. Purrington of Wakefield in 1949.

STURBRIDGE

Oliver Wight house. Owned by Old Sturbridge Village, used as a motel, built 1783. Gray-green monochrome frescoes in hall, c. 1830–1835, formerly papered over; in very poor condition when restored in 1948 by Robert Atkins.

TOWNSEND

Frescoes, c. 1830–1835.

Charles A. Smith house. Gray monochrome frescoes, in fair condition.

Reed mansion. Townsend Historical Society, built shortly after 1800. Frescoes in an exceptionally fine state of preservation in upstairs room; lower room papered over well before 1950. Grained decoration on many door panels, and mantel in upstairs landscaped room stippled or sponged in dark green.

WAKEFIELD

Frescoes, all c. 1835–1840.

Emerson house. Owned by Mr. and Mrs. Robert N. Duffie, built 1749. Mural with waterfall signed "R. Porter, painter" on rock at right of waterfall. Outside walls of parlor damaged by humidity, covered with wallboard as owners did not want to undertake restoration but cared to preserve what remained; two inside walls in exceptionally fine condition, though panels framed with gilt molding to look like large pictures rather than murals (Figs. 89, 90, Color Plate 11).

Winn house. Owned by Mr. and Mrs. Howard E. Melanson, built 1817 by Samuel Winn. Gray monochrome frescoes, well restored in 1910 when house owned by Elwin I. Purrington (Figs. 87, 88).

Franklin Poole house. Owned by Mr. and Mrs. Ronald S. Lancaster, built before 1795 by Elias Emerson. Frescoes entirely repainted before 1950, now papered over.

Lilly Eaton house. Built 1804, demolished 1913. Second floor hall frescoes in good condition at time of demolition.

Thomas Walton house. House moved, remodeled, no trace of frescoes left.

Kenneth Odiorne house. Frescoes in very poor condition and papered over in 1951.

WEST BOXFORD

Frescoes, all c. 1838.

John A. Andrew house. Owned by Mr. and Mrs. John F. G. Eichorn, Jr. Frescoes in upstairs and downstairs halls, said to have been painted shortly after 1837 when Andrew family bought house. A doorway cut through one mural, others in good, unrestored condition (Color Plate 12).

Joseph Burgson house. Owned by Mrs. Dorothy A. Chadwick. Frescoes entirely destroyed.

Hovey house. Burned.

WESTWOOD

Frescoes, all c. 1838 and all probably by Porter with his son Stephen Twombly. (There is verbal tradition about a painter named Swift who worked on some of the Westwood murals.)

Dr. Francis Howe house. Built 1818, demolished 1965; walls purchased from owner, Robert Smith, and removed by Benjamin M. Hildebrant and Francis Holland; owned by Louis DiGiovanni. Stairway mural signed "R. Porter, 1838" on rock halfway up the stairs, and above it "S. T. Porter." Frescoes in an exceptionally fine state of preservation when this house, with the only signed and dated mural by Porter, was demolished. The dozen wall panels (priced for sale at approximately $40,000) were exhibited in Boston at the First Annual New England Antiques Show in 1967, and at the Whitney Museum of American

Art on the occasion of the publication of this book in 1968 (Figs. 81–84, Color Plate 16).

E. A. West house. Formerly owned by Boyden and Allen families, presently owned by Mr. and Mrs. Allen D. Badger, built in the late 1700s. Stairway and upstairs hall frescoes papered over before 1950; those in lower hall in good condition, cleaned and one small area restored (Figs. 78, 79).

Reuben Guild house. Owned by E. E. Baker, built 1818, demolished 1961 (Fig. 80).

Storer Ware house. Owned by Whiting and Colburn families, presently owned by Mr. and Mrs. George Frick; built before 1835, decorated by Porter during ownership of William P. Colburn. Frescoes, which had been wallpapered after 1925, now in fair condition, restored (Fig. 77).

Allen house. Built some time before 1818, burned 1905 when owned by William V. Tripp.

WOBURN

Shaker Glenn Inn. Owned by Shaker Glen Associates, Inc., built 1800–1810. Frescoes, c. 1835–1840, repainted and varnished before 1950. Umber monochrome frescoes in hall, parlor in color. Two signatures of "R. Porter."

Tidd house. Demolished.

NEW HAMPSHIRE

BRADFORD

Joshua Eaton house. Owned by Mr. and Mrs. Eldred M. Keays (formerly owned by William Taylor Morson), built 1814; after 1818 was a Masonic meeting place for a number of years. Frescoes and decorations, recorded as by "two young men," probably Porter and Moses Eaton, Jr., c. 1824; all in an exceptionally fine state of preservation. Stencil designs and frescoes well restored where necessary about 30 years ago; at that time the front hall, originally decorated with a sun on one side and a moon on the other but covered with a coat of red paint some time ago, was wallpapered. Landscapes and fireboard attributed to Porter, stenciling to Moses Eaton, Jr. (Fig. 60, Color Plates 3–5).

DOVER

Neighborhood house. Owned by Alcide Turgeon, built c. 1820. Frescoes, c. 1825–1830, largely repainted before 1950.

EAST JAFFREY

Frescoes, c. 1824.

Prescott Tavern. Built 1803 by Oliver Prescott, torn down about 1940. Frescoes with stenciled border and stenciled floor removed to Goyette Museum, Peterborough, New Hampshire; museum closed in 1960 and frescoes, now owned by Mortimer Zuckerman. All in excellent original condition (Figs. 55, 56, Color Plates 1, 2).

Don Pierce house. Frescoes in fair condition.

GREENFIELD

Frescoes, all c. 1825.

Squire Craigin house. Owned by Ornan S. Cook, 3rd, built c. 1820. Frescoes restored in 1941, then papered over; paper recently removed. Frescoes in color, dados gray monochrome (Figs. 65, 66).

James T. Garvin house. Owned by Mrs. Hazel O. Cary. Frescoes papered over before 1950.

Eliot Hutchinson house, owned by Mrs. Haydn Pearson, built 1773. Frescoes papered over in late 1940s.

HANCOCK

Frescoes, all c. 1825

Patricia Holsaert house, built 1790 by Robert Matthews. Owned by Mr. and Mrs. Charles Cobb. Frescoes in an exceptionally fine state of preservation (Color Plates 6, 7).

Cynthia Porter Weston house. Owned by Mr. and Mrs. H. Thorne King. Frescoes papered over until late 1940s, now in fair condition, unrestored.

John Hancock Inn. Owned by Mr. and Mrs. Charles Marsh. Frescoes poorly repainted before 1950.

Miss Mary and Dr. Fredrika Moore house. Owned by Mrs. Earl Hamilton, recorded as decorated about 1824. Frescoes discovered under 12 layers of wallpaper, in fair condition; all but one wall restored.

HAVERHILL

Grace D. Wilson-Lavery house. Built c. 1815. Frescoes covered by many layers of wallpaper, removed 1914, and frescoes photographed by workmen employed by owner, Miss Ada Fitts. After seeing photographs owner ordered frescoed walls repapered. Paper removed in 1955 and frescoes restored by an elderly primitive painter; remains of Porter's landscapes virtually hidden under repaint. Hall landscape features a French château, identified as deriving directly from an engraved view of "La Grange the Residence of the Marquis Lafayette." Lafayette visited Vermont and New Hampshire on his second trip to America, in 1824, and could have been in Haverhill. It seems likely that the mural was done shortly after his visit; suggested dating, c. 1825–1830.

LANGDON

Bidwell Tavern. Burned c. 1927. Frescoes, c. 1824. Dado gray monochrome, rest in color; walls in one room decorated with spongework (Figs. 63, 64).

LYME

Frescoes, all c. 1825–1830.

Frederick Wagner house (formerly George Wittenborn). Built 1811 by Moses Kent; frescoes in an exceptionally fine state of preservation (Figs. 45, 69).

Dennis house (Latham Tavern). Burned several years ago.

Dennis-Culver house. Owned by John S. Eaton, built 1790. Said to have landscaped walls, at present wallpapered; reports of murals may have confused Dennis house, above, with Dennis-Culver house, as present owner has found no trace of murals under paper.

Perkins-Simmons house. Built c. 1795 for Samuel Perkins who was owner of house when murals were painted. House partially burned and demolished in 1963. Two sections of frescoes, each about 5 feet long and in fair condition, removed and stored by William Hart at West Wind Farm, Lyme.

Kent-Mativia house. Burned.

MASON

Frescoes, all c. 1825.

Asher Tarbell house. Owned by William T. Clark, built c. 1822. Frescoes said to have been done for Asher Tarbell and his wife shortly after house finished. Frescoes in parlor, papered over in 1949; floor in this room grained.

Jonathan Batchelder house. Owned by Tracy A. Eaton, built c. 1800. Lower floor rooms landscaped, one wall destroyed; upstairs stenciled bands around doors and windows, same tulip design as in Solomon Russell house in New Ipswich. Frescoes in fair condition.

Joseph Saunders house. Built in the 1790s, burned 1917 when owned by Herbert Russell. Frescoes in a downstairs room, in fair condition when burned.

NEW IPSWICH

Frescoes, all c. 1825.

Solomon Russell house (formerly Davis). Owned by Alfred Hobbs. Frescoes upstairs, in good condition until destroyed recently when larger windows installed; scenes above stair rail and stenciled band at top were in color, dado gray monochrome.

Gardner Davis house. Frescoes with stenciled border, destroyed before 1952 (Figs. 58, 59).

Gould-Chickering house. Owned by Warren E. Legsdin. Frescoes in front hall, papered over.

NORTH HAVERHILL

Frescoes, all c. 1825–1830.

Daniel Carr house. Owned by Robert Graham Chase. Wing containing frescoes built in 1816. Frescoes in an exceptionally fine state of preservation (Figs. 67, 68).

Harold Kimball house. Frescoes in fair condition.

Leslie Lackie house. Frescoes destroyed.

ORFORD

Beale house (old Dyar T. Hinckley house). Owned by Mrs. Howard K. Beale, built 1822–1824. Frescoes in two upstairs rooms, c. 1824, had been papered over, discovered in 1964; restored by Carroll Wales, a professional Boston restorer, in 1964 and 1966.

VERMONT

TOPSHAM

Elwin Chase house. Owned by Seymour Browne. Built prior to 1800. Frescoes datable c. 1831–1834 based on identification of the frigate *Potomac*, whose circumnavigation of the globe in those years was of great public interest. A wall with landscape said by owners to resemble the hilltop city in the Squire Craigin house in Greenfield, New Hampshire, now destroyed; upstairs and downstairs hall frescoes in good condition (Color Plate 10).

MAINE

BETHEL

Dr. Moses Mason House. Owned by Mrs. Ada Durell, built c. 1812. Frescoes, attributed to Jonathan D. Poor, c. 1835–1840. Murals in front hall in an exceptionally fine state of preservation; those in parlor almost entirely destroyed and papered over before 1950. An observatory in one of the scenes was labeled "Portland" by Dr. Mason in 1863 (Color Plate 18).

BRIDGTON

Deacon Libby house. Stairway murals, c. 1830–1835, wallpapered many years ago.

BRYANT POND

Whitman homestead. Burned in late 1940s. Frescoes, said to have been similar to those in the Dr. Moses Mason house in Bethel, probably by Jonathan D. Poor, c. 1835–1840.

BUXTON

Frescoes, c. 1830–1835.

Carroll Rounds house (former stagecoach tavern). Owned by Robert Johnson. Frescoes in an exceptionally fine state of preservation.

A. I. Poulsen house. Frescoes in fair condition.

CHESTERVILLE

Frescoes, all locally remembered as Jonathan D. Poor's work, datable c. 1834.

Professor Diller house (old Benjamin Bachellor house). Built 1805 by Allen Wing, now abandoned and in poor shape. Walls removed by Professor Eliot Diller to his house, a short distance away. Murals considerably weathered; one was signed "J. D. Poor—1834."

Fuller Dyke house. Burned 1905. The late Mrs. Abigail Hodgkins Knowlton remembered that her father had the walls decorated by Poor, and his initials were found on one of the frescoes; murals in excellent condition when house burned.

Captain Thomas Williams homestead. Built c. 1780 by Captain Williams. Frescoes papered over, paper removed and frescoes restored in 1952 by Jack Robertson, a Chicago artist, for owner, Mrs. Nettie M. Ingham; lost much of Poor's coloring and style in restoration.

Lyman Whittier house. Frescoes papered over before 1950.

Thomas Austin house (old Benjamin S. French house). Burned some time after 1950.

CORNISH

Tompkins house. Demolished about 10 years ago. Frescoes, as described, by Porter or Porter school, probably c. 1830–1835.

EAST BALDWIN

Lorenzo Norton house. Owned by Mr. and Mrs. Stephen Butler. Frescoes by Jonathan D. Poor in a number of rooms, one initialed "J. D. P." and dated 1840, in fair condition.

FAIRBANKS

Frescoes, traditionally ascribed to Jonathan D. Poor, datable c. 1835–1840.
(There is evidence that Paine also worked in this town.)
Milton Gay house (former tavern). Owned by Mrs. Emily Scribner, built by Samuel Emery in 1820. Ballroom frescoes attributed to Paine and Poor, now papered over (Fig. 97).
Gerald York house (formerly Carrie Archabald). Frescoes papered over before 1950.
Benjamin Stanley house. Owned by Mrs. Elizabeth Gray Hood, built by Sanford Davis c. 1818. Frescoes in an exceptionally fine state of preservation, papered over before 1950 (Figs. 98, 99).
David E. Currier house. Owned by Mr. and Mrs. Tyler Currier, built c. 1828 by Ephraim Green. Frescoes papered over, paper removed and frescoes in fairly good condition, restored in 1967.

FARMINGTON

Frescoes, all attributed to Jonathan D. Poor working with Paine, datable c. 1830–1835.
Jonathan Cushman farm. Built 1830, burned 1944; formerly the town poorhouse. Frescoes in good condition when house burned.
William Gilman farm. Owned by Richard Adams. Frescoes papered over before 1950, house burned 1967.
David Ingham farm. Owned by Robert Schultz. Frescoes destroyed in 1940s.
Robert C. Bruce house. Frescoes discovered under wallpaper, in fair condition.

FARMINGTON FALLS

Russ house (Jeremiah Stinchfield store). Built c. 1795, torn down 1914. Frescoes, traditionally ascribed to Jonathan D. Poor, datable c. 1830. Evidence that Paine also worked in this house (Fig. 96).

FAYETTE

Lieutenant John Lovejoy house. Owned by Clyde Wells, built c. 1795. Frescoes, traditionally ascribed to Jonathan D. Poor, datable c. 1835–1840, papered over some time after 1950.

FRYEBURG

Frescoes, c. 1830.
Barrows homestead. Owned by Mrs. Georgiana Steadman, built 1809. Tradition records date of 1830 for frescoes. The style suggests the possibility that Porter was assisted here by Jonathan D. Poor. The murals are in an especially fine state of preservation (Color Plates 14, 15).
Warren-Towle house. Owned by Mrs. George C. Young, built early 1800s. Frescoes papered over before 1950; paper removed, frescoes in fair condition.

GORHAM

Dr. Files house. Owned by Mrs. James Godfrey, built in late 1700s. Downstairs bedroom frescoes and stenciled frieze repainted, evidently with some improvised reconstruction, and too highly colored; attribution cannot be more definite than to Porter or Porter school, probably c. 1830–40.
Fox house. Owned by Professor and Mrs. James Whitten, built in 1700s. Frescoes in downstairs hallway, in good condition, recently retouched; stairway frescoes papered over; those in upstairs room considerably repainted. Murals related to

Porter's, but not attributable to him, Poor, Paine, Wood, Gilbert or Bennett; may possibly be attributed to Granville Fernald, c. 1851–53. A unique element is a looped curtain painted as if hanging from the ceiling; it runs as a continuous frieze around the ceiling and occupies almost a quarter of the frescoed walls.

Hollis Center

Quillcote. Home of Kate Douglas Wiggin, purchased by her in 1893, presently owned by Mr. and Mrs. Ralph W. Turner. Frescoes, painted during occupancy of first owner, Jabez Woodbury, between 1823 and 1835, probably c. 1830. (A date on one mural repainted in 1910 reads 1820; the 2 could well have been misread by restorer—an 1830 date seems more likely.) Front hall frescoes upstairs and downstairs practically demolished by early architectural changes and now covered with wallpaper; upstairs bedroom restored in 1910 by B. P. Lee. Hall and frescoes still in good condition (Figs. 70, 71).

Lewiston

Frescoes, attributed to Orison Wood, c. 1830.

H. O. Wood house. Owned by Mrs. E. Mechot, built c. 1813. Frescoes in an exceptionally fine state of preservation.

Howard W. Mann house. Frescoes removed from another Lewiston house before it was demolished and set up in the Mann house before 1950.

Limerick

Frescoes, traditionally ascribed to Paine, datable c. 1830.

McDonald Inn. Owned by C. Sadler, built early 1800s. Frescoes entirely repainted before 1950.

Furlong house. Demolished before 1950.

Monmouth

Simon Martson house, owned by Marius B. Péladeau, built 1809. Porter-style frescoes in downstairs hall in such poor, worn condition that attribution must be general: to Porter possibly with one of his assistants, c. 1830–1840 when they were working in this area.

Mt. Vernon

Frescoes, traditionally ascribed to Jonathan D. Poor, c. 1835–1840.

Burbank house. Owned by Mr. and Mrs. Chris Huntington (in the 1800s by Dr. Silas Burbank), built c. 1820. A mural in each of two downstairs rooms uncovered when wallpaper removed a year ago; painted wall in large room in fair condition, in smaller room, poor.

Arthur Gordon house. Frescoes papered over some time after 1950; house burned several years ago.

New Sharon

Robert C. Bruce house. Built c. 1839. Frescoes, attributed to Jonathan D. Poor, c. 1835–1840, found under old wallpaper; in poor condition.

North Parsonfield

Frescoes, all attributed to Paine working with Jonathan D. Poor, c. 1830–1835.

Curtis M. Sweat house. Owned by Dr. and Mrs. George E. Doe, built c. 1814–1816. Signature "J. D. P." on one wall. Frescoes in an exceptionally fine state of preservation (Color Plates, 19, 20).

Frank Chapman house. Frescoes in poor condition.

Helen Cating house. Frescoes papered over except one panel about 5 by 7 feet.

Dr. William Reid house. Built c. 1814–1816. Frescoes papered over before 1950.

Parsonfield

Dalton house. Owned by Mrs. Blanche Marcionette Kingsbury, built 1805–1816. Frescoes, traditionally ascribed to Paine, c. 1830; in an exceptionally fine state of preservation.

Chillis house. Owned by Edward H. Stann, built before 1785. Staircase mural by Jonathan D. Poor, c. 1830–1835, signed "J. D. Poor"; staircase and hall frescoes in an exceptionally fine state of preservation.

Portland

Deacon John Bailey house. Owned by Mr. and Mrs. Howard U. Heller, built c. 1760. Frescoes, recorded as dating between 1815 and 1827, can be placed after

1824 when Porter began mural painting; c. 1827 probably accurate. Last owner began to retouch frescoes but stopped; still in good, original condition.

Ellis Place (Blackstrap area). Burned. Frescoes probably approximately same date as Deacon Bailey house (above).

READFIELD

Frescoes, attributed to Jonathan D. Poor, datable c. 1835–1840.

Captain Dudley Haines house. Owned by Mr. and Mrs. A. H. Saunders, built in late 1700s. Frescoes in an especially fine state of preservation (Color Plates 21, 22).

Judge Bean house. Owned by Mr. and Mrs. Edward Dodge, built in late 1700s. Signature "J. D. Poor" on a ship in one of murals. Frescoes in excellent condition in upstairs and downstairs halls; a front bedroom papered over.

RUMFORD

Phil Baker house. Frescoes, similar to those in Dr. Moses Mason house in Bethel, probably by Jonathan D. Poor; said to have been done c. 1840.

SEBEC

Ellerton Jetté house (old Burgess house). Built 1785, added to in early 1820s. Frescoes and stenciled walls attributed to Porter and Moses Eaton, Jr., c. 1824. Every wall in the house originally ornamented with freehand or stenciled decoration, probably shortly after completion of the addition. Some walls replastered, some badly faded, but many in an exceptionally fine state of preservation (Figs. 61, 62).

SOUTH BRIDGTON

Ingalls house. Owned by Carl Dadmun. Porter-style frescoes in a second-floor bedroom, papered over, described by South Bridgton people; probably c. 1830–1835.

STANDISH

Frescoes, c. 1830–1835.

Warren Pederson house (former tavern). Now occupied by Mr. and Mrs. Jackson E. Blake. Owned by Mrs. Pederson. Frescoes in two upstairs rooms, originally the long ballroom, said to have been done by Jonathan D. Poor; in excellent condition, though some repainting of trees in room with stenciled frieze (Color Plate 17).

Barbara E. Parker house. Built by a Paine, according to the Standish town clerk, before 1800; the house is situated in what is known as the Paine Neighborhood at Watchic Lake. Frescoes attributed to Paine on wall of one room found under 7 layers of wallpaper; in fair condition, somewhat touched up.

STRONG

William McClary homestead. Owned by Mrs. Arline Curtis, built 1826. Frescoes, attributed to Jonathan D. Poor, c. 1835–1840, in good condition.

TURNER

Frescoes, attributed to Orison Wood, c. 1830.

Captain Leavitt house. Owned by Mr. and Mrs. Roger Prince, built c. 1800. Wallpaper stripped off some years ago with great damage to frescoes; two walls still papered; alterations in living room cut into murals; stairway paintings in relatively good shape.

Unidentified house. Burned recently. Frescoes, as reported by Roger Prince, similar to those in his house (above).

VIENNA

Frescoes locally remembered as by Jonathan D. Poor, datable c. 1833 when Poor is recorded as living in Vienna.

Nathaniel Whittier house. Owned by Otis Foss. Frescoes in very poor condition when house burned several years ago.

Gilman Bachelder house. Frescoes papered over, house recently burned.

Unidentified house. Burned. Frescoes, as described, in fair condition before house burned.

WEBSTER CORNER

Cushman Tavern. Owned by Mr. and Mrs. Minot C. Morse, built 1826. Frescoes by Orison Wood, c. 1830. Murals in one room papered over, those in hall in an especially fine state of preservation (Fig. 93).

WEST AUBURN

Otis B. Tibbets house. Frescoes by Orison Wood, c. 1830. Parlor frescoes in an exceptionally fine state of preservation, other room restored by Mrs. Mary Preble before 1950 (Fig. 94).

WESTBROOK

Frescoes, c. 1830–1835.

Zebulon Trickey house. Owned by Frank Bovine, built 1754. Front parlor frescoes in excellent condition, but with only flaw some cracking of plaster near mantel.

Pride house. Owned by Herbert E. Erskine, built by Nathan Harris c. 1828. Frescoes in front hall and parlor, in quite good condition, related to but not attributable to Porter or Porter school; painted drapery similar to that in the Fox house in Gorham suggests possible attribution to Granville Fernald, c. 1851–1853.

WEST MT. VERNON

Frescoes, attributed to Jonathan D. Poor, c. 1835–1840.

Leon H. Marr house. Built c. 1830. Frescoes in fair condition when house recently demolished.

Unidentified house. Demolished before 1950.

WINTHROP

Frescoes, all c. 1830–1835.

Frank Hanson house. Signature "E. V. Bennett." Frescoes varnished before 1950, badly discolored.

Knowlton house. Owned by Mr. and Mrs. Harold Olsen, built by Dr. Peleg Benson c. 1795. Frescoes in very good condition; two walls signed "E. J. Gilbert" (Fig. 100).

Captain Samuel Benjamin house (telephone building). Built by Captain Benjamin c. 1819. Frescoes, in an upstairs room, probably by Porter and an assistant (indication that there may have been other decorated rooms, replastered). Murals slightly repainted in parts but in pretty good condition; one wall, attributed to Porter, in excellent condition; two in bad shape from leaks. When house was scheduled for demolition in 1967, the Maine State Commission removed murals; they are now in the collection of the Maine State Museum, Augusta (Color Plate 13).

✿   ✿   ✿

UNIDENTIFIED TOWNS

An unidentified house is recorded in photographs owned by the Society for the Preservation of New England Antiquities, Boston. Fresco style, close to the late eastern Massachusetts group of Porter murals, suggests done for a Massachusetts house by Porter, c. 1835–1840.

A panel, 4 x 5 feet, origin unknown, is owned by the Society for the Preservation of New England Antiquities, Boston. Style suggests attribution to Paine, possibly with Jonathan D. Poor, c. 1830–1835, most likely from a house in the vicinity of Parsonfield, Maine.

✿   ✿   ✿

Postscript

RESEARCH IS ALWAYS an ongoing project. In the case of Rufus Porter, the investigation I began in 1940 has accelerated year by year. Since the first edition of this book in 1968, hundreds of informative letters, documents, and photographs have been sent to me; and as this edition goes to press they are still coming in.

It has been impossible to check in person the latest information, to view all the material myself, in order to verify dating, condition, possible signatures, etc. The following summary presents the most recent data in brief, as accurately as possible, listed now as an aid to continuing research.

MURALS (attributed to Rufus Porter unless otherwise noted. Those attributed to Jonathan D. Poor printed in *italics*.)

MASSACHUSETTS

AMESBURY
Parsonage of Main Street Congregational Church.

ANDOVER
Edmund W. Fredericks house.

GROTON (frescoes attributed to Jonathan D. Poor)
Groton Inn (old Richardson Tavern).
Robert M. May house.

LINCOLN
Mrs. Gordon A. Donaldson house.

NEWBURYPORT
Marie A. Carlson house.

WESTWOOD
Sylvester Wells house. One mural moved to Westwood Public Library.

NEW HAMPSHIRE

EAST JAFFREY
Richard A. Grodin house.

HANCOCK
Mrs. Margaret Perry house.

KEENE
Howard W. Kirk house.
Charles Norwood house (frescoes and stairway stenciled wall).
Lawrence MacKenzie house (old Captain Isaac Wyman house).
Ellen Faulkner house.

LYME
    Jack Schriever house.

SURREY
    Robert Likins house.

THORNTON
    Walls removed from unidentified house, owned by John Walton, Inc.; Jewett City,
    Connecticut.

TROY
    Robert R. Devoid house.

MAINE

DENMARK
    Mrs. Baron P. Mayer house (old Cyrus Ingalls house).

FARMINGTON FALLS (frescoes attributed to Jonathan D. Poor, probably with Paine)
    Gordon M. Grigsby house (old John Russ house). Frescoes and stenciled walls.
    Reverend G. Ernest Lynch house.

MERCER (frescoes by Jonathan D. Poor)
    Ralph Tree house (old Walton homestead). Fragment signed *J. D. Poor, 1842* re-
    moved for display at Cutler Memorial Library.

NEW SHARON (frescoes attributed to Jonathan D. Poor)
    Richard Handrakan, Jr. house.
    Linwood C. Currier house (old Christopher Dyer house).

ROCKLAND
    Raymond C. Keefer house.

HOUSE DECORATION

Fireboard attributed to Rufus Porter, Mr. and Mrs. Samual Shaer, Manchester, New
    Hampshire.
Bears and Pears fireboard New York State Historical Association, Cooperstown, attributed
    to Rufus Porter.
Fireboard attributed to school of Rufus Porter, John H. Martin, Woodstock, Vermont.
Overmantel panel attributed to Rufus Porter, formerly Mr. and Mrs. Jerome Blum,
    Lisbon, Connecticut.
Mantelpiece attributed to Rufus Porter, Abby Aldrich Rockefeller Folk Art Center,
    Williamsburg, Virginia.

PORTRAITS

Small watercolor profile portraits, unidentified unless otherwise noted.

Three members of the Robbins family of Lexington, Massachusetts, Lexington Historical
Society; pair, Bucknam Tavern on the Green, Lexington, Massachusetts; seven children
of Rufus and Martha Merriam of Concord, Massachusetts, Mrs. Charles Lund, Concord,
Massachusetts; New England Lady, Maine State Museum, Augusta; Lady and Gentleman, National Portrait Gallery, Washington, D.C.; single portraits, pairs and groups
owned by Mr. and Mrs. Norbert H. Savage, Kildeer, Illinois; John F. G. Eichorn, Jr.,

West Boxford, Massachusetts; Roger Bacon, Exeter, New Hampshire; Joy Piscapo Antiques, Portland, Maine; Phyllis Kirkpatrick, Shelburne Falls, Maine; Barbara Johnson, Princeton, New Jersey; Caroline Stevens, North Andover, Massachusetts; Mrs. E. C. Sterling, New York, New York; Mr. and Mrs. Victor Carapella, Glen Ellyn, Illinois; Mr. and Mrs. Frank Pollack, Highland Park, New Jersey; Mr. and Mrs. Joseph Keown, Glen Ellyn, Illinois; Mr. and Mrs. Gary Stass, New Canaan, Connecticut.

Three small watercolor full-face portraits of members of the Mills family, one signed *Drawn by Rufus Porter*, dated 1835, all owned by Robert Thayer, New York, New York.

MISCELLANEOUS

Pair of oil landscapes, Brandegee Antiques, Pittsburgh, Pennsylvania.
Painted box, Nina Fletcher Little, Brookline, Massachusetts.
Family register, Mrs. Robert M. Barclay, Reading, Massachusetts.
Measuring instrument, Old Sturbridge Village, Sturbridge, Massachusetts.

DOCUMENTS

Xerox reprint of essays on various kinds of painting by Rufus Porter as they appeared in *Scientific American*, September 11, 1845, to April 9, 1846, assembled by Louis C. Jones for the Library of the New York State Historical Association, Cooperstown. This Xerox edition has been microfilmed by the Archives of American Art and is available in its six offices in New York, Boston, Detroit, San Francisco, Houston and Washington, D.C., and is also available through Inter-Library Loan to libraries throughout the world.

Xerox reprint of the first issue of *Scientific American*, for the *Scientific American* library, New York City.

Rufus Porter material collected by the Minnesota Historical Society, St. Paul: Stock Certificate for Porter's Aerial Navigation Company; letter from Porter to Markoe, in William Markoe Papers file; vol. 1, no. 8 of *Aerial Reporter*; printed prospectus for shares in the development of the "Steam Farmer"; *An Aerial Steamer, or Flying Ship*; *Aerial Navigation*.

Articles published in the *San Diego Union* in the 1870s, recorded by Mrs. Thomas C. Webster, President of the Spring Valley Historical Society, California (copies sent for the author's file). The articles show that three of Porter's children were living in San Diego in the latter half of the nineteenth century; that Porter was "a correspondent of the *San Diego Union*"; and that his son, Captain Rufus K. Porter, also wrote for the *Union*. One article quotes a clipping from *Harper's Weekly* about his father; others quote long letters to him from Rufus Porter, with details about his daily life when he was in his eighties.

A letter sent to the author from Mrs. C. Bruce Campbell, Rufus Porter's great-granddaughter, about her grandmother Nancy Adams Porter. Describes her grandmother's recollections of accompanying her father on many of his painting trips.

A thesis titled "The *Scientific American* in Nineteenth Century America," written by Michael Barut for his Ph.D. degree from New York University in 1977, was brought to my attention just as this edition was going to press. The thesis is based on fifty years of the diaries of Orson D. Munn, who bought *Scientific American* from Rufus Porter in 1846, and so includes firsthand background for Porter's career as a journalist. A copy of Barut's thesis is in the possession of the present Orson D. Munn, who had made his great-grandfather's diaries available for the thesis research.

Chronology of Rufus Porter's Life

1792	Born May 1 in West Boxford, Massachusetts.
1796	Entered the Fifth District School in West Boxford.
1801	Moved with his family to Flintstown (Baldwin), Maine.
1804	Living with his family in Pleasant Mountain Gore, Maine.
	November 8, entered Fryeburg Academy, Maine, where he remained six months.
1805–1807	Farming, fiddling and making various mechanisms in Pleasant Mountain Gore.
1807	Shoemaker's apprentice in West Boxford.
1807–1810	Playing fife and fiddle in Portland, Maine.
1810–1811	House and sign painter in Portland.
1812	Private in the Boxford West Parish company of foot soldiers.
	May 25, drafted as a private from West Boxford to guard Atlantic seaboard.
	Painting gunboats in Portland.
1813	In Denmark, Maine, painting sleighs and drums, playing drum, teaching drumming and drum painting.
1814	September 7–November 25, private and musician in three Portland companies of the state militia.
1814–1815	Teaching school in Baldwin and Waterford, Maine.
1815	Building wind-driven gristmills in Portland.
	January 24, copyrighted title of music book, *The Martial Musician's Companion*.
	October 16, married Eunice Twombly of Portland.
1816	Moved to New Haven, Connecticut.
	Started portrait painting.
	Conducting a dancing school in New Haven.
	August 16, son, Stephen Twombly, born in Portland.
1817–1819	Trading voyage to the Northwest Coast and Hawaii.
1818	Painting in Hawaii.
	July 29, daughter, Mary Broadbury, born in Portland.
1819	Painting portraits in Boston after return from Hawaii.
	Painted portraits of John and Mehitable Tyler in West Boxford.
1819–1820	Traveling southward on foot painting portraits—from Boston, through New York and New Jersey, to Baltimore, then to Harrisonburg Hot Springs, Virginia.
1820	August 9, son, Rufus King, born in Cambridge, Massachusetts.
	In Alexandria, Virginia, made a camera obscura to facilitate portrait painting.
	Traveling with camera and handcart, painting portraits, to Harrisonburg Hot Springs, Virginia.
	Boring for source of perpetual heat at Harrisonburg Hot Springs.
	Invented main features of his "aerial locomotive."
1821–1822	Traveling northward painting portraits and inventing various mechanisms. (Continued as part-time itinerant inventor and portrait painter until near end of life.)
1822	Invented, manufactured and sold a revolving almanac in Billerica, Massachusetts.

1823	Traveling through New England with "Joe" (probably nephew Jonathan D. Poor) as portrait painter.
	Painting portraits in New York.
	Worked on project of a horse-propelled twin boat in Hartford, Connecticut.
	June 29, twin sons, Sylvanus Frederick and Francis Augustus, born in Billerica, Massachusetts, where Porter maintained legal residence from 1823 to 1843.
	July 2, son, Francis Augustus, died in Billerica.
1823–1824	Stagecoach trip to Philadelphia.
	On foot from Philadelphia to New York as silhouette cutter.
	Sold camera and tried itinerant landscape painting in New England.
1824	Began traveling through New England painting mural landscapes, which he continued on and off until c. 1845 (see Checklist of frescoes for details).
	Built a horsepowered flatboat which he worked on the Connecticut River for a short time and then sold.
c. 1824–1825	Painted murals in East Pepperell, Massachusetts; in Bradford, East Jaffrey, Greenfield, Langdon, Mason, New Ipswich and Orford, New Hampshire; and in Sebec, Maine.
	Published *A Select Collection of Approved, Genuine, Secret and Modern Receipts, For the Preparation and Execution of Various Valuable and Curious Arts* in Concord, Massachusetts.
1825	December 5, son, John Randolph, born in Billerica.
1825–1826	Published four editions of *A Select Collection of Valuable and Curious Arts, and Interesting Experiments* in Concord, New Hampshire.
c. 1825–1830	Painted murals in Dover, Hancock, Haverhill, Lyme and North Haverhill, New Hampshire.
1827	July 31, son, Edward Leroy, born in Billerica.
c. 1827	Painted murals in Portland, Maine.
1829	July 16, daughter, Nancy Adams, born in Billerica.
c. 1830	Painted murals in Fryeburg and Hollis Center, Maine.
c. 1830–1835	Painted murals in Amesbury, Bedford, Billerica, East Haverhill, Groveland, Harvard, Lexington, Lunenburg, Merrimac, Merrimacport, Sturbridge and Townsend, Massachusetts; and in Bridgton, Buxton, Cornish, Freyburg, South Bridgton, Westbrook and Winthrop, Maine.
1831	June 19, daughter, Ellen Augusta, born in Billerica.
c. 1831–1834	Painted murals in Topsham, Vermont.
1832	Patented a clock.
c. 1832	Painted murals in Georgetown, Massachusetts.
1833	Constructed first model of his airship in Bristol, Connecticut.
1834	Published plans for its construction in *Mechanics' Magazine*.
	Patented a boat improvement.
	October 1, son, Washington Irving, born in Billerica.
1835	Patented a floating dry dock and a self-adjusting cheese press.
c. 1835–1840	Painted murals in Boston, Charlestown, North Reading, Wakefield and Woburn, Massachusetts.
1836	January 7 son, Washington Irving, died in Billerica.
	Patented a distance measuring appliance, and a horsepower mechanism.
1838	Patented a churn and a corn sheller.
	Painted murals in West Boxford and Westwood, Massachusetts; assisted in Westwood by son Stephen Twombly.
1840	Patented a life preserver, fire alarm and cheese press.
	Bought interest in the *New York Mechanic*.
1841–1842	Publishing and editing the *New York Mechanic* in New York (changed to the *American Mechanic* in 1842 and published in Boston). In this journal published his plans for the rotary plow, hot air ventilation system, "American Telegraph," etc., and advertised his general patent agency run in connection with the paper.
1843	Learned and practiced electroplating in Boston, and probably painted murals (there is one frescoed house in Boston).
1844	Invented a revolvin rifle and sold it to Colonel Colt.

	Joined the militia at the outbreak of the Mexican War.
1845	Painted murals in East Weymouth, Massachusetts.
	Went to New York City to engage in the electrotyping business.
1845–1847	Publishing and editing the *Scientific American* in New York. In this journal published his plans for the elevated railroad, "Steam-Carriage for Common Roads," etc.
1847	Constructed and publicly exhibited a small working model of his airship in New York. (The small model was again exhibited in New York in 1849, and a larger and improved model was shown in Boston and New York in 1850.)
1847–1848	Publishing and editing the *Scientific Mechanic* in New York and Washington.
1848	November 15, wife, Eunice Twombly Porter, died in Billerica where she had resided since 1823.
1849	Residing in New York City.
	Married Emma Tallman Edgar of Roxbury, Massachusetts, in Brooklyn, New York.
	Patented method of working the valves of auxiliary engines for feeding boilers.
	Published *Aerial Navigation* in New York.
1850	October 6, son, Stephen Twombly, died in Billerica.
	Published *An Aerial Steamer, or Flying Ship* in Washington, D.C.
1850–1860	Maintained legal residence in Washington, D.C.
1851	January 23, petitioned Senate, 31st Congress, 2nd session, for appropriation to extend experiments in practical aviation.
	Organized a stock company, the Aerial Navigation Company, to promote his airship, and shortly thereafter began construction of a full-sized machine, which was never successfully completed.
1852	Published *Essential Truth* in Washington, D.C.
1852–1853	Published and edited the *Aerial Reporter* in Washington, D.C.
1853	Exhibited a twenty-two-foot working model of his airship at Carusi's Hall in Washington.
1854	Patented a cord-making machine and a chair-cane.
1855	Residing in Springfield, Massachusetts.
1856	Patented a punching machine and a fog whistle.
1857	Patented two automatic grain-weighing machines.
c. 1857	Circulating flyer to promote his "Steam Farmer" by offering shares in the invention.
	Invented a prefabricated movable house; constructed one in Baltimore and one in Washington, D.C.
1858	Patented a steam engine.
1859	Patented a blind fastener.
	Son, Frank Rufus, born.
1861	Patented apparatus for elevating liquids by retained power.
1861–1863	Residing in Melrose, Massachusetts.
1863	Patented an air pump.
1865	Residing in Malden, Massachusetts.
	Patented a fan blower.
1869	Residing in New York City.
	Making plans for construction of an improved airship.
1871	Residing in Bristol, Connecticut.
	Patented a vise.
1872	Residing in Plantsville, Connecticut.
	Writing on religious subjects.
	Invented and sold a cam lever vise.
1873	Living in West Birmingham, Connecticut. Soliciting shares for his airship.
1878	Living on Water Street, West Haven, Connecticut.
	Applied for and received pension as veteran of War of 1812.
1879	Manufacturing and selling improved clothes driers.
c. 1880–1884	Residing in Bristol, Connecticut.
1884	Visited son, Frank Rufus, in West Haven, Connecticut, and died there August 13.
	Buried in Oak Grove Cemetery, West Haven, Connecticut.

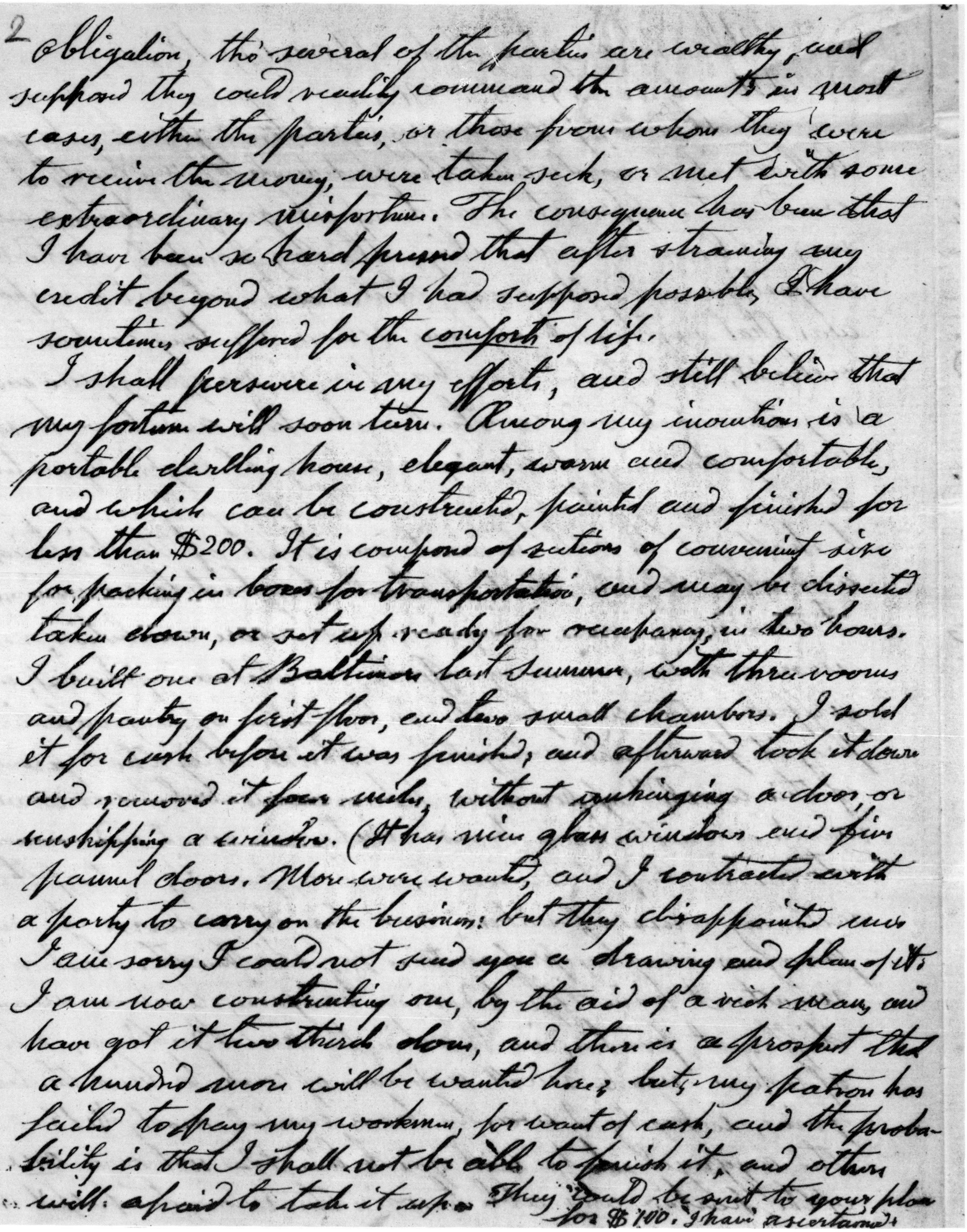

2

obligation, tho' several of the parties are wealthy, and suppose they could readily command the amounts in most cases, either the parties, or those from whom they were to receive the money, were taken sick, or met with some extraordinary misfortune. The consequence has been that I have been so hard pressed that after straining my credit beyond what I had supposed possible, I have sometimes suffered for the <u>comforts</u> of life.

I shall persevere in my efforts, and still believe that my fortune will soon turn. Among my inventions is a portable dwelling house, elegant, warm and comfortable, and which can be constructed, painted and finished for less than $200. It is composed of sections of convenient size for packing in boxes for transportation, and may be dissected taken down, or set up ready for occupancy, in two hours. I built one at Baltimore last summer, with three rooms and pantry on first floor, and two small chambers. I sold it for cash before it was finished, and afterward took it down and removed it four miles, without unhinging a door, or unshipping a window. (It has nine glass windows and five pannel doors. More were wanted, and I contracted with a party to carry on the business: but they disappointed me. I am sorry I could not send you a drawing and plan of it. I am now constructing one, by the aid of a rich man, and have got it two thirds done, and there is a prospect that a hundred more will be wanted here; but, my patron has failed to pay my workmen, for want of cash, and the probability is that I shall not be able to finish it, and others will afraid to take it up. They could be sent to your place for $400. I have ascertained.

Fig. 104. Page from a Porter letter written in 1857 to his friend and patron William Markoe, in which he describes, among other inventions, his prefabricated portable house. *Minnesota Historical Society, St. Paul.*

Selected Bibliography

"Academies of Art," *North American Review*, LVIII, article X (1828), 207–24.

"An Aged Inventor," *New Haven Daily Palladium* (August 14, 1884), 3.

Allen, Edward B. *Early American Wall Paintings 1710–1850*. New Haven, Connecticut: Yale University Press, 1926.

————. "Interior Decoration a Hundred Years Ago," *House Beautiful* (March, 1929), 380–84.

————. "The Quaint Frescoes of New England," *Art in America* (October, 1922), 263–74.

————. "Some Historic American Frescoes," *Antiques* (July, 1928), 46–48.

The Artist's Assistant in Drawing, Perspective, Etching, Engraving, Mezzotinto Scraping, Painting on Glass, in Crayons, in Water Colours, etc. Philadelphia: printed by Benjamin Johnson for Benjamin Davis, 1794.

The Artist's Companion and Manufacturer's Guide. Boston: J. Norman, 1814.

Auer, May Hale. "Rufus Porter," *The Decorator* (April, 1951), 12–17.

Banks, William N. "History in towns: Temple, New Hampshire," *Antiques* (October, 1975), 712–29.

Barrows, J. S. *Fryeburg, Maine*. Fryeburg, Maine: Pequoit Press, 1938.

Beard, Charles A. and Mary. *The Rise of American Civilization*. New York: The Macmillan Company, 1930.

Brazer, Esther Stevens. *Early American Decoration*. Springfield, Massachusetts: Pond-Ekberg Co., 1940.

Brooks, Van Wyck. *The Flowering of New England*. New York: E. P. Dutton & Co., 1936.

————. *The World of Washington Irving*. New York: E. P. Dutton & Co., 1944.

Burlingame, Roger. *Engines of Democracy*. New York: Charles Scribner's Sons, 1940.

————. *March of the Iron Men*. New York: Charles Scribner's Sons, 1938.

Burton, Reverend Warren. *The District School as It Was*. Ed. Clifton Johnson. Boston: Lee & Shepard, 1897. (First published, Boston, 1833.)

Butler, Ben and Natalie. *Farmington Historical Society Pilgrimage No. 2*. Farmington, Maine, 1966.

The Charter and By-Laws of the American Academy of the Fine Arts with an account of the statues, busts, paintings, etc. belonging to the Academy. New York: David Longworth, 1817.

Cummings, Thomas S. *Historic Annals of the National Academy of Design*. Philadelphia: George W. Childs, 1865.

"Death of Rufus Porter," *New Haven Union* (August 14, 1884), 4.

Dimon, Eugenie. "A Visit to Hancock House," *The Decorator* (Autumn, 1954), 23–26.

Discover America/Poems 1976. San José, California: San José Studies, San José State University, 1976.

Drepperd, Carl W. *American Pioneer Arts and Artists*. Springfield, Massachusetts: Pond-Ekberg Co., 1942.

Earle, Alice Morse. *Stage Coach and Tavern Days*. New York: The Macmillan Company, 1938.

"To Exhibit Westwood Murals of Rufus Porter at Antiques Show," *Westwood Press*, Massachusetts (September 6, 1967), 44.

"Farmington's House of the Painted Walls," *Lewiston Journal*, Maine, magazine section (October 31–November 4, 1908), 3.

Fenerty, Marjory R. "Story of Westwood Murals Reflects History of Town," *The Westwood Press*, Massachusetts (August 12, 1964), 1, 4.

Finn, Matthew D. *Theoremetical System of Painting*. New York: James Ryan, 1830.

"The First American Art Academy," *Lippincott's Magazine* (February, 1872), 143–53; (March, 1872), 309–21.

Fish, Carl Russell. *The Rise of the Common Man*. New York: The Macmillan Company, 1927.

Forbes, Esther. *Rainbow on the Road*. Boston: Houghton Mifflin Company, 1954.

Forsyth, David P. *The Business Press in America, 1750–1875*. Philadelphia: Chilton Book Company, 1964.

Fryeburg Academy 1792–1942 Sesqui-Centennial. Fryeburg, Maine: Fryeburg Academy, 1942.

Hamilton, Thomas. *Men and Manners in America*. Philadelphia: Carey, Lea & Blanchard, 1833.

Hands that Built New Hampshire. (Compiled by the New Hampshire workers of the W.P.A. writers' program.) Brattleboro, Vermont: Daye Press, 1940.

Hayes, Alvah G. "Have Idea; Will Travel," *Yankee* (May, 1962), 58, 59, 120, 122.

Hibben, Paxton. *Henry Ward Beecher: an American Portrait*. New York: Doran Co., 1927.

Howells, John Mead. *The Architectural Heritage of the Merrimack*. New York: Architectural Book Publishing Co., 1941.

Ingalls, Albert G. "A Century of Scientific American," *Scientific American* (December, 1945), 327–32.

Isaacson, Doris. "Rufus Porter: 19th Century Painter-Inventor-Publisher," *The Maine History News* (January, 1968), 2, 8.

Johnson, R. (ed.). *Twentieth Century Biographical Dictionary of Notable Americans*. Vol. 8. Boston: Biographical Society, 1904.

Karr, Louise. "Old Westwood Murals," *Antiques* (April, 1926), 231–36.

————. "Painted Walls and Panels," *The Antiquarian* (August, 1925), 26–30.

Keyes, Frances Parkington. *Also the Hills*. New York: Julian Messner, 1943.

Kouwenhoven, John A. *Made in America*. New York: Doubleday & Company, 1948.

Lewis, A. F. and C. W. *The Illustrated Fryeburg Webster Memorial*. Fryeburg, Maine, 1882.

Lipman, Jean. *American Primitive Painting*. New York: Oxford University Press, 1942.

————. "A Critical Definition of the American Primitive," *Art in America* (October 1938), 171–77.

————. "Primitive Vision and Modern Design," *Art in America* (January, 1945), 11–19.

————. "Rufus Porter, Yankee Wall Painter," *Art in America* (October, 1950), 133–200.

————. *Rufus Porter: Yankee Pioneer*. New York: Clarkson N. Potter, 1968.

————. "The Study of Folk Art," *Art in America* (October, 1945), 245–54.

———— and Tom Armstrong. *American Folk Painters of Three Centuries*. New York: Hudson Hills Press in association with the Whitney Museum of American Art, 1980.

———— and Alice Winchester. *The Flowering of American Folk Art, 1776–1876*. Viking Press in cooperation with the Whitney Museum of American Art, 1974.

Little, Nina Fletcher. *American Decorative Wall Painting 1700–1850*. New York: Studio Publications (with Old Sturbridge Village), 1952.

————. *Floor Coverings in New England Before 1850*. Sturbridge, Massachusetts: Old Sturbridge Inc., 1967.

————. "Itinerant Painting in America, 1750–1850," *New York History* (April, 1949), 210–11.

Longfellow, Samuel. *Life of Henry Wadsworth Longfellow*. Boston: Ticknor & Co., 1886.

Lord, Alice Frost. "Century Old House at Webster Contains Original Wall Sketches," *Lewiston Journal*, Maine (January 27, 1927), magazine section A–2.

Malone, Dumas (ed.). *Dictionary of American Biography*. Vol. 15. New York: Charles Scribner's Sons, 1935.

Markoe, William. Papers in the collection of the Minnesota Historical Society, St. Paul (in connection with Markoe's financial support of Porter's airship) include: two letters from Rufus Porter to Markoe written in 1853 and 1857; letter books belonging to Markoe containing several letters to Porter written in the 1850s and numerous references to him in other correspondence; copies of Porter's *Aerial Navigation* and *An Aerial Steamer;* a stock certificate in Porter's Aerial Navigation Company; a flyer headed "Liberal and Interesting Proposition" advertising Porter's "Steam Farmer."

(McCartney, Charlotte). "Rufus Porter and the Topsham Murals," *Rural Vermonter* (Fall, 1963), 10–11.

McClelland, Nancy. *Historic Wall Papers*. Philadelphia: J. B. Lippincott Co., 1924.

McCluer, C. E. "Rufus Porter and his 'Flying Ship,'" *Scientific American* (January 8, 1910), 30.

McGrath, Robert L. "Rediscovery: Rufus Porter in Vermont," *Art in America* (January–February, 1968), 78–79.

Morison, Samuel Eliot. *The Maritime History of Massachusetts*. Boston: Houghton Mifflin Company, 1921.

Morson, W. T. "Another Old New England Farmhouse Restored," *Antiques* (July, 1948), 32–35.

Moulton, Alphonso, and Howard L. Sampson and Granville Fernald (eds.). *Centennial History of Harrison, Maine*. Portland, Maine: Southwork Printing Co., 1909.

Nichols, L. T. *Forty Years of American Life*. London: Longmans Green, 1874.

Noyes, Reginald Webb. *A Bibliography of Maine Imprints to 1820*. Stonington, Maine: printed for Mr. and Mrs. R. Webb Noyes, 1930.

"Old Russ House Is Rich in Memories," *Franklin Journal*, Maine (September 15, 1944), 6.

One Thousand Valuable Secrets in the Elegant and Useful Arts. Philadelphia: printed for B. Davies and T. Stephens, 1795.

Paine, Thomas. *The Age of Reason* (1794–1796). Indianapolis: The Bobbs-Merrill Co., undated paperback.

Park, Edward. "Old Murals to be Shown at Bedford 'Open House,'" *Boston Daily Globe* (October 2, 1952), 13.

Parrington, Vernon Louis. *Main Currents in American Thought*. New York: Harcourt, Brace & World, 1927.

Peachem, Henry. *Graphics of the Most Ancient and Excellent Art of Drawing and Limning*. London: printed for John Browne, 1612.

Perley, Sidney. *The Dwellings of Boxford*. Salem, Massachusetts: Essex Institute, 1893.

————. *The History of Boxford*. Boston: Franklin Press, 1880.

Philpott, A. J. Articles about Rufus Porter, *Boston Globe* (June 12, 1936), 6; (July 5, 1936), 46; (July 28, 1936), 3; (September 20, 1936), 50; (December 19, 1936), 3.

Porter, Frank Rufus. Manuscript letters written to the *Scientific American*, 1938–1940, *Scientific American* office file.

Porter, Joseph Whitcomb. *A Genealogy of the Descendents of Richard Porter and John Porter*. Bangor, Maine: Burr & Robinson, 1878.

Porter, Rufus. *Aerial Navigation, the Practicability of Traveling Pleasantly and Safely from New York to California in Three Days*. New York. H. Smith. (Only three known copies: in Yale, Harvard and the Minnesota Historical Society libraries. Reprinted in an edition of 200 with an introduction by Lieutenant Commander H. V. Wiley, San Francisco, L. R. Kennedy, 1935.)

———— (ed.). *Aerial Reporter*. Washington, printed by Kirkwood & McGill, 1852. (Only known issues extant: Vol. 1, No. 6 (August 14, 1852), in the Library of Congress, Washington; Vol. 1, No. 8 (September 11, 1852), in the Minnesota Historical Society, St. Paul.

————. *An Aerial Steamer, or Flying Ship*. Washington, D.C.: W. Greer, 1850. (Only one known copy extant, in the Minnesota Historical Society, St. Paul.)

———— (ed.). *American Mechanic*. Boston, 1842.

————. *Essential Truth*. Washington, D.C.: Kirkwood & McGill, 1852.

————. "The Flying Ship," *National Intelligencer* (March 20, 1852), 4.

———— (ed.). *New York Mechanic*. New York, 1840–1841.

———— (ed.). *Scientific American*. New York, 1845–1847.

———— (ed.). *Scientific Mechanic*. New York and Washington, D.C., 1847–1848.

————. *A Select Collection of Approved, Genuine, Secret and Modern Receipts, For the Preparation and Execution of Various Valuable and Curious Arts*. Concord, Massachusetts: J. T. Peters, printer, undated—probably shortly before 1825. (Only one copy known, in the collection of Old Sturbridge Village, Sturbridge, Massachusetts.)

————. *A Select Collection of Valuable and Curious Arts, and Interesting Experiments*. Concord, New Hampshire: J. B. Moore, printer, 1825. (Reprinted in four more editions in Concord, New Hampshire, 1826: second and third editions by J. B. Moore, fourth and fifth by William Brown.)

————. "Traveling Balloon, or Flying Machine," *Mechanics' Magazine,* American Edition (November 8, 1834), 273–75.

————. *A Yankee Inventor's Flying Ship.* Reprints *Aerial Navigation* and *An Aerial Steamer,* ed. and with introduction by Rhoda R. Gilman. St. Paul: Minnesota Historical Society, 1969.

Rawson, Marion Nicholl. *Candle Days.* New York: Century Co., 1927.

————. *From Here to Yender.* New York: E. P. Dutton & Co., 1932.

Reynolds, N. J. *Voyage of the United States Frigate Potomac, under the Command of Commodore John Downes, during the Circumnavigation of the Globe, in the Years 1831, 1832, 1833, and 1834.* New York: Harper & Brothers, 1834.

Reynolds, Stephen. *The Voyage of the New Hazard.* Ed. F. W. Howay. Salem, Massachusetts: Peabody Museum, 1938.

Roberts, Kenneth. *Rabble in Arms.* New York: Doubleday & Company, 1933.

"Rufus Porter's Aeroport," *Scientific American* (November 20, 1869), 325–26.

"Rufus Porter, Founder of the Scientific American," *Scientific American* (September 6, 1884), 144–45.

"Rufus Porter Paid For Keep By Painting Wall Murals," *Norwood Free Press,* Massachusetts (September 19, 1947), 30.

"Rufus Porter.—A Representative of American Genius," *Scientific American* (November 8, 1884), 297.

Scharf, J. T., and T. Westcott. *History of Philadelphia.* Philadelphia: C. H. Leverts & Co., 1884.

The School of Wisdom or Repository of the Most Valuable Curiosities of Art. New Brunswick, New Jersey: printed for W. Lawson & J. Dunham, 1787.

Sears, Clara Endicott. *Some American Primitives.* Boston: Houghton Mifflin Company, 1941.

Svinin, Pavel Petrovich. *Picturesque United States of America.* New York: W. E. Rudge, 1930.

Tocqueville, Alexis de. *Democracy in America.* New York: J. & H. Langley, 1840.

Towne, Richard R. "The Mysterious Murals," *Yankee* (March, 1968), 86–88, 156–161.

Trollope, Mrs. (Frances Milton). *Domestic Manners of the Americans.* 3rd edition. London: Whitaker, Treacher, & Co., 1832.

U.S. Congressional Globe, 31st Congress, 2nd Session. Washington, D.C., 1851, Vol. 23, 310, 369.

U.S. Senate Journal, 31st Congress, 2nd Session. Washington, D.C., 1850–1851, 105, 127.

Verplanck, G. C. *An address delivered at the opening of the tenth exhibition of the American Academy of the Fine Arts.* New York: G. & C. Carvill, 1825.

Vital Records of Boxford, Massachusetts, to the End of the Year 1849. Topsfield, Massachusetts: Topsfield Historical Society, 1905.

"Wall Paintings Found Hidden Under Paper," *Boston Sunday Globe* (September 27, 1925) 40.

Waring, Janet. *Early American Stencils on Walls and Furniture.* New York: William R. Scott, 1937.

Warrington, Francis. *Cruise of the United States Frigate Potomac Round the World, During the Years 1831–34.* New York: Leavit, Lord & Co. (Boston: Crocker & Brewster), 1835.

Washburn, Gordon. *Catalogue of Old and New England, an Exhibition.* Providence: Museum of Art, Rhode Island School of Design, 1945.

Williamson, Joseph. *A Bibliography of the State of Maine.* Portland: Thurston, 1896.

Wilson, J. G., and J. Fiske (eds.). *Appleton's Cyclopedia of American Biography.* Vol. 5. New York: D. Appleton & Co., 1900.

Winchester, Alice. "A Painted Wall," *Antiques* (May, 1946), 310.

"Winthrop Murals Suggest What New Maine Museum Will Contain," *Press Herald,* Portland, Maine (January 9, 1968), 6.

Wood, E. Henry. *The Genealogy of the Wood Family.* Clinton, Massachusetts: printed by W. J. Coulter, 1890.

Wright, Richardson. *Hawkers and Walkers in Early America.* Philadelphia: J. B. Lippincott Co., 1927.

Yates, Elizabeth. *Patterns on the Wall.* New York: Alfred A. Knopf, 1943.

Zahm, A. F. *Aerial Navigation.* New York: D. Appleton & Co., 1911.

Acknowledgments

THE PUBLICATIONS THAT WENT into the making of this book are listed in the bibliography, but as very little had been recorded about Rufus Porter himself it could never have been written without the cooperation of countless people, generous with their time and interest over a period of twenty-five years. My Rufus Porter file contains over a thousand letters from librarians, officers of historical societies, museum directors, town clerks, owners of frescoed houses, and other people of all kinds from all parts of New England who had some information to give me about Porter's life or work. Many of them loaned photographs, clippings, record books. I wish it were possible to thank them all, instead of the small number I had to select from among them for special acknowledgments. (Some of these people, whose help dates back twenty-five years, are no longer living.)

For information about Porter's life and career: Dorothea Porter, Frank Rufus Porter's widow; Frederick Buechner and his cousin Edith R. King—Rufus Porter and Jonathan D. Poor were among their ancestors; Mary A. Andrew of West Boxford whose husband's great-grandfather was a townfellow and friend of Rufus Porter's and who corresponded with me regularly for one year about Porter material she gathered from Boxford people, old records and publications; Frank A. Manny, a Boxford historian, who gave me many valuable suggestions for hunting information about Porter; Elroy O. LaCasce, principal of Fryeburg Academy, who provided me with early Fryeburg history and searched the Academy records for the items pertaining to Porter's attendance there; Carl W. Mitman of the Smithsonian Institution who had written about Porter for the *Dictionary of American Biography* and who sent me important additional material which had since come to his attention; Milton E. Lord, director of the Boston Public Library, who volunteered to track down the facts about Porter's music book; Edward N. Waters of the Music Division of the Library of Congress whom Mr. Lord set on the hunt and who carried it to a conclusion, and then located the only extant copy of Porter's *Religious Truth*; James Tanis, Yale University head librarian, who located Porter obituaries; Rhoda R. Gilman of the Minnesota Historical Society who brought to my attention the William Markoe—Rufus Porter papers in the Society's collection; A. J. Philpott of the *Boston Globe* who had written a series of articles on Porter and sent me his personal scrapbooks to examine and use; Albert G. Ingalls of the *Scientific American* who loaned me the sheaf of letters Frank Rufus Porter had written to the editors of that magazine.

For data on the portraits: Florence M. Bryant who allowed me to have her Porter portraits photographed for reproduction, and loaned me photographs of the old Tyler homestead and a batch of newspaper clippings about Rufus Porter which she had collected; Esther Doane Osman who reported on two pairs of portraits no longer in existence; Alice Winchester, editor of *Antiques* magazine, who cooperated by publishing a notice requesting information about Porter portraits; Bert and Gail Savage who helped locate a number of newly discovered portraits.

For the chapter on Porter as an art instructor: the late Carl W. Drepperd who lent me his copy of Porter's rare *Curious Arts*, allowed me to browse among his collection of early art instruction books, and gave me the benefit of his extensive research in this branch of early Americana; Etta Falkner, Old Sturbridge Village librarian, who clarified various questions connected with Porter's art instruction books.

194

For locating frescoes: Ben Stinchfield who, about 1950, conducted a systematic search for frescoed houses in the vicinity of Vienna, Maine, located not only the frescoes but information about them, old newspaper clippings and photographs, and, without consulting me, sent out a typed questionnaire to owners of old houses asking about possible frescoes, their subject, authorship, date and condition, then in 1967 loaned his photographs of murals for study and illustration; A. Warren Stearns who did much the same thing in the vicinity of Billerica, Massachusetts, and who on his own initiative inserted an advertisement requesting information in the local newspapers; Martha H. Stearns who took me on a tour of the frescoed houses of Hancock, New Hampshire; Ruth W. Ledward of the Hancock library who conducted a telephone campaign to locate more houses in neighboring towns; Elwin I. Purrington who steered my search for Porter frescoes in and around Wakefield, Massachusetts; William H. Ilsley who had restored the old Pingree house in Georgetown, Massachusetts, and who wrote numerous letters to owners of houses in the vicinity to verify the locations of other frescoes; Mary Preble who restored the Orison Wood frescoes in the Tibbets house in West Auburn, Maine, and who was largely instrumental in reconstructing Wood's oeuvre; Frances Parkinson Keyes who, having woven one of the New Hampshire frescoes into *Also the Hills*, gave me permission to quote from her book and was instrumental in locating photographs of these frescoes and of others in the neighborhood; Bartley A. Jackson, who had followed with his camera this author's itinerary for Porter frescoes in Maine, found quite a number of other frescoed houses en route, and loaned his entire slide collection for study and half a dozen for reproduction; Nina Fletcher Little, the authority on early wall painting, who had taken a lively interest in Rufus Porter since my published accounts of his career, and as this book was in final stages helped most generously with all sorts of added information and a number of photographs of murals, and of the only family register which has been found.

Also, for photographs of the frescoes and various details about them: William Sumner Appleton, Abigail Bacon, Mabel L. Badger, Mary D. Bartlett, Barbara C. Blanchard, Louise K. Brown, Benjamin and Natalie S. Butler, Sadie R. Carr, Frances E. Chase, T. A. Eaton, Wilhelmina Farrand, Marjory R. Fenerty, Frances E. Foster, Ethel M. Fredrick, Milton Gay, Hazel Goyette, Henry J. Harlow, William Henry Harrison, Thomas Hayes, Alice Doan Hodgson, Patricia Holsaert, Nettie M. Ingham, Ellerton Jetté, Virginia A. May, Samuel L. Meulendyke, M. C. Morse, John Pancoast, Marjorie S. Parker, Marion Nicholl Rawson, Katharine M. Rolfe, Clara Endicott Sears, Barbara Sessions, David Sheehan, Glen B. Skillin, Bradley Smith, Elinor J. Smith, Edith M. Tibbets, Creigh Wagner, Ida F. Ward, Dorothy C. Waterhouse, John Wilmerding, George Wittenborn, Ruth Woodbury—and all the owners of the frescoed houses who allowed visits and photography.

For special photography: George M. Cushing, Jr., A. W. Merwin, Perron Studio, Phelps Photo, Inc.

For help with picture planning: Elton Robinson.

For editorial assistance: Mary Ann Haxthausen, Margaret Aspinwall.

For constant interest and assistance: my husband, Howard Lipman; the editors of Clarkson N. Potter, Inc.; the Whitney Museum of American Art; and The Hudson River Museum.

List of Illustrations

COLOR PLATES

Index

Note: Italicized page numbers refer to illustrations.